D1422691

The WATERWAYS REVOLUTION

The WATERWAYS REVOLUTION

From The Peaks To The Trent

1768-1778

CHRISTINE RICHARDSON

Published in 1992 by
The Self Publishing Association Ltd
Units 7/10 Hanley Workshops
Hanley Swan, Worcs.

A MEMBER OF

in conjunction with
Christine Richardson

British Library Cataloguing in Publication Data

A catalogue record for this book is
available from the British Library

ISBN 1 85421 161 7

Designed & Produced by Images Design & Print Ltd, Hanley Swan, Worcs.
Printed & Bound in Great Britain by Hartnolls Ltd, Bodmin, Cornwall.

CONTENTS

Page No

Acknowledgements

Foreword   11
Background   13

PART ONE   **PLANNING & FINANCE**

Chapter 1   A Canal for Chesterfield   27
Chapter 2   What about Retford?   46
Chapter 3   Selling the Idea to the Public   59
Chapter 4   An Act of Parliament   73
Chapter 5   Final Arrangements   89

PART TWO   **CANAL CONSTRUCTION**

Chapter 6   Start at the Top   101
Chapter 7   The First Crises   127
Chapter 8   Norwood and Retford   154
Chapter 9   Through Norwood Hill   186
Chapter 10   Financial Crises   206
Chapter 11   Final Stages   242
Epilogue   255

Location of Source Documents   260
Source References   261
Table of £.s.d / £.p equivalents   268
Appendix A   269
Appendix B   270
Appendix C   273
Appendix D   274
Appendix E   277
Appendix F   278
Appendix G   279
Bibliography   280
Index   285

LIST OF ILLUSTRATIONS

	Page no
Map of Chesterfield Canal	10
Map of Chesterfield's Geographical location and the river system	17
Map of Chesterfield c1762-7	20
Portrait of James Brindley	22
Typical dress of 1760/70	29
Map – Crossing the hills between Chesterfield and Bawtry	36
Map – East end of Varley's Route to Bawtry (1769)	
– Rise/Fall of Canal	39
Varley's hand drawn map	40-41
Map of Eastern end of the canal – Three route options	52
Map of Chesterfield Canal Route as Built	56
Map of Influential Landowners along the Canal	64
Map of Rivers flowing north to the Humber	79
Map of Water Supply to Staveley Forge	81
Cross Sections of the Canal near Staveley	82
Illustration of Company Seal	97
Map of progress to date 1771	100
Canal Company Receipts. Notts Univ. Ki 77/130, Ki 77/13	110
Map of progress to date 1772	137
Map of progress to date 1774	182
Map of Extra Water Supply at Retford	193
Map of progress to date April 1776	222
Map of progress to date Aug 1776	229
Map of Water Supply at Western End of Canal	231
Canal Lock	269

For Mal – For Everything

ACKNOWLEDGEMENTS

His Grace the Duke of Norfolk, and the Director of Libraries, for access to the Arundel Castle Manuscripts in the Archives Division, Sheffield City Libraries.

His Grace the Duke of Devonshire, for access to the Cavendish family archives, Chatsworth House.

Olive, Countess Fitzwilliam's Wentworth Settlement Trustees, and the Director, for access to the Wentworth Woodhouse Muniments in Sheffield City Libraries.

Mr. K. Gascoyne, for access to the map illustrated on pages 40-41

University of Nottingham Library for the illustration on page 110.

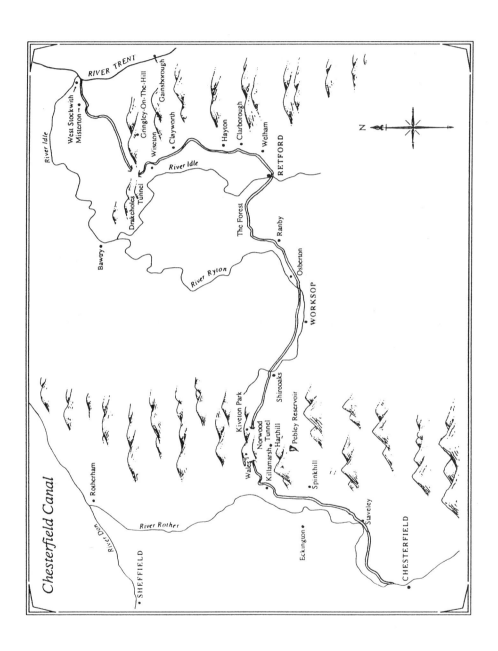

Chesterfield Canal

FOREWORD

The men who planned, financed and created the Chesterfield Canal in the eighteenth century were people like us. They had families to support, health problems, uncertain careers and futures. They had personality clashes with those they worked with, they complained about the weather, they went on tourist trips to London and came home with souvenirs.

These men were real living people, as real as you. They did not think of themselves as "history" any more than you think of yourself that way. To them the 1770s were the present, and very advanced in comparison with what had gone before.

They did not miss telephones, mechanical diggers, computers, railways, or fast road transport any more than you feel the loss of whatever will have been invented in two hundred years time.

BACKGROUND

It winds its way up from the River Trent; a small, narrow, shallow waterway lined with reeds, wild flowers and old buildings. It appears to be a natural feature that has been there forever – but looks can be deceptive. In 1777 the Chesterfield Canal was new, raw, and intrusive; its banks were uncovered clay and mud, the buildings, bridges and fences were stark and unweathered. It had slashed its way across the landscape with scant regard to local inhabitants, either human or animal. It was the latest achievement of a progressive age. So there is nothing natural about the Chesterfield Canal; it was created by men, part of a transport revolution. This book is the story of those men, the age in which they lived, and their new canal.

ᨶ ᨶ ᨶ

Today only a small percentage of the general public notice hills and valleys. To the majority a hill is only acknowledged as a semi-automatic decision to increase the pressure on the accelerator, to others it is a loss of scenery as their train rushes through a tunnel or a cutting. We give very little thought to the hill thus conquered, or that the land newly opened to our gaze is probably a valley containing a river. To be noticed the river has to be a major waterway, in which case we look down from our comfortable seat to see the water as we speed over a wide, strong bridge. Lesser rivers are hardly seen at all, their bridges simply supporting a length of motorway indistinguishable from other endless miles.

Valleys that we can name tend to have become familiar not as geographical features but as labels; Thames Valley Police, Don Valley Sports Stadium, Rother Valley Country Park, Trent Valley Bus Company. Few people think of such names as land features. But in the 18th century the physical shape of the local area was well understood by everyone. It was familiar because even the lowest hills and the shallowest valleys exerted a strong influence on the pattern of life in two ways – travel and the supply of water. All land transport was powered by two feet or four, either way hills were a tiring experience avoided whenever possible. And water was a valuable commodity channelled by the hills into the valleys; not only needed for drinking and agriculture, but as the major power source of an age only just becoming aware of the potential of steam. It was into such a society that canals came. They answered the need of the fledgling Industrial Revolution; trade could no longer accept the confines of geography. The hills and valleys had to be beaten.

In one area the challenge was taken up by the residents of a small Derbyshire town. By 1768 Chesterfield had become a busy market centre; the houses squeezed together, the roads unpaved and unlit, the smells strong and natural. The compressed buildings huddled around the two natural centres of influence, the Market Place and St. Mary's church; the latter visible for many miles from all approach routes, its famous crooked spire proclaiming the identity of the town to all visitors. But for all the prestige and dominance of the church, both as a building and an authority, the centre of commerce and power was the Market Place. Almost anything could be traded there; fruit, vegetables, bread, cheese, horses, cattle, clothes. The busy inns, such as the Angel and the Falcon, provided accommodation as well as food and drink; the adjacent Post Office was the centre not only for mail deliveries but also for property sales and auctions. The Market Place was the site of noise, activity, colour, litter, odours, wagon-jams and money; as a result the surrounding streets housed many merchants and the lawyers attracted by commerce and contracts.

These leading inhabitants were an ambitious and slightly roguish group and it was from amongst these opportunists that the advanced idea of a canal was first advocated. That these men, in only ten years, were to succeed in promoting, financing, planning, and completely constructing over forty miles of canal remains a testimony to their drive and energy. But in displaying such attributes they were by no means unique. The spirit of the time was venturesome, patriotic, confident, and the inhabitants of the two major towns involved in building the canal, Chesterfield and Retford, revealed the same characteristics. But before going on to identify individuals it is important to know something of their background and the

14

circumstances which nurtured such progressive plans.

Nationally, it was a busy time. London was four years into a building boom in which thousands of houses had been built, the Royal Crescent at Bath had been started, Edinburgh was building a New Town. Throughout the country there was great activity; improvements to harbours, the bridging of rivers, land drainage, road building. This activity was the legacy of the century before when long-held views on religion and fundamental beliefs had been challenged. It was no longer thought that God closely controlled society, instead Newton had proposed new concepts and scientific principles that put control of the world into the hands of men. Now it was felt that anything could be achieved without waiting for divine intervention. Internationally, the previous century had also created a new trade empire; India, and the settlements in the West Indies and America, had a profound impact upon England's commerce and wealth. Recently there had been a few disagreements with the American colonies but nothing that worried anyone – it was confidently expected that the matter would be sorted out. After all, colonies were there to expand British influence and trade, not to make their own rules. Nobody saw any clouds on the economic horizon.

Many foreign visitors repeatedly stated the comfortable life style of most of the English population, the joy they took in making money (and spending it) and the confidence they had in their own country. It did not take long before such visitors also discovered that these attributes were only surpassed by a distrust of foreigners, especially the French; the popular modern songs of the time included "Rule Britannia" and "God Save the King" and they amply stated the certainty of the nation.

But all this business activity was revealing new problems, the most important being the movement of goods and raw materials. The roads were atrocious. It is difficult to envisage a society where transport was so basic; in all but perfect summer weather a journey was tiring, dangerous and time-consuming. The dirt roads became water-logged very quickly and the steep camber used to drain the water made the passage of wheeled vehicles even more difficult. The carriages and wagons made axle-deep ruts which added to the problems and the mud on many roads was almost beyond modern comprehension. It was not unknown for horses to flounder belly-deep in the mire after a rainy spell. Many accidents happened. The wagon drivers did not always take as much care as they should; inadequate bridges often spilled horses, vehicle and passengers into the river below; the iron-work of the wagons was not of a high standard and often failed; many more over-turned because of the road surfaces. And heavy traffic volumes are not a new problem. The difference is that our roads are worn out by wheels, in the 1760s they were worn out by feet. In addition to the horses that were the main means of transport great herds of cattle, pigs, geese and goats staggered down from the north to local and London food markets. Thousands upon thousands of animals used the roads; in wet weather their feet turned the unsurfaced roads into quagmires, their "deposits" added a full-bodied aroma to the mixture. As well as all these difficulties road atlases were only just becoming available and signposts and milestones were unreliable guides. Some areas had hardly any and the mileages stated were as likely to have been measured in local versions of a mile as in the new standard measurement.

The roads never had been any good but now, for the first time, industries were becoming large, centralised and efficient. As a result, they needed raw materials from further afield and, of equal importance, the distribution of manufactured output to their customers. The main method available for goods transportation was pack-horse, especially in hilly areas such as Derbyshire. Obviously each horse could only carry a small amount of a heavy cargo such as lead and as a result large trains of such animals were needed for the movement of raw materials. In most winters, or very wet weather at any time, it was virtually impossible to move such items. Usually heavy goods loads went as directly as possible to the nearest navigable river or the coast, carriage by water being much the easier and cheaper option. Not that this alternative was perfect. Rivers were unreliable and affected by flood or drought. When water was scarce there were many disputes between the owners of water-powered mills and boatmen. In times of flood the rivers were often unusable. When proposals were made for controlling the water flow there were objections from the powerful pressure groups of the day, the landowners, mill-owners, and wild-fowlers. Even so between 1660 and 1750 several hundred miles of river

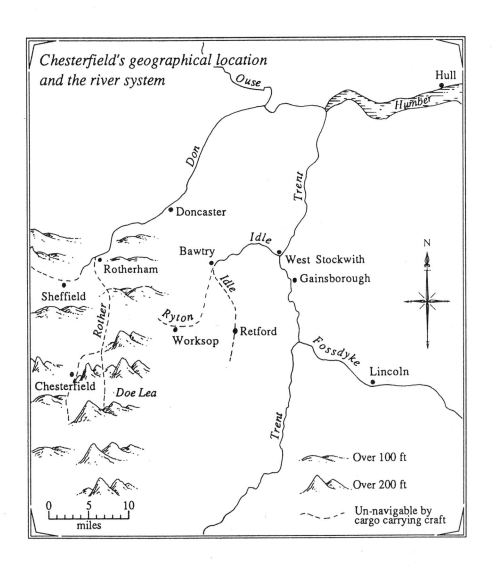

Chesterfield's geographical location and the river system

Over 100 ft

Over 200 ft

Un-navigable by cargo carrying craft

0 5 10
miles

N

Hull

Ouse

Humber

Don

Trent

Doncaster

Idle

Bawtry

Rotherham

West Stockwith

Gainsborough

Sheffield

Idle

Rother

Ryton

Retford

Worksop

Fossdyke

Lincoln

Chesterfield

Doe Lea

Trent

navigations were created in England. Imperfect though they were they formed the country's main transport system for heavy goods, giving the rivers an importance in national affairs which is now difficult to comprehend. They were the "motorways" of the time and the majority of early canals were built to link into this extensive network.

The area with which we are concerned was served by the thriving inland port of Bawtry on the Yorkshire/Nottinghamshire border. Bawtry had used its position on the River Idle to great effect. At its many wharfs goods were loaded onto boats which took the cargoes down to West Stockwith, the Idle's junction with the great, but tidal, River Trent. From here larger boats plied the Trent, going upstream and inland, or downstream to Hull and the even greater River Humber. The Humber gave access to the North Sea and coastal shipping to and from London, Newcastle, and Scandinavia.

In spite of the logistical problems, wealth was being generated by the booming trade conditions. It comes as no surprise that the aristocracy and the gentry built themselves imposing houses and travelled in even finer carriages than they had before. But of greater importance was the growth, both in finance and influence, of what historians generally refer to as "the middling sort". These were ambitious men who had taken advantage of the new opportunities and had made substantial amounts of money. With their new riches they usually bought land – ownership of which was the ultimate powerbase – and sometimes married into the gentry. But new-found wealth was one thing, status another. At the very top of the social ladder was the aristocracy – mainly consisting of the various influential Dukes and their families – who still owned a large percentage of the land in England. Many of them resented, or ignored, the pretensions of the newly rich up-start traders and these social pressures could have caused considerable unrest. But compromise came to the rescue. Social and political development ensured that the new spirit of the entrepreneurs worked together with the aristocracy's influence and political knowledge. A classic example of such a partnership of interests and abilities was the construction of the Chesterfield Canal.

ða   ða   ða

Chesterfield was not far from the centre of the thriving nation, situated on the eastern edge of Derbyshire's lead-producing hills and on the north-south London/Derby/Sheffield road. The men who were to build the Chesterfield Canal were merchants and lawyers of influence in the town, influence that was mainly channelled via the Market Place and their membership of the Corporation and the Manor Court. The Corporation's chief functions were to manage its own property and over-see the financial affairs of local charities. These responsibilities seemed to entail the organisation and attendance of a fair number of banquets and the claiming of subsequent expenses. Also some of the charity money does seem to have been used with "imagination". By its self-perpetuating nature the Corporation became a secretive and closed organisation that could be described as having been inept or corrupt; the verdict depends on the charitable nature of those making the judgement. Other canal promoters, if not members, served the Corporation in various ways, either as favoured suppliers or as legal advisers.

The second institution was the Manor Court which met once a year and passed and upheld the town's bye-laws. Of course the jury was formed from local men and the Foreman was usually an influential member of the Corporation. But it must be said that the Manor Court showed no favouritism and often made judgements against influential citizens. For example, telling them to clear the open drains outside their house, or to remove their rubbish heaps from outside the Shambles; although it did little to enforce compliance. It is the records of this Court that have left us a picture of neglected property, insanitary conditions, over-flowing ditches, dung-hills, open sewers, traffic congestion, booming trade. But to judge any society by its court records results in a distorted image with only the negative aspects being revealed. So it is likely that Chesterfield was no worse than most of the towns in England at that time. Certainly its local administration was by no means unique in its financial dealings.

ð&   *ð&*   *ð&*

Twenty-two miles away was Retford, the second major town in the history of the canal. In some ways it was similar to Chesterfield; a busy market

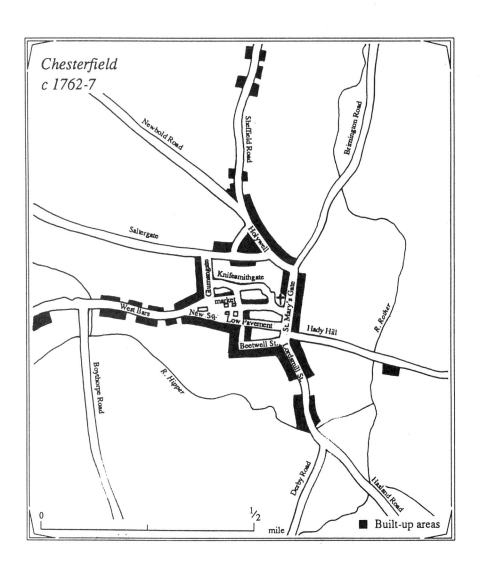

Chesterfield
c 1762-7

Newbold Road

Sheffield Road

Birmington Road

Saltergate

Holywell

Knifesmithgate

Glumangate

market

West Bars

New Sq.

Low Pavement

St. Mary's Gate

Hady Hill

R. Rother

Beetwell St.

St. Mary's Port

Boythorpe Road

R. Hipper

Derby Road

Haslend Road

0   ½

mile

■ Built-up areas

20

centre for a wide area and on a north/south road, but geographically its location was very different. Chesterfield was in a valley in the foothills of Derbyshire's High Peak district; Retford was surrounded by the flat fertile farmlands of north Nottinghamshire. There was also the important feature of the River Idle dividing the main town of thriving East Retford from the smaller and quieter West Retford. As with Chesterfield there was a form of local government; the Corporation consisting of two Bailiffs, a Town Clerk, two Sergeants at Mace and a Recorder. The Bailiffs were chosen annually by the Aldermen and Freemen of the town, the senior of the two being the equivalent of a Mayor. This organisation seems to have been of a rather more open nature than that of Chesterfield. It is true that the same names reappear in the different offices, if only for one year at a time, but it should be remembered that in a small market town the number of men educated enough to hold such offices was limited. And these men were no less ambitious or resourceful than their counterparts in Chesterfield. For many years they had been trying to improve Retford's transport links by making the River Idle navigable to the inland port of Bawtry, but to no avail. However, a major success had been achieved just two years before. In 1766, after much Parliamentary lobbying, they had obtained an Act to divert the Great North Road through the centre of Retford instead of by-passing the town a few miles to the west. Strange as this may seem to modern minds – their aim being the complete opposite of the hopes of many of today's small towns – the passing coaches and wagons brought the trade and wealth that was to allow Retford to become financially involved in the new canal. With a major highway going north/south and a new canal going east/west Retford would be well situated to make a wealthy future for itself and, of course, its influential citizens.[*]

৯ ৯ ৯

Another important basic difference between the two towns was that

---

[*] For obvious reasons Retford ensured that when the Great North Road was diverted through the town the great herds kept to the old road and continued to by-pass the Market Square. Carriages, wagons and stage-coaches would bring wealth and trade – thousands of animals would bring less beneficial blessings.

21

James Brindley

Retford was an agricultural market-town lacking in raw materials, especially coal, but rich in arable produce. Chesterfield, on the other hand, had an additional important trade in heavy raw materials dug from the hills of Derbyshire – coal, lead, stone – the transport of which was expensive and difficult. The supply of such commodities was crucial to the expansion of the nation's fledgling industries and, of course, to Chesterfield's ambitions. As to imports, both towns wished to have the good things of life that their new wealth would make possible; fine materials, porcelain, exotic food. In simplistic terms what was needed in both towns was a method of transporting heavy or bulky goods out, and desirable consumer goods in. Of course it was not a unique problem, in fact it was national.

A few years before, in Lancashire, the Duke of Bridgewater had had exactly the same transport problems. Chiefly, how to move the coal from his mines at Worsley to the neighbouring, and booming, city of Manchester. And not simply to move the coal but to be able to do so in enough bulk and at a cheap enough price to undercut other suppliers and make a good profit. The water transport in the area was controlled by the proprietors of the Mersey & Irwell Navigation. They had made improvements to the rivers to aid boat traffic but their toll charges reflected their monopoly, by paying them the Duke could not undercut the price of coal in Manchester. His solution was to become the source of a revolution in goods transportation in this country and the start of the canal age. The Duke employed the talents of a millwright who had locally built a high reputation for harnessing the power of water and channelling it to and from various locations. His name was James Brindley and he built an artificial waterway between the Duke's coal mine and Manchester, therefore bringing the ease of water transport to the whole journey. This was the Bridgewater Canal. By using the canal the Duke drastically reduced his transport costs and he sold his coal at half the price previously charged. To the Duke this brought huge financial rewards; to Brindley a career as the nation's foremost canal engineer. There were other civil engineers of the time who could have done the work but such was the fame of the Bridgewater Canal that Brindley took the chance to make his name known throughout England. From then on most of the future Canal

Companies considered that he was "the" engineer for their project. He did surveys for, or gave advice to, the Chester Canal, the Lower Avon Navigation, the Calder & Hebble Navigation, the Grand Trunk Canal (Trent & Mersey) and others in Bradford, Rochdale and Darlington; all these in addition to being involved in extensions to the Bridgewater. Eventually there were so many being built at the same time that he trained assistants to be the on-site engineer of each project whilst he travelled between each enterprise in the role of consultant engineer. Nevertheless, these canals are all known as Brindley's work, and one of them was the Chesterfield Canal.

PART ONE

PLANNING AND FINANCE

1769

The King is George III – Lord Grafton is Prime Minister – There has been a series of bad harvests – Captain Cook is on his first voyage of discovery – James Watt has patented improvements to his steam engine.

August, 1769

It is also certain, that the Ministry have promised to repeal the American Duties on Paint, Paper, and Glass, with a View to quiet, for the present, the Minds of the People in that Country; but the Duty on Tea is to remain. Those who best know the Dispositions of the Americans say, that their Jealousies and Fears will never subside, not even in Part, till every iota, real or nominal, of Taxation is wholly repealed.

Borough of Derby,

11th Sept 1769

Whereas Complaints have been made to us against persons leaving their Waggons, Carts, and other Nuisances in the public Streets and Highways leading to this Town, and the Owners thereof being sent to remove the same, have promised Time after Time to do, but have neglected. It is therefore Ordered, That whatever Carts or Carriages are found standing in the said Streets any longer than is necessary for the Loading or Unloading the same, the Penalty of Ten Shillings, according to Act of Parliament, will be levied upon the respective Owners thereof.

WILLIAM EVANS, Mayor

STRAY'D or CONVEY'D, from WORKSOP, on Tuesday Morning the 5th of September,

A Strong Brown MARE

about 14 Hands high, aged, with a cut Tail, a little White in the Forehead, her hind Legs both white, goes pretty well on her Legs, and rather offers to leer when any Body come nigh her.

Whoever can give Notice of the above Mare so as she may be had again to John Mason of Worksop, shall receive One Guinea Reward, and all reasonable Charges.

October 1769

On Saturday five Prisoners were tried at the Old Bailey, one of whom was capitally convicted, viz. John Maycock, a Blacksmith, for robbing Luke Shirbourn on the Highway between Stepney and Bow, of 13s. One was cast for Transportation, and three acquitted.

CHAPTER ONE

A Canal for Chesterfield

By June 1761 the Bridgewater Canal had become a national monument to business acumen, hard work, and ingenuity. It had taken civil engineering into realms of achievement previously thought impossible, if thought of at all. The canal became a tourist attraction with visitors from all over England. The incredulity caused by the sight of the canal passing 39ft over the River Irwell on the spectacular Barton Aqueduct is difficult to accept now. But eminent engineers had poured scorn on the possibility of such a feat which, when successful, only added to the prestige of the construction. Over the next five years the business and financial lessons taught by the Bridgewater Canal permeated into the thinking of merchants and manufacturers throughout the country – if it can be done there, why not here? High transport costs had been accepted as unavoidable for generations but there was now a way they could be substantially reduced, thereby opening up new markets and increasing profits. By 1766 the first canal-building boom had started.

Chesterfield was not immune to this first flush of canal fever. As early as 1768 the business community began to discuss the construction of a canal to carry the trade of the town and the surrounding districts. For as long as anyone could remember the main trade route from the area had been by road to Bawtry, the goods being carried by pack-horse trains or on lumbering wagons. This was very unsatisfactory. For instance in winter, just when the market for coal was at its peak, the road conditions were usually so bad that the poor beasts could not make the journey at all. The output of Derbyshire's lead-mines was wanted at all times but again it could not be moved for many months of the year. At Bawtry the heavy loads were transferred to boats on the River Idle for further passage via the substantial river systems of eastern England. There had been some previous plans to offer alternative trade routes. For instance in pre-canal days, about 1731, there had been a proposal to make Chesterfield's own river, the Rother, navigable to within six miles of the town. The engineer, William Palmer, did a survey and reported that there would not be any great difficulties or expense in bringing the river up to navigable standards as far as Beighton.[1] Presumably the more hilly terrain beyond that point would have made it prohibitively expensive to extend the works to Chesterfield itself, or perhaps it was technically beyond the expertise of those pre-Brindley years. This plan, which would have given Chesterfield's goods access to the river system via the Rother and the Don, was promoted by the Don Navigation Company who had long cast envious eyes on Chesterfield's rich mineral trade. But it came to nothing and the pack-horses continued to struggle to Bawtry. This kind of aggressive business challenge was indicative of the age, those who assumed that things would always be done in the traditional way often lost out in these battles. Bawtry had already lost a considerable amount of business when the Don Navigation had taken the Sheffield, Rotherham and Doncaster trade, much of which had previously gone via the busy inland port. But the lesson was not learnt and very soon the Chesterfield Canal was to deal a death-blow to Bawtry's waterborne trade.

➚ ➚ ➚

Because of the heavy weight of its product the initial impetus for a canal came from the lead-mining industry, the figure-head of which was William, 5th Duke of Devonshire. The Duke was a member of the powerful Cavendish family who had continued to exert a tremendous amount of local influence ever since the days of their great Elizabethan, Bess of Hardwick. Their Chatsworth mansion continues to stand in a beautiful part of Derbyshire, just eight miles from Chesterfield. Cavendish power was also felt in Parliament, but their Royal prestige was at a low ebb, the previous Duke having resigned from all his Court offices in 1763. And for all his status the present Duke was only an unmarried man of nineteen. He had inherited the title as little as four years before so it is likely that the main influence for the canal came from his advisers. Of these his uncles, Lord George and Lord John Cavendish, were strongly in

Typical Dress of 1760/70

favour and their Parliamentary expertise was to become very useful in the near future. The Duke's main adviser on lead-mining was Alexander Barker whose family had used the industry to become rich and commanding; Barker was also an advocate of a canal. These opinions were crucial as objections by the Duke of Devonshire would have effectively ensured that the embryonic canal would have been still-born. Also significant were the business links between Alexander Barker and the Wilkinson family of Chesterfield. The latter were financiers and shareholders in various lead-mines, including 50% of the Gregory mine in Ashover which was one of the richest in Derbyshire at that time. The Wilkinson's also owned smelting mills, were merchants and exporters of some significance and later, when financial services became more organised, developed into Chesterfield's earliest bankers. Two Wilkinson's, Isaac and Allwood, were eventually to play central roles in the Canal Company – Allwood being appointed to the joint post of Treasurer as soon as the Company was formed.

A second vital link between the Duke of Devonshire and Chesterfield was Godfrey Heathcote, a solicitor in the town who had been Chief Steward and Auditor to successive Dukes for the last fifteen years. But of equal consequence to the canal scheme was the fact that Heathcote also held the office of Clerk of the Peace for Derbyshire, the top administrative post in the county.[2] In addition he ran a flourishing law practice in an office near the Market Place in Chesterfield, so flourishing that his house had six acres of land, a garden, and a coach-house and stables. These combined circumstances made Heathcote a vital participant in the early stages of planning the canal, but his many years of legal and administrative experience also meant that his age would not allow him to be physically active. Travelling to meetings and discussions via the infamous roads was not easy for him because he was sixty-seven, a reasonably old age for the eighteenth century. His wife Dorothy had died two years before and their two children had died when young, Ralph when he was thirteen and little Dorothy when she was only one year old.[3] Heathcote himself was not in the best of health and the lonely old man may have found comfort in his strong connections with the church.

Godfrey Heathcote shared his Chesterfield law office with a junior partner who, because of his senior's age and ill-health, was to take on the central and vital task of the Canal Company's chief administrator and legal adviser. He was to have a key involvement in the canal's construction and his name was Anthony Lax. A young man, only twenty-six, he was originally from North Yorkshire but now lived in Glumangate, Chesterfield.[4] He was somewhat officious, tended towards pomposity, was careful about his appearance, low on humour, high on ambition; but most importantly he was efficient and energetic. To him would fall most of the arduous travelling involved in organising a large project in an age with bad roads and no telephones. He was ten years younger than his wife Dorothy who was the favourite niece of his childless senior partner. Obviously this was an advantageous marriage for the young lawyer but the passage of time hinders any judgement on whether it was based on love or ambition. Lax was the eldest of ten children and his parents were still alive, his family attachment being mainly to his mother. She was of the opinion that she had married beneath her status, indeed as soon as her husband died she began the legal proceedings to revert to her single name of Maynard.[*] Her son's ambitions – for status and influence as much as money – may have stemmed from this base of family pride and the classic scenario, seen so often in history, of a strong mother promoting her eldest son to achieve the success she could not.

Other leading residents of Chesterfield were also involved at this early stage, most of them going on to become leading members of the Canal Company. In general, the principal participants were wealthy and successful men, mostly Corporation members or county officials, who were often linked by firm friendships and the marriage of their children. For example, John Frith owned a substantial amount of property on the southern side of the Market Place as well as his lead-mine shares and was a friend of Joseph Storrs. Samuel Jebb, a merchant, had been made Deputy Lieutenant of Derbyshire in 1762 and was to become Chief Magistrate (Mayor) of Chesterfield next year (1769). He had a "good farm home" at Walton where he lived for many years and the practiced flamboyance of his signature would be of interest to graphologists. There were two

---

[*]   After 1784 Lax used the name Anthony Lax Maynard in her honour.

Richard Milnes. One was a merchant and a Derbyshire JP, the other was a doctor with a fine large house at the north-west corner of New Square. Adam Slater was thirty-four, an apothecary and surgeon, and had been a Derbyshire JP. He probably lived at Durant Hall (part of the manor of Tapton). Samuel Towndrow was thirty-eight and had been the Chief Magistrate of Chesterfield the previous year (1767). Nevertheless, he was continually being told by the Manor Court to remove various types of detritus which his grocery business had left about the town - hogsheads and casks from outside his warehouse in the Shambles, dung and stone from Glumangate. His record of rubbish dumping was so bad that he still had judgements made against him when he was Foreman of the Jury. Nicholas Twigg lived at Dronfield near the Sheffield turnpike road and he had already been Chief Magistrate twice. His substantial house was of two storeys, with six rooms on each floor, and had a garden, orchard and eleven acres adjoining. William Cowley was the landlord at the Angel Inn where a good many of the Corporation's banquets were held and, he hoped, future Canal Company meetings.

The initial discussions about a canal probably took place during the second half of 1768 and it must have been agreed there was sufficient local interest to make the project feasible. However, it would be a mistake to assume that what they envisaged was the canal route we can see today. In fact they made the very human assumption that what they needed was an improvement to the trade route they had always used; taking goods to Bawtry had been the accepted practice for generations. As a result the canal was seen as an alternative method of reaching the same destination, a method which would avoid the dreadful roads. From Bawtry there were some problems with the Idle so they also considered the possible inclusion of navigational improvements to the river.[5]

Having come to these conclusions the next step was to engage a civil engineer to carry out a survey of the proposed route and to produce costings and time-scales. With this information they would be able to decide on the business viability of the plan and proceed as appropriate. Informal funds were raised to pay for the survey, after which the easiest decision was which engineer to approach. It had to be James Brindley. Almost all canal proprietors wanted the status of being involved with a Brindley waterway, it was fashionable and financially prudent, a hard combination to beat. Indeed such was Brindley's fame at that time it is possible that many parties would only become financially involved in such an advanced scheme if they were given the confidence of Brindley's hand on the helm.

ֵ֤א   ֵ֤א   ֵ֤א

Brindley was probably contacted during the autumn or winter of 1768. As he was so busy with various enterprises he delegated the initial survey to one of his assistants, all of whom had been trained on-site at the various work-camps. This way they became thoroughly imbued with Brindley's working methods, and could be trusted to carry out the work assigned to them in accordance with his perfectionist standards. The initial survey for the Chesterfield Canal was entrusted to John Varley. He was a young man and this would be his first big challenge, an opportunity to make a name for himself in the thriving and prosperous canal construction industry. If the survey was accepted and the project went ahead he could probably rely on Brindley suggesting to the Canal Company that he be appointed on-site engineer for the actual construction work. Brindley's suggestions were rarely ignored.

At the start of his great challenge in 1769 John Varley was only twenty-nine, his original training having been as a surveyor.[6] He may have been chosen because he was a Derbyshire man, originally from Heanor, a small town seventeen miles south of Chesterfield. But he had probably been trained by Brindley in Cheshire, at the work-camps of two of the master's major projects, the Bridgewater and the Trent & Mersey Canals. Certainly Hannah, his wife, was from Dutton which was just south of Runcorn. Up to now John's nomadic work had not allowed them to settle down. But if he got this job . . . well then it would be different, they would have to stay in the area for some years and a family home would be possible. Varley would not have brought Hannah with him in 1769; horseback was the most efficient form of personal transport but women rarely travelled in such a way. Also, it would be a long time, even if the initial survey was accepted, before construction could begin and he would be expected to do other work in the meantime. Settling in the Chesterfield area was not yet a viable proposition for John and Hannah Varley.

ﺰ   ﺰ   ﺰ

It can only be surmised but Brindley probably met the Chesterfield promoters of the canal in the early spring of 1769, as soon as travel was again possible after the winter. It is also likely that he introduced Varley and took the opportunity to look at the geography of the area together with his assistant. About April 1769, not later, Varley carried out a survey of the land between Chesterfield and Bawtry. His resultant proposal was for the canal to follow a quite obvious route and an independent survey done a few years later did not disagree with his findings.

Chesterfield's location was in the Rother Valley which at that point ran almost due north/south. Bawtry was twenty-four miles away to the north-east in a totally different river valley, the hills to the east of Chesterfield being the main barrier between the two. Varley had found that between one and two miles to the north of Chesterfield the Rother turned to the east and as a consequence its valley widened and the river flowed in a very useful north-east direction. Varley had no intention of actually using the river to form the canal, that was certainly no part of Brindley's doctrine. His opinion on unregulated flowing water was not open to discussion; Brindley liked water to be organised and for it to move as he wished, not otherwise. But it was Brindley practice that canals should follow the contours of the land wherever possible, therefore maintaining a reasonably level course that was easy to build and use. Making water climb or descend steep hills was to be avoided whenever it was cost effective to do so.*

---

* This philosophy has resulted in the phrase "a typical Brindley Canal", now used when describing early waterways. Their history is still distinguishable by their winding routes, quite different from later canals. By then engineering techniques had been developed to create large embankments over valleys and deep cuttings through hills, resulting in much straighter canals.

A second vital reason for using valleys was to obtain a substantial water supply for the canal. This could only come from local rivers and streams, either directly into the canal or via storage in reservoirs. Either way it is important to realise that water was a valuable commodity in a century without plumbing and public supplies. As a result it was not allowed to simply flow away to the sea and almost all rivers and streams had already been put to some use. A canal needing millions of gallons each day was bound to disrupt someone's supplies. As we shall see later the political problems caused by water were intense and hard-fought.

So for these basic reasons Varley followed the Rother. The flow of the river showed that the valley floor was not level and the canal was planned to fall 60ft from its beginning to where it would cross the Rother's tributary, the Doe Lea. From the Doe Lea to Killamarsh the canal was to be kept level, which must have meant small embankments being used. Near Killamarsh the Rother passed into Yorkshire and ceased to be of use to Varley, its course going due north to Rotherham where it flowed into the River Don. The great ridge of high ground to the east could no longer be avoided. It did end a further ten miles to the north but taking the canal that far out of its way to avoid hills was not cost effective. Even if it had been there was another important reason for not going that way. At the end of the hills was the valley of the River Don, and that was the territory of the already powerful Don Navigation Company. They would not countenance any opposition to their river trade although they would probably have welcomed Chesterfield's canal joining the Don and going no further. The boats from the canal would then have to use their river for the rest of their journey and increased traffic meant increased toll revenue. But Varley knew that his proprietors in Chesterfield wished to have the independence of a waterway of their own linked with Bawtry. What he may not have known was that the canal promoters intended to rival the Don Navigation Company by under-cutting the cost of coal supplied to the markets. So for the two reasons of construction costs and commercial politics Varley had to find another way.

There was no alternative. The proposed canal would have to cross the eastern hills so Varley looked for the most suitable location. He had

35

Crossing the Hills between
Chesterfield and Bawtry

Kiveton Park

R. Ryton

Wales

Norwood

Killamarsh

Harthill

Shireoaks

Pebley Reservoir

River Rother

Eckington

Spinkhill

Staveley

CHESTERFIELD

Doe Lea

N

0   1   2
MILES

━━   VARLEY'S ROUTE FOR THE
     WESTERN END OF THE CANAL

═ ═   NORWOOD TUNNEL (630 YDS)

36

three main considerations. Firstly, to choose a route that could be crossed using the engineering skills of the day. Secondly, to keep construction costs to a minimum. And thirdly, to ensure that water could be made available to supply the canal where it climbed to its greatest height. Just beyond Killamarsh, at Norwood, he found what he was looking for. Here the hills began to lose height on their descent to the Don valley and, of crucial importance, the width of the barrier was substantially less because long before in the ice age a glacier had gouged a deep valley into its eastern flank. Even so, crossing the hills would still be a substantial challenge and on a par with the boldest schemes of the day. Varley planned to have the canal climb 120ft from the valley bottom by using flights of locks, how many and in what configuration is not known.[*] The remaining height, 28ft, was to be bypassed by excavating a tunnel, 630yds long, to carry the canal under the hill tops and into the head of the convenient glacial valley on the other side.[7] Tunnelling was fraught with problems, danger and expense. But Varley judged it to be necessary because the water supply would have to flow down to the canal from reservoirs in the higher hills, and the reservoirs would need adequate catchment areas higher than themselves. If the canal had climbed to the summit there would not have been many higher points from which the water could have been supplied. The important decision from a cost point of view was how high to climb using locks and therefore at what height to tunnel? The lower down the hillside the longer the tunnel would have to be as it passed through nearer to the wider base of the hills.

Once he had made his decisions on crossing the hills Varley had a much easier task in planning the rest of the route to Bawtry. He followed the glacial valley, locking down 120ft whilst doing so, and when that petered out near Shireoaks he crossed the remaining low lands in an almost straight line, falling a further 152ft along the way, and approaching Bawtry from the south-west. He must also have surveyed from Bawtry to the Trent, but it is not known if he planned to improve the Idle or build a separate canal across the flat land, most of which was below sea level and latticed with drainage ditches. From the few papers remaining it may be

---

[*] For general description of a canal lock, see Appendix A.

judged that a separate canal was intended, and certainly this would have avoided any connection with the owners of the Idle navigation rights. But no definite proof has yet been found, only that it was to meet the Trent at West Stockwith which is where the Idle also ends. Even so it cannot be assumed the plan was to use the Idle, there were other good reasons for a canal to go to West Stockwith, as we shall see later.[8]

The survey would have entailed Varley spending a considerable amount of time riding throughout the area on horse-back, "taking the levells", and writing his findings in a note book. Varley would have used the basic land surveying principle of triangulation and would have had the use of a theodolite, an early example having been made fifty years before. The levels were taken with a spirit level attached to a telescope through which two staffs with movable markers on them were sighted. By moving the markers up and down the staffs until they met in the cross wires of the measuring instrument the difference between the two markers was the difference in the height of the land at those points. Although the surveying instruments of the time were accurate they did not measure the curvature of the earth, an allowance for which had to be manually calculated. It was not until the early 1780's that the first theodolite capable of measuring the curvature of the earth was made for the infant Ordnance Survey. Such was its importance that its development was paid for by the King and it is now known as the "father of accurate theodolites".[9]

The next step would have been for Varley to discuss his findings and decisions with Brindley and then, when accepted, to produce a map of the route. This would then be shown to the proprietors in Chesterfield when Brindley made his presentation to them. The professional training of a surveyor such as Varley was expected to include an ability to create hand-drawn maps of great quality, and Varley's skill in this field was of a very high standard.[*] His original map for the Bawtry route of 1769 has survived and when recently shown to the staff of the Map Room at the

---

[*] The original was then taken to a printer who produced as many copies as required. The design was engraved into a copper plate and printed in a roller press, by exerting considerable pressure the ink was squeezed from the incised lines on the plate and transferred to the paper.

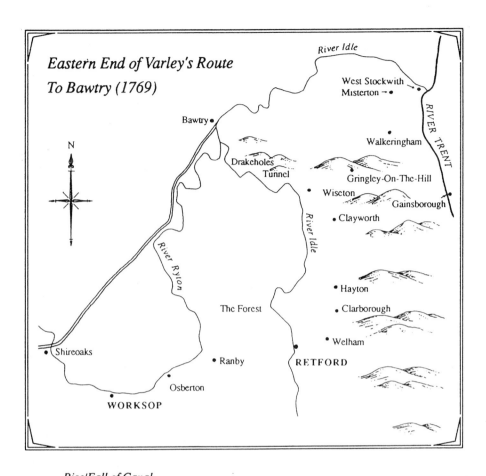

Eastern End of Varley's Route
To Bawtry (1769)

River Idle

West Stockwith
Misterton →

Bawtry ●

Walkeringham

Drakeholes
Tunnel

Gringley-On-The-Hill

Wiseton

Gainsborough

● Clayworth

N

River Ryton

River Idle

RIVER TRENT

● Hayton

The Forest

● Clarborough

● Welham

● Shireoaks

● Ranby

RETFORD

Osberton

WORKSOP

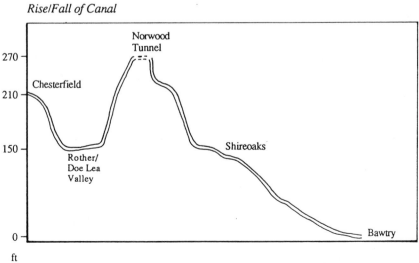

Rise/Fall of Canal

Norwood
Tunnel

270 –

Chesterfield

210 –

150 –

Rother/
Doe Lea
Valley

Shireoaks

Bawtry

0 –

ft

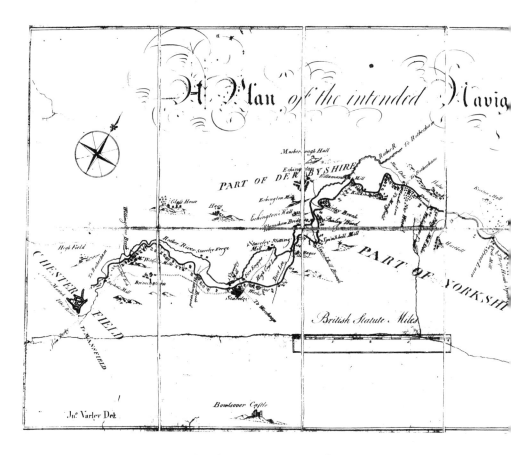

Varley hand-drawn map[10]

British Library it took their experienced eyes to confirm that it was indeed hand-drawn and not printed. They also said that in their opinion the quality, style and complexity of the content pointed to Varley trying to make a very good impression on Brindley and the Chesterfield proprietors. Certainly it is much more flamboyant, intricate and involved than subsequent maps he was to produce and it must have taken a considerable amount of time and patience. This seems to tie in with Varley being keen to make a good impression; to show that he was up to the challenge of this, his first great project, and that the Chesterfield Canal would be safe in his hands.

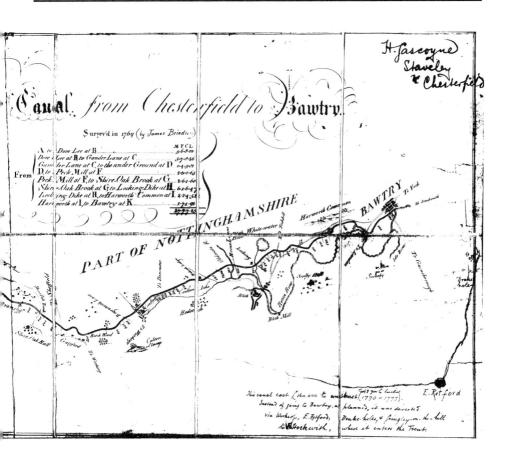

At a subsequent meeting, probably held in Chesterfield, the interested parties were told that the canal to Bawtry would be 28 miles long, within its banks it would be over 28ft wide, the banks themselves being a further 12ft on each side. It had been designed to carry boats 70ft long, 7ft wide, which would be horse-drawn with a crew of two. It was thought that a boat would "make a voige in 4 days" and that every 24hrs it would need six men and three horses to navigate each boat.[11] This may have meant two men and a horse doing eight-hour shifts and three crews covering the 24hrs, in which case they appear to have expected the boats to be worked throughout the night, summer and winter. Or it could have meant less hours for each crew and the boat stopped at night, although short hours of work are not usually associated with the eighteenth century. Certainly some of the old boatmen living now can remember working through the night, but only in the summer if they had an urgent cargo or just wanted to get home. In the winter they did not consider it possible, the dark, long nights and ice and snow being a dangerous mixture.

Brindley also announced that the cost of building the whole route would be £100,000, a suspiciously round figure which may indicate a lack of detailed costings.* Whatever basic figures it may have lacked Brindley had allowed for 25% higher costs than he had ever done before.[12] Why he should have done that is not clear; a prudent contingency allowance, a feeling that the tunnel at Norwood might give problems, astute knowledge that suppliers always increased their costs to large schemes? Probably a mixture of many reasons, mostly his already wide experience of the problems that could be caused by the volatile mixture of human nature, politics, profits and high-risk engineering. Although he had been born in Derbyshire Brindley's knowledge of the business world of Chesterfield must have been limited, so it is more likely that the extremely optimistic figures for projected cargoes and profits that were published were the work of the local promoters of the canal. Of course they had good reasons for projecting an image of high financial rewards for imminent investors. But the variety of cargo, and the amounts of each, that they forecast would have been difficult to achieve even if the thriving national trade conditions of 1769 had continued, which, in hindsight, they did not. So there was an element of either uncontrolled enthusiasm or devious exaggeration. As will be the case in many situations in the canal's creation the judgement at this distance in time must be a personal opinion.

So that was the package presented to Chesterfield's business men. Now they could discuss the merits of the scheme, try to ascertain the likelihood of adequate investment and decide whether or not to proceed further. By this time the normal procedure for raising funds for canal construction was to form a private Company and issue shares to the public. The Duke of

---

*   To convert financial amounts to current values, multiply by 50.

Bridgewater had financed his canal himself but even his wealth had almost given out before the project became a success, so a share issue was now the usual option.

Meanwhile John Varley took the opportunity to go off and do some surveying work in his own right. After all, he was Brindley's man in the area and might as well cash in on the reflected glory and earn some money for himself. He had not much to do while Chesterfield was making up its mind on his future employment. The Marquis of Rockingham was another of the very powerful men of the time and he wanted a short canal, less than two miles, to link the road from Rotherham to the Don Navigation. About April or May 1769 Varley surveyed two routes, drew a map and produced written costings.[13] This venture is interesting as it gives us a second viewpoint from which to judge Varley and his work and it also reveals more details of his paperwork. The map was again very well drawn but nowhere near as ornate as his Chesterfield-Bawtry example, even though the work was being done for the Marquis of Rockingham. His report on the costings was brief, almost inadequate. If it reflects the way Brindley had taught him to make financial estimates, and there is no reason to suppose otherwise, it may explain why the cost of the Chesterfield Canal was a nice, round £100,000. The Marquis did not immediately build his canal but he did resurrect the idea in 1775 and then, possibly because Varley was otherwise employed, he engaged John Smeaton who was one of the country's most illustrious civil engineers. Smeaton based his proposals on the previous work done on the project and his comments on Varley's findings give us a valuable example of one 18th century engineer commenting on another. They may also throw light upon Varley's original thinking for the Chesterfield Canal and the initial mistakes he may have made. Smeaton found no fault with the surveying, a reflection of Varley's original profession and prime skill. But he did find that the idea of using a few deep locks would give water supply problems. By making more, but shallower, locks this would be solved. Also Smeaton's costings were much more detailed in their construction estimates. He had also allowed for possible future changes in the business markets and for flood protection against the River Don, neither of which had been taken into account by Varley.[14] To sum up, Varley's work seems to have been a good survey but he lacked insight into other important aspects. He should have considered the need for detailed reports, an understanding of business costs, the geographical problems of the local area, his proprietor's needs and requirements. Altogether it appears to have been the work of a young surveyor with engineering ability, but not much experience of commercial reality.[*]

---

[*] Now known as the Greasbrough Canal it was eventually built by William Jessop to a survey done by William Fairbank in 1778.

1769

October 1769

They write from Jamaica, that Commodore Forest had dispatched two Frigates of War to the Bay of Honduras, to demand Satisfaction of the Spanish Governor, for some Insults offered to the British Logwood Cutters on the Bay.

It is said that an Order has been sent to Portsmouth and Plymouth to take into the King's Service an additional Number of Seamen, to be distributed on board several Guard Ships till draughted for Service.

A Detachment from the First (or Royal) Regiment of Foot, was ordered, on Saturday Morning to be embarked at Portsmouth for Jersey immediately, to quell some Disturbances, which have arisen on that Island.

Advices is said to be received, that some of the East India Company's Ships had destroyed a Number of armed Grabs belonging to the Marattas; by which the Naval Force of these Pirates had been greatly weakened.

December 1769

We hear that there is to be a total Change in the Government of America, and that shortly there will be a Viceroy sent thither, who is to be empowered to preside, similar to the Lord Lieutenant of Ireland, and that the Administration of Affairs will be new modelled in such a Manner, as to put an End to the present alarming Disputes between Great Britain and the Colonies.

CHAPTER TWO

What about Retford?

The diversion of the Great North Road through Retford two years before had been a great success and the busy little Nottinghamshire town had gained considerable trade and affluence. The Saturday market was well stocked with malt, barley, meat, vegetables and hops; the hops being grown in large plantations around the town. The River Idle was a problem though. If it could have been made navigable downstream to Bawtry it could have been of great benefit but it continued to defy all attempts to do so. All it did do was make the land to the south of Retford marshy, almost useless, and with distressing regularity it flooded the town itself. The water level usually rose very quickly and quite a torrent often raced into Retford tearing up what paved areas there were. Sometimes the Market Square was covered as deep as three feet and the receding flood always left stagnant water and bad smells.

As the Idle stubbornly refused to allow itself to become an alternative to the bad roads – and in low-lying north Nottinghamshire they could be very bad – it was not surprising that when rumours of Chesterfield's canal plans reached Retford men of vision saw possibilities for their own town. In fact it would be more accurate to say that one visionary realised the magnitude of the potential gains. His foresight eventually made him a central character in the story of the Chesterfield Canal; the Reverend Seth Ellis Stevenson.

A prominent Retford personality, Stevenson was headmaster of the Grammar School and was later described as "a real gentleman and scholar, generous, public-spirited, a conscientious teacher and a good father". In his youth he had been thought over-confident and aggressive but by 1768 he was forty-four and had been mellowed by age and a comfortable life-style. He was a typical parson of the 18th century. Hardly zealous in his church duties, doing just enough but certainly not negligent; he took snuff, gambled at cards, and enjoyed brandy and wine. He dressed well. His stockings were black and made of "superfine cotton" or silk, more than once he bought silver buckles for his shoes, his gloves were leather, his handkerchiefs silk, and he regularly paid for his shoes to be cleaned. But he was no dandy. Instead he was an avid gardener and farmer who did much of the work himself, his most popular line being the pigs he fed and fattened with his own recipes. He was a Cambridge graduate and a man of wide interests. As the secretary of a circulating library he undertook the distribution of periodicals like The Universal Magazine, The Gentleman's Magazine and various Reviews to the gentlemen of the neighbourhood. He took an active interest in local politics and also had a general awareness of the great changes that were happening in the country. His first wife had died six years ago but now he was happily married to Elizabeth, and his five children ranged from seventeen year old Billy to little Beth who was three.

In the previous April (1767) Seth Ellis Stevenson had travelled to the north-west of England with his friend, Mr Shilleto. Stevenson's curiosity to see the area had been aroused during the winter. He had read a recently published pamphlet about the controversial new concept of canals and, as a result, he had wanted to see the canal sites for himself and to form his own opinion. He and his friend had waited for the roads to become safe after the winter ice and spring floods, not willing to risk an accident as the winter had already been marred by one tragedy in the Stevenson family. Their new-born son Henry had only lived for three weeks, Seth Ellis baptising him at a private service on the first day of the year. Little Henry died ten days later. By the middle of April the dark days had receded and the Reverend Stevenson and Mr Shilleto had set out on horseback for Manchester, Liverpool, Chester and Shrewsbury, returning via Litchfield and Derby. The tour took nine days, during which time Seth Ellis Stevenson enthusiastically learnt about the new engineering thresholds and general information about canals. This was knowledge that was to have a radical effect on the Chesterfield Canal.

⁂

By December 1768 Stevenson had heard the rumours about Chesterfield's plans. Others may not have seen any relevance in what was going on in Derbyshire, but the facts learnt on his tour enabled him to see the potential business opportunities for Retford. But only if the proposed route was changed. Stevenson used to dine regularly, both as host and guest, with the other leading citizens of Retford and on Boxing Day he invited twelve of the most prominent to dinner. It may be that during the evening he outlined his proposal for the canal; still to go from Chesterfield to the River Trent, but this time via Retford and not Bawtry. Certainly the twelve men invited that evening all became leading members of the Canal Company and were involved in the earliest planning and promotion.

The Retford men were similar to their Chesterfield counterparts in age, background, influence and experience. John Bright was typical. An orderly, tidy man, he was a solicitor and had spent many years as a member of the Corporation of East Retford and had been a Bailiff twice. He had been to Parliament to lobby the Borough's MPs about diverting the Great North Road and was of enough stature to visit the Duke of Newcastle at nearby Clumber Park. (His social stature we can only surmise but his weight was 11st 11lbs in his boots . . . the Duke had a set of new-fangled scales and insisted on weighing all his family and guests!).[1] Thomas Brumby was an Alderman and Bailiff who had a "manufactury" and was currently advertising for weavers to make various types of cloth. Thomas Cockshutt was the rector at Ordsall. Captain George Brown owned a considerable amount of land to the west of Retford, the canal eventually going through a large section of it. (Another of the Duke of Newcastle's weighing machine victims . . . he was 14st 4lbs in his boots). Lindley Simpson's home was Babworth Hall which was to benefit greatly from a private canal wharf. Robert Sutton was a senior member of the community and a great benefactor to Retford. He was sixty-nine and had amassed a fine collection of titles during his long career; Alderman, Bailiff, Master of the King's Staghounds in Sherwood Forest, Gentleman Usher to Queen Caroline, a JP and Deputy-Lieutenant of Nottinghamshire. Anthony Eyre lived at Grove Hall, his 1500 acre estate giving extensive views from its elevated position just south of Retford. He and his family frequently visited the Duke of Newcastle at Clumber Park. (15st 11lbs in his shoes). Others were

William Kirke, "a gentleman, originally from Liverpool". John Mason, already a Bailiff four times, soon to become a JP. Sampson Mosman, supplier of cloth and clothes but most famed for being the father of triplets. George Mason, agent to the Duke of Newcastle in Nottinghamshire (a booted 11st 8lb). John Parker, Alderman and Bailiff. And George Poplewell, Bailiff, Alderman and financier, in the future he was to hold the office of joint Treasurer to the Canal Company.

The idea of a canal for Retford was embraced enthusiastically. It was felt that it would fit in so well with the town's ambition of expanding to become a trading centre for a much larger area. The Great North Road already gave access to London and the north, and now the possibility of a canal link to coal-rich Derbyshire and the strategically important River Trent. As had been done in Chesterfield, where the Duke of Devonshire and his Cavendish family held much influence, Retford was also careful to involve its equivalent grandee, the Duke of Newcastle, who lived just six miles away. The Duke had inherited the title only the year before but since 1760 he had been developing Clumber Park into a country seat for his eventual succession. By 1769 he had already built most of the house but the creation of the landscape and the lake were to take another twenty years. The new, raw Clumber Park visited by the Retford canal promoters was far different from that now enjoyed by the public.* Another important contact was Sir Cecil Wray, a wealthy Lincolnshire Baronet who had been elected MP for Retford a year ago (1768). At that election one of his most enthusiastic canvassers had been Seth Ellis Stevenson whose main motivation had been the curtailment of the Duke of Newcastle's influence in local affairs.

Sometime in 1769, probably about May, a delegation suggested to Chesterfield that a route via Retford would be of great benefit to both towns. There was really no reason for Chesterfield to disagree. They would still have a link to the River Trent, Retford would become a market for their goods carried on the canal (especially the coal), the financial burden would be halved, and Retford's experience of Parliamentary lobbying

---

* Clumber Park is now a National Trust property of 3,800 acres, six miles south-west of Retford.

would be valuable. The new route would also remove the problems likely to be caused by the owners of the very low-lying land on the approach to Bawtry. In the past this land had been the flood-plain of the Trent and only a complicated drainage system kept it usable. It was a common opinion that canals going across low land paid little heed to such practicalities and as a result often ruined the drainage and drowned the surrounding meadows. All things considered, the least Chesterfield could do was investigate the possibilities and Brindley was asked to suggest a new route. On 15 June 1769 Varley arrived in the Retford area to carry out the survey.[2] He was accompanied by some of the Chesterfield gentlemen who had come to discuss matters further and they were wined and dined by Seth Ellis Stevenson. Varley stayed in the district for at least six weeks as he carried out his surveying duties. An anomaly of his situation was that he was not paid a salary until later when the Canal Company was formed. In the meantime he needed several loans from Stevenson to pay his living expenses, no wonder he was unable to bring his wife to the area and build a home.

The first section of the original route to Bawtry – from Chesterfield, along the Rother valley, across the hills at Norwood and along the glacial valley to Shireoaks – was still valid. The change would be after that when the new route would go further east to Worksop and then to Retford, using slightly higher ground to skirt the edge of the controversial low-lying areas. From Retford it was to progress as appropriate to the original destination, West Stockwith on the River Trent. The survey showed that such a route was feasible and the Bawtry option was forgotten. There would be further disagreements about the site of the canal's junction with the Trent but it was beyond dispute that the canal would pass through Retford. Privately it had been agreed that the Canal Company would be tightly controlled by joint representatives from Chesterfield and Retford, and there were two good reasons for this. Firstly, it would ensure that no other group could interfere with their plans. Secondly, it would balance the influence that could be exerted by making sure there would be an equal number of committee appointees and salaried officials from each town. Partners they may have been but both groups saw a need to stop the other gaining dominance in the Company –

they did not equate trust with business convenience. This was to be the pattern throughout the construction of the canal. The participants from each of the two towns did not really know each other, travelling for any reason other than business was not often undertaken, they were very much separate partners in a venture that just happened to benefit both areas.

By early August 1769 the proprietors had completed their private arrangements for the Company and were ready to make the first declaration of their intentions. Advertisements in local newspapers announced that on 24 August a public meeting would be held at the Red Lion in Worksop at 11.00am. The famous Mr Brindley would be present to make his report on the route surveys and "landowners, merchants, traders and manufacturers – of the counties of Derby, York, Nottingham and Lincoln" were invited to attend, either as prospective investors or objectors. The canal was to terminate at West Stockwith.[3]*

Despite the private arrangements made by Chesterfield and Retford a third powerbase did develop and by the date of the public meeting the influential men of Lincolnshire had already scored a significant victory. They suggested that if much of the canal's cargo was to be destined for sale to national markets at Gainsborough then why not have the canal join the Trent opposite that town, and not four and a half miles further downstream.[4] If the canal ended at West Stockwith cargoes would then have to be taken up the tidal section of the Trent to Gainsborough, increasing costs and transportation problems. If the canal ended opposite Gainsborough then extra wharfs on the west bank of the Trent would mean that cargo could be marketed without any further delay. Of course, it would also ensure that most of the canal's goods were sold via Gainsborough, increasing the town's trade and the gentlemen's profits. Not only had they advised Brindley of their ideas but the great man had quickly surveyed the route they were advocating (probably Varley's work again) and had decided in Lincolnshire's favour! Sir Cecil Wray MP may have represented Retford but he was a Lincolnshire man

---

* The use of Worksop for early meetings is interesting. The reason may be that it was on the proposed route but "neutral territory", neither Retford nor Chesterfield allowing the other to gain "home" advantage? Perhaps the inn had the largest room?

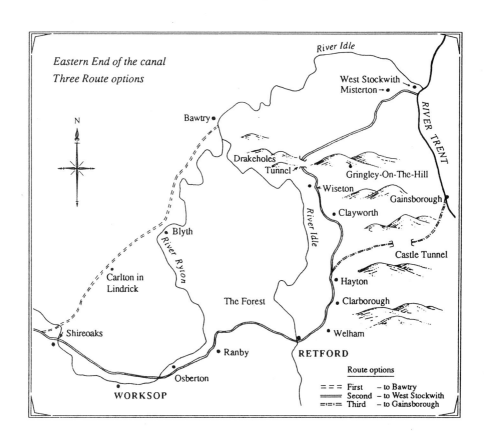

Eastern End of the canal
Three Route options

N

River Idle

West Stockwith
Misterton →

RIVER TRENT

Bawtry

Drakeholes
Tunnel

Gringley-On-The-Hill

Wiseton

Gainsborough

River Idle

Clayworth

Blyth

River Ryton

Castle Tunnel

Carlton in
Lindrick

Hayton

The Forest

Clarborough

Shireoaks

Welham

Ranby

RETFORD

Osberton

WORKSOP

Route options

=== First   – to Bawtry
─── Second – to West Stockwith
=ı=ı= Third   – to Gainsborough

52

and he could see a way to benefit both areas. But these changes did not please the Retford interests, it was true the canal would still go through the town but a strong Lincolnshire influence in the Company was not appreciated.

On 24 August 1769, the day of the first public meeting, the Red Lion at Worksop was crowded. Some people had travelled that morning – 11am was a popular time for meetings for that reason, allowing some hours of daylight travel on the unlit roads – others had arrived the night before and stayed at the inn. Almost all the Canal Company's public and private meetings would be held at inns, the usual practice of the time. Such establishments were easy to find by visitors; they had the large rooms necessary for public meetings; overnight accommodation was available, especially useful in the winter when there were few daylight hours for travelling. Food was available after a long, arduous journey; postal collections and deliveries were often made there; and the inns could easily stable the large number of horses that had transported the gentlemen to the meeting. Now many had been drawn to the Red Lion by the chance to see the famous Mr Brindley and some may have been surprised by his appearance. On other occasions it was reported that he was "in appearance and manners a mere peasant. Unlettered and rude of speech, it was easier for him to devise a design than to communicate his ideas to others". Nevertheless, he was the nation's most illustrious canal engineer and the crowd listened avidly as he reported that a canal from Chesterfield to West Stockwith, via Retford, was viable and practicable and would cost £95,000. He then went on to say that he recommended that the canal finish not at West Stockwith but near Gainsborough, and this option would cost £105,000.* The meeting, as was to be expected, agreed

---

* How Brindley came to these totals is not known. One clue we do have are Varley's estimates for the Marquis of Rockingham, most likely to have been done in accordance with Brindley's training. The cost of locks was worked out by allowing a price for each foot of rise/fall for the entire canal, eg 25ft 8ins at £66.13s per ft = £1710. When Smeaton wrote his report in 1775 he allowed £500 per lock, considerably higher than Varley and said "experience teaches me that even in a country where stone is plentiful they (locks) cannot be made good sound work, even without any finery, for less . . ." Smeaton costed a stone road bridge at £150, an aqueduct over a dyke at £60, and timber bridges over the lock-tails at £30 each. Smeaton also added 10% for contingencies which Varley did not. These costs appear to be for a wide canal.

with the great man and voted to officially promote the route to Gainsborough even though it would mean a long tunnel being built through Castle Hill, east of Retford. They also agreed that a further meeting be held on 12 October at the same venue. Attendees would be asked to pay a subscription towards the costs, sign a petition to Parliament, and agree the wording of the Bill to follow the petition.[5] They were full of enthusiasm, and no wonder when they had heard Brindley and the others painting such a glowing picture of post-canal life. Tradesmen would save 12s in every £ on carriage costs. Farmers would be able to reduce greatly the cost of lime to spread on their fields, meaning they could use more of the fertiliser and increase yields. The Nottinghamshire towns on the canal would get coal at half the current price. And as a result old trades would flourish, new trades would be started, the population and, more to the point, land values would increase. Interest on their investment should be 5% and even if this could not be paid in the early years of the Company 3% should be possible. This was not expected to be any great hardship as every tradesman would have increased his business and would also have a warm glow from having provided a public utility for the general benefit of the community. If they needed any more convincing they were told that the Don Navigation proprietors were threatening to link their river with Chesterfield and bypass Worksop and Retford completely.[6] To sum up . . . the bandwagon was leaving now and only poor fools would be left behind.

The remaining four months of 1769 were busy for the canal promoters; there were further public meetings but many more private discussions and agreements. As anticipated the ploy of linking Brindley's name to the project had proved to be of considerable advantage. Many local cases of "canal fever" had been diagnosed and although there were anti-canal opinions Brindley's presence seems to have quelled most of them. There was definitely going to be a canal, the only minor point yet to be resolved was its exact route. The advocates of the two Trent termini, West Stockwith or Gainsborough, both put their case without pulling any punches. There was considerable support in Gainsborough for their option adding as it would an extra dimension to that already busy town's trade. The Trent brought substantial business from Hull and the coast and from further inland. A canal reaching into coal-rich Derbyshire would open up further opportunities and for these reasons Gainsborough businessmen had been early investors in the canal. Supporters in other towns considered that there was much to be said for easy access to the trade of an already established port and that, as a bonus, large amounts of marketable rock would be found whilst tunnelling through Castle Hill. The promoters of the Stockwith route stressed the lower cost of their option but, more importantly, that a long tunnel on the canal would greatly add to the engineering difficulties, and this at a time when canal tunnelling was a very new skill. It was at the forefront of the available technology and should be undertaken only when there was no alternative, as with the 630 yard tunnel planned at Norwood. So why go through Castle Hill? By going to Stockwith there would be a very short tunnel at Drakeholes and the rest of the line would be across basically flat and easy countryside. The discussions raged on for the rest of 1769 with both camps promoting their route with guile and energy.*

Seth Ellis Stevenson wanted the canal to end at West Stockwith as originally planned. The little town had grown at the junction of the Rivers Idle and Trent and there were many wharves where cargoes were moved from small craft to larger coastal vessels, there were boat-building yards, and many craftsmen such as sail-makers, carpenters, shipwrights and rope-makers. Most of the large vessels on the Trent stopped there so the canal would be able to take advantage of these facilities, for trans-shipping and building boats, without the extra expense of going to Gainsborough. As usual Stevenson spared no effort in achieving his objective, often riding his horse Jockey – in the depths of winter – to the homes of various influential people to put his point of view. And by the first week of December he had also written a pamphlet with the snappy title "Seasonable Hints relating to The Intended Canal from Chesterfield in Derbyshire to The River Trent below Gainsborough" this he took to a printer and subsequently distributed 1000 copies in Chesterfield, Retford

---

* John Varley was not allowed to waste his time during this period of discussions, politics and indecision. Brindley was involved with the Leeds & Liverpool canal and some re-surveying was necessary in Lancashire. Varley was sent to do the work during the cold winter months of November and early December 1769.

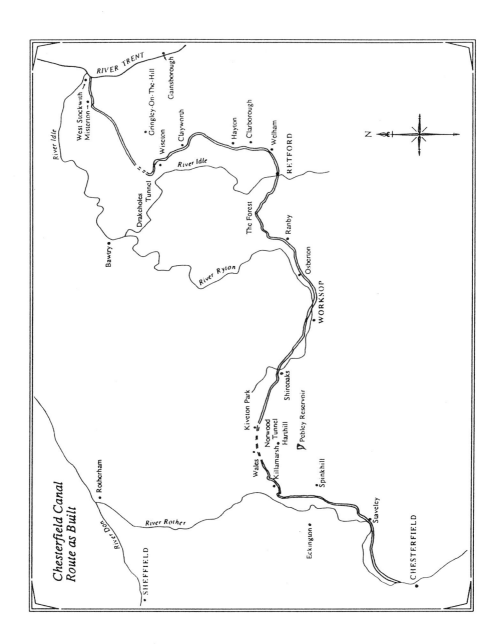

Chesterfield Canal
Route as Built

and the surrounding areas.[7]

On 14 December another public meeting was held at the Red Lion. The route was still officially to Gainsborough and on this basis the public had already been invited to make investments at any one of three locations; the Heathcote/Lax office in Chesterfield, Seth Ellis Stevenson's in Retford, and at a Mr Maddison's in Gainsborough.[8] But Stevenson was slowly winning the battle for West Stockwith and on 26 December he cleared one of that route's last obstacles when he dined with Jonathan Acklom at Wiseton Hall. The canal would pass close to the Hall and Acklom's agreement was vital. He was a keen farmer and had made many improvements to his estate. Obviously a noisy, public canal being built through his land was not immediately appealing and he also had good Parliamentary contacts. However, during their meal Stevenson was able to allay Acklom's fears and agreement was reached. Two days later a crucial meeting at The Crown in Retford was attended by many businessmen from that town and Gainsborough and a final decision was made. Seth Ellis Stevenson's efforts were rewarded. The canal was to go to West Stockwith. Three days before the start of the new decade the route of the canal had finally been agreed and was never again to be opposed.

On 25 January 1770 Brindley made the public announcement to another crowded meeting, this time at The Crown in Retford. He now recommended the route Chesterfield-Worksop-Retford-West Stockwith. The official reasons given were lower construction costs, faster completion time, and easier usage of the canal because of the smaller number of locks and the avoidance of a long tunnel.[9]

1770

The new Prime Minister is Lord North – The American colonies are causing serious trouble – Spain has invaded the Falkland Islands, strong fear of war – Press gangs as near as Nottingham and Newark.

His MAJESTY's most Gracious SPEECH to both HOUSES of Parliament on Tuesday the Ninth Day of January, 1770.

It is needless for Me to recommend to the serious Attention of My Parliament the State of My Government in America. I have endeavoured, on My Part, by every Means, to bring back My Subjects there to their Duty, and to a due Sense of lawful Authority. It gives Me much Concern to inform you that the Success of My Endeavours has not answered My Expectations; and that, in some of My Colonies, many Persons have embarked in Measures highly unwarrantable, and calculated to destroy the Commercial Connection between them and the Mother Country.

January 1770

At the General Quarter Sessions for this County, held here Yesterday, John Tugby and Richard Smallwood were found guilty of stealing two Dozen Plates, and one Dozen Dishes (Earthen Ware) from the Warehouse at Willington, and ordered to be transported for seven Years. – It is hoped this will be a Warning to all such Offenders.

February 1770

They write from Portsmouth, that great Encouragement is given to Sailors, Orders having been sent down to man the Men of War as soon as possible. They likewise assure us, that various Appearances in that Port strongly indicate War to be at hand.

January 1770

VACANT

THE CURACY of ASHBOURNE, in the County of Derby. The Stipend Fifty Pounds a Year. The Duty easy.

February 1770

The Estate of his Grace the Duke of Devonshire, on his lately coming of Age, amounts to no less than £52,000 per Annum.

CHAPTER THREE

Selling the Idea to the Public

The public meetings had been very well attended but promotional pamphlets were the main method used to reach a wider audience.[1] Their writers, one of whom was Seth Ellis Stevenson, included every persuasive technique they could think of to convince people of the merit of the proposals. They had to assure possible investors that sufficient cargoes would be carried to cover the capital cost of the construction and provide profits. As a result the cargoes they said the canal would carry were of a great variety. They included not only the heavy materials from Chesterfield but also easily-broken earthenware which suffered grievously from the jolting of the pack-horses. The lead could be supplied to all the areas along the canal as well as going to the Trent for onward shipping; it was even said that the boatmen would find it useful as ballast as well as cargo. They estimated the price could be substantially reduced and that extra trade and profits would inevitably be the result. So as not to appear too grasping, it was also stressed that although extra trade meant more profits for the lead-mine owners and investors it would also "assist in the support of many thousands of poor families".

Timber, especially mature oak, was plentiful around Chesterfield and along the route as far as Worksop. This would be taken to the Nottinghamshire end of the canal, where wood was not so plentiful, and to Gainsborough for ship-building and many other useful purposes. Any landowner with some forestry would be bound to make a great profit. Also it would encourage owners of waste lands to cultivate plantations which "will afford a growing patriotic pleasure to themselves and wooden-walls (ships) to the nation". A clever ploy; the French were greatly mistrusted at this time and any appeal to nationalistic support of the Royal Navy was bound to be popular.[*]

If timber and lead were difficult to transport by road there was a product of Hathersage, and other parts of Derbyshire, which must have been a nightmare to move: millstones. For as long as anyone could remember, the enormously heavy and unwieldy stones had been moved overland, slowly and expensively, to many distant parts of England. Now the canal's supporters were claiming that once a millstone had reached Chesterfield it could go via the canal and the river system almost to the mill where it was required. They predicted that the reduced carriage costs and the speed of delivery would be sure to increase trade and profits. Also marble was produced at Ashford and cheaper transport would allow it to compete with the imported stone from Italy.

In Yorkshire the area between Kiveton and Shireoaks was known to be rich in limestone for about four miles on both sides of the intended canal. It was used to produce lime which was then highly thought of as a fertiliser for spreading on farmland; in fact it was so popular that farmers were finding supplies difficult to obtain. There were also vast areas of low-priced land near Retford which were thought capable of being transformed into rich forest land if enough lime was added, the quantities needed not being possible via land transport. For the landowners this was another opportunity for financial gain.

Further along the canal Retford had many makers of roof tiles. These were popular as they were lightweight and smaller timber could be used for roof supports, unlike Chesterfield where the roof tiles available were of "a ponderous kind of coarse slate, at a great expense in carriage and strong timber". If to this market was added the roofing of farmhouses and outhouses along the actual line of the canal it was bound to be of great benefit to the tilemakers of Retford.

Retford, and its surrounding area, was rich in an excellent sort of gravel which was thought to be very useful for road building. Of course, the roads

---

[*] The poet William Wordsworth always remembered that when he was very young he and the other boys at school killed the white butterflies they caught because "they were thought to be Frenchmen". The French flag was predominantly white until the Revolution.

of the day were unsurfaced and often in disrepair as the responsibility for maintaining them was not always clear. Areas where the soil was naturally soft and yielding, such as those near the Trent, had more problems than most in refurbishing their roads. The gravel from Retford would answer all their problems, so said the confident canal pundits. The high-quality white stone near Anston was already famous and would be available to a wide area and this is one forecast that did come true. About one hundred years later the stone was selected to rebuild the Houses of Parliament after a great fire, and the water transport via the canal, Trent, Humber, sea and Thames was one of its main advantages.

But coal was to be the main cargo. Derbyshire had large coalfields around Chesterfield and along the line of the canal. By contrast from Worksop onwards, and into Lincolnshire on the opposite side of the Trent, there was hardly any – the coal at Shireoaks and in Nottinghamshire not yet having been discovered. The market for Derbyshire's coal was thought to be enormous, the supply inexhaustible. Brindley thought it would undersell the Yorkshire coal coming via the Don Navigation to Gainsborough, in addition the market in Gainsborough itself was thought to be "inconceivably great". Seventy towns and villages had been counted on the Nottinghamshire side of the Trent where coal could be delivered almost to the doorstep, as well as to "four noblemen's palaces" – the homes of the Dukes of Norfolk, Newcastle, Leeds and Portland. This was an obvious appeal to the four Dukes but again, to soften the hard sell and widen the target, it was pointed out that "such extensive public benefits cannot fail to receive the applause of the rich, and the grateful blessings of many thousands of poor inhabitants".

Having dealt with local produce, and the fortunes to be made from it, thought was also given to the canal's ability to bring into the area items on which all this new found wealth could be spent: fine wool, rice, oils, wines, sugar, tobacco, groceries. Not only would the prices be lower but water transport would mean these items would be available throughout the year; no longer would the bad roads mean waiting until the summer. It seems the shopkeepers and dealers were also to share in the available wealth.

Just in case anyone was not convinced by the bounteous benefits of a canal from Chesterfield to the River Trent, the promoters wound up their case by stating that it would be of national importance – "therefore it seems a duty incumbent on every man of property, who would be esteemed a lover of his country, strenuously to aid and assist in promoting this great design". A little moral blackmail did not go amiss.

But even though every persuasive argument had been used, even though benefits had been promised to every sector of the local population, there was still one group who were not convinced, one group who remained intransigent in their doubt. The farmers could not see the logic of it. They argued that in times of plenty prices went down and the farmers suffered, in times of scarcity prices went up and farmers suffered, everyone knew that. It had always been so. So how could it be that these copious supplies of everything coming and going were going to make them rich? Farmers would not be able to get a decent price for their produce if the market was flooded with cheap imports. It was all very well saying that lime would be cheaper so more land could be made productive. All very well to say that tools would be cheaper and that farms could be managed with less horses, farmhands and wagons. And it was no good saying that these lower production costs would mean they could sell at a cheaper price. That was the quickest way to poverty, you always tried to get the highest price you could. And on top of everything else, whoever heard of boats floating to Derbyshire, through hills as well as up and down them? It was not possible. It had never been so.

In the face of these time-honoured opinions the canal promoters took to quoting examples to prove their hypothesis, farmers elsewhere who did grow rich in times of plenty. Nevertheless, the farmers were still not convinced. Eventually the canal men stopped trying to change such deep-rooted fears and ignored their further objections with condescending grace.

"It is by no means surprising that men whose forefathers for ages have been inured to rugged and deep roads, to wade after their beasts of burden up to the knees in mire, to see their loaded wagons stick fast in dirt; men, who from their interior inland situation, are almost totally unacquainted with all objects of navigation. It is by no means strange that people so accustomed should consider an attempt to introduce a navigable canal up to the town of Chesterfield, and within the air of the Peak Mountains, with alarming ideas, with suspicion, and with amazement".[2]

But generally the methods of the canal promoters worked. There was no shortage of interested parties, from Dukes to small traders, and all were agreeable to making a financial commitment to the project. The next major step was to obtain an Act of Parliament. This would authorise the construction of the canal, sanction the creation of a Canal Company in which shares could legally be sold to the public, and designate the power to purchase the land across which the canal was to be built.

ᴈᴀ ᴈᴀ ᴈᴀ

For the last three months of 1769 the publicists had been the most obvious of the canal's promoters but many hours of work had also been done by the legal representatives, quietly and in the background. It was crucial that the groundwork for the Act of Parliament covered all the legal contingencies that could be foreseen. Not only the rights of land purchase but also the ongoing rights of water supply, access to the canal from nearby roads, the tolls that could be charged for cargoes carried, and the penalties for criminal acts against the canal such as vandalism or obstruction. At the same time the current owners of land or water rights told their lawyers to guard against the Canal Company gaining any advantage over them. In most areas of the country the opinions of the local landowners had only a marginal effect on a canal's progress. Perhaps one or two more prominent figures may insist that a special clause be added to protect their interests but generally the Act would be reasonably straight forward. But the Chesterfield Canal was due to pass through an area near Worksop still known as "The Dukeries".[*] In addition to the Duke of Newcastle at Clumber Park there was the Duke of Portland at neighbouring Welbeck and most important of all, from the canal's point of view, the Duke of

---

[*] Worksop is not an obvious location for such a collection of aristocratic power but it is the result of the dynastic dreams of Elizabeth of Shrewsbury, better known as Bess of Hardwick. The Dukes of Devonshire, Newcastle, Portland and Norfolk could all trace their line back to the great Elizabethan and the families had not moved far from their Derbyshire and Nottinghamshire roots.

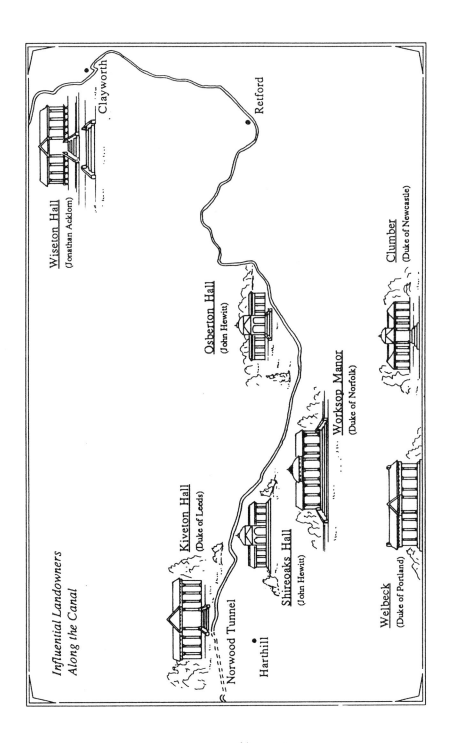

Influential Landowners Along the Canal

Wiseton Hall
(Jonathan Acklom)

Clayworth

Retford

Osberton Hall
(John Hewitt)

Worksop Manor
(Duke of Norfolk)

Clumber
(Duke of Newcastle)

Kiveton Hall
(Duke of Leeds)

Shireoaks Hall
(John Hewitt)

Welbeck
(Duke of Portland)

Norwood Tunnel

Harthill

Norfolk at Worksop Manor. These grandees were in addition to the Duke of Devonshire and his large Derbyshire estates, the Duke of Leeds at Kiveton Hall which was near where the canal was to tunnel under the hill at Norwood, and the Archbishop of York in whose name the Church controlled much of the land needed for the canal near the River Trent.

Dealing with the rights of landowners such as these, via their expensive and experienced legal representatives, was always going to be a major task. An injudicious clause, once it was enshrined in an Act of Parliament, could cause problems not only with the construction of the canal but also the ongoing operation of the Canal Company and result in diminished profits or bankruptcy. So it is surprising that at the Red Lion in January 1770, when Brindley announced the canal route had eventually been defined, it was also decided that an application for an Act be made to the present session of Parliament.[3] It may have been that the Chesterfield promoters were quite frustrated by then. Their idea of a simple canal to Bawtry had been hijacked by Retford and the resultant disputes about the Nottinghamshire end of the route had seemed to be never ending, even though it was only just over a year since the scheme began. Now they wanted progress. Work on a draft Act had been going on for some time and Godfrey Heathcote and Anthony Lax had probably laboured away in Chesterfield defining the clauses for the un-disputed Derbyshire section. But there had been very little time to incorporate the ramifications of building the canal to West Stockwith. It had only been one month since Jonathan Acklom had agreed to the route passing near Wiseton Hall and in that time he had been unable to obtain legal advice on protecting his interests. But paperwork is dull compared with actively promoting a canal. They were involved in a brilliant new scheme. Their enthusiasm over-came their business sense, and their common sense. They had achieved a great deal in just over a year. If they got the Act passed the first soil could be dug in the spring. Now the ball was rolling no one seemed to be able to stop it – that is until the age-old brake on any progress was applied. They formed a committee.

It was no ordinary committee.[4] They elected no less than seventy members to serve on it and, in the status conscious ways of the time, noted that they had mustered:

1 Baronet

19 Esquires

1 Doctor in Physick

4 Churchmen

45 Gentlemen

Almost every one of the Chesterfield and Retford promoters was included except Anthony Lax who was always considered to be an employee rather than one of the gentlemen, his only qualification being his junior partnership with Heathcote. This was certainly not enough status to warrant inclusion on a committee of this quality.

⁂ ⁂ ⁂

The money to pay for building the canal was to be raised by the public sale of £100 shares. For some months the public had been able to enter their names as subscribers but no money could change hands until the Act authorised such sales. However, to alleviate the expenses, both legal and travel, of applying for the Act it was privately agreed that all the interested parties already involved would pay a first instalment of £2 for each share they intended to purchase later.[5]

On Monday, 5 February 1770 a General Meeting was held at The Angel in Chesterfield. On the Friday of the same week a petition was laid before Parliament for "a Cut or Canal for the Navigation of Boats and other Vessels . . . to be made from a convenient Part of the said Town of Chesterfield, through or near the Towns of Worksop and Retford, to join the River Trent at or near Stockwith . . ." The House of Commons – as they would today – referred the matter to a Committee of the House which was told, with a commendable sense of urgency, to hold the first of its series of meetings at 5.00pm that same evening – probably not as they would do today. They were to report their findings back to the House at a future date.[6] As had been planned the MP to whom the leadership of the Commons Committee was delegated was the Duke of Devonshire's uncle,

Lord George Cavendish.* But the unwise haste with which the canal promoters had approached such a major task quickly became evident. It may have been that the draft Act was unsatisfactory, although it must be assumed that the advice of Lord George would have been sought during its writing. Or it may be that the braking-power of a seventy-strong committee had eventually moderated the speed of progress. In this instance the committee was correct. The petition was withdrawn as little as two weeks after it had been placed before Parliament and was "laid aside for this year".[7] So not only was the draft found to be wanting it was also recognised that at least eleven months of work would be needed to correct its shortcomings.

Jonathan Acklom at Wiseton Hall was told of these developments by his Parliamentary contact, George Saville MP. Saville advised Acklom that he should change his method of ensuring the canal did not come too near to the Hall. Instead of having the Act give him the choice of where the canal should go, which was his original intention, Saville advised him that "it is a more usual way, and I think rather better, to fix (the Canal Company) . . . to such & such a track or line for their canal as shall not come too near, or be a hurt or nuisance to the landowner".[8] Acklom took the hint, as can clearly be seen today at Wiseton.

A public announcement of the delay in obtaining the Act was not made until early May although the committee of seventy had met a month before at The White Hart in Retford.[9] A major problem appears to have been the definition of the exact route; landowners had been told it would go through their land but where exactly? Which fields would be split? Which paths were to be crossed? Other users of the paths were also unaware of the canal's impact. Probably a great number of people who would be affected still knew nothing about the scheme at all. In their excited haste to build a canal it seems that the most basic information had not yet been advised, if it were known at all. As a result John Varley reappeared on the scene. During May he was told to go along the entire route and mark it with stakes so that landowners and other interested

---

*   Lord George Cavendish was MP for Derbyshire and an experienced Parliamentarian. When he died in 1794 he was the oldest member of the House of Commons.

parties could see how they would be affected by it.[10] Even if people did not read the newspapers they would see the route marked over the land and would therefore know something was going on. Plans of the route could also be obtained from Heathcote and Lax in Chesterfield, from Seth Ellis Stevenson or John Bright in Retford, and from the Reverend John Peacock in Worksop. For the next six weeks the local newspapers carried notification of a meeting at The Black Bull in Worksop on 28 June which the public could attend to make known any objections.

And the staking out of the route certainly did awaken some people who appear to have been oblivious of the canal and the threat it would be to their livelihood. John Lister, the owner of the navigation rights on the River Idle, eventually realised what was going on. If the substantial amount of goods from Chesterfield, Derbyshire and the Peak District could go to West Stockwith on the canal they would not use his river to reach the same destination. Not too long ago that fellow Varley had been round Bawtry surveying a route for their canal to meet the Idle – that was going to be very satisfactory - but now they had staked out a route that was going to miss Bawtry altogether. Business was bad enough now that the Yorkshire trade from Sheffield, Rotherham and Doncaster had been lost to the Don Navigation. If the Derbyshire trade disappeared as well it would be disastrous. It was urgent that something be done about it.

を を を

The "something" that John Lister did was to contact John Grundy, a surveyor with a fine reputation in Lincolnshire, just the other side of the River Trent. Grundy was asked to define a line for the new canal which would go from Chesterfield via Bawtry and somehow also include Worksop and Retford, a sort of amalgam of Varley's various routes. As a Lincolnshire man Grundy had vast experience in dealing with flat low-lying land with intricate drainage requirements; Bawtry's position in such an area made him an excellent choice for the task. By contrast both Brindley and Varley were from hilly Derbyshire, a background which left them lacking the special skills needed to deal with land below sea-level. And John Lister's need to have Bawtry included in the canal scheme was urgent. The canal proprietors had reached an advanced point in their planning and there was very little time to advocate yet another route. Grundy immediately left his home in Spalding and was in Bawtry by the beginning of June 1770. He spent the next two months examining the condition of the River Idle and mapping out a course for a canal to meet the requirements of his patron.

John Grundy carried out a diligent and detailed investigation. He had done some drainage work in the area just two years before so he had some local knowledge. He could see the current line of the canal staked-out over the countryside but Grundy had no knowledge of the earlier discarded route to Bawtry. So he started from scratch. Varley's work from Chesterfield, over the hills, and along the glacial valley to Shireoaks was accepted without change. Unknowingly Grundy then surveyed a route to Bawtry that covered almost the same ground as Varley had chosen before, and why not? Two good surveyors had independently come to the same conclusion, it was the obvious line to follow. There was a minor difference in that Grundy would have deviated from the current route a mile further east than Varley but generally they had made the same judgements. Of course, Grundy's instructions were to include Worksop and Retford and the only practical way he could see was to have side-cuts to those towns. He published his report on 22 August 1770, a detailed document with a map for further clarity.[*] But it was all wasted work, it was far too late. The canal plans had progressed beyond the contemplation of yet another route, especially as the only reason for its proposal was to save Bawtry's trade. Bawtry had no influence amongst the canal promoters, it would have to survive the best it could.[11]

Grundy's report may have only gathered dust on a Bawtry desk but it did include another valuable insight into Varley's work as seen by a contemporary. Again, the same picture emerges. Varley's surveying is accepted without correction, although by not knowing about the past discord Grundy was puzzled about the current route. He could see nothing in its favour compared with the simple line to Bawtry. He looked at it clearly through his surveyor's eyes; his vision unobscured by the mist of

---

[*] See Appendix B for full details of Grundy's report and the route options identified.

politics, financial interests, the old-boy network, local power and intrigue. From a professional viewpoint it is likely that Varley was of the same opinion, but he was not in a position to write an analysis as critical as Grundy's. His job depended on making the best of his proprietors' decisions. Grundy's objections covered three main themes. First, cost. Although the canal on its way to Retford was to follow the general contours of the land it would still need many small embankments, cuttings and aqueducts; without these the canal would twist and turn so much that it would almost unusable. Therefore the construction costs per mile were estimated to be much higher than crossing the low-lands, even taking into account Grundy's allowance for land drainage. Two, soil suitability. Between Worksop and Retford the canal was to pass through an area known as "the Forest". Grundy judged the ground to be loose and sandy, "extremely ill adapted to hold water". He feared that unknown cavities would swallow large volumes. On other stretches he found the land was "hard, gravelly and stoney", much harder to excavate than the plain, pliable soil of the low-lands. Third, the impact on local residents. The route was to dissect valuable lands and grounds, homesteads and gardens, Grundy said they would be "mangled". Not only would this be very inconvenient to the owners but many bridges would have to be built by the Canal Company, resulting in more expense.

Varley's surveying skills had received a second plaudit from Grundy, matching that of Smeaton the year before, but his paperwork received a second condemnation. The cost estimates contained no details, only gross figures, and there was nothing to show how the totals had been arrived at. In addition, the actual building plans were vague. There was nothing about how many locks there would be; their location, widths, depths. The construction methods and capacities of aqueducts and bridges were not listed. The quantity of stone, brick, wood and iron required was unspecified. Even the boats, the vital reasons for building the canal, were of an unknown length, width, draught and capacity. Grundy had expected every detail to be listed for individual lengths of the waterway, and then totalled to give an overall estimate. But he could find nothing.

Grundy's plans included an optional canal from Bawtry to West Stockwith so that the shoals of the Idle could be avoided. He said it would be capable of taking boats large enough to safely go out onto the Trent and along the Yorkshire river system, thereby saving trans-shipping costs at the end of the canal. His report is a masterful piece of work and there is no doubt that if the gentlemen of Chesterfield had appointed Grundy for the first survey they would have been unlikely to listen to Retford's later blandishments. But Brindley it had to be. And it may be that the Lincolnshire man would have had trouble dealing with the hilly aspect of the Derbyshire end of the project. Perhaps a canal across two such different types of terrain would have been best served by a partnership between Derbyshire's Brindley and Lincolnshire's Grundy. The infant canal-age had not yet produced an engineer with such all-round experience. Even so, it was no excuse for the paltry paperwork.

1770

Birmingham, Lichfield, Burton, Derby and Nottingham

NEW FLY, in one day

SETS out from the CASTLE INN in Birmingham, and the Feathers Inn in Nottingham, every Tuesday, Thursday, and Saturday Mornings, at Six o'Clock. The Birmingham Coach meets the Leeds and Wakefield Coaches at Nottingham; and the Nottingham and London, Bath and Bristol Coaches at Birmingham. Each inside Passenger from Birmingham to Nottingham 14s. Outsides, Half Price. Short Passengers to any part of the Road, 3d per Mile. All Parcels under 12lb Weight 1s; above to pay 1d per Pound, and so in proportion to any part of the Road.

N.B. The first Coach set out from Nottingham on Tuesday last, at Six o'Clock in the Morning.

*** The Proprietors will not be answerable for any Plate, Money, Watches, or Writings, unless entered, and paid for as such. Perform'd by

CAMDEN, the Castle, Birmingham
JACKSON, the Coach and Horses, Lichfield
WALLIS, the New Inn, Derby
CLARKE, the Feathers, Nottingham

At the above Proprietors Houses, neat Post Chaise, to accommodate Gentlemen and Ladies to any places adjacent to the Main Roads.

THE celebrated ORMSKIRK MEDICINE: Being the most noble and safe Antidote for the Bite or any Infection of a mad Dog, or any other mad Animal, ever yet discovered, which is allowed by all in the Profession of Physic, who have seen its Effects, and Thousands can testify it Success, who have had Occasion to take it, is now sold by Mr Stephenson, Druggist (and not other person) in Derby.

Friday a Woman, known by the Name of THE WANDERING SHEPHERDESS, with 40 Sheep, made her Appearance in Sheffield. She gives out that she is the Daughter of a Knight who resided in the North of England, and that having fallen in Love with a Shepherd of her Father's he immediately ordered him to be shot, but surviving the same a few Days, bequeathed to her such a Number of Sheep, with which he told her she must travel 30 YEARS, 28 of which, it is said, are already expired. She is about 60 Years of Age, takes no Money, and is dressed in a very whimsical Manner.

CHAPTER FOUR

An Act of Parliament

Less than a month after the publication of Grundy's report the canal advocates had completed their re-draft of the proposed Act of Parliament; on 13 September 1770 it was read to a meeting at the White Hart in Worksop and generally accepted.[1] There were still some loose ends to tie down; one important aspect was that the Church owned large tracts of land near the Trent and final clarification of sale agreements was needed. The seventy-strong committee asked two of their four churchmen to negotiate on their behalf: The Rev. John Peacock from Worksop and, of course, Seth Ellis Stevenson. Peacock had been involved in the canal project since its earliest days and was usually regarded as the representative of the enterprise in Worksop. Later he was to be appointed Paymaster of the Canal Company, responsible for paying the contractors and navvies. On 11 December the two Reverends set out on horse-back for a cold winter ride to see the Archbishop of York at Brodsworth, eighteen miles away near Doncaster. They stayed overnight and left the next day, Stevenson making a slight detour to call on the Dean of York at Melton. Dinner was preceded by further discussions. In the morning, as soon as it was light, Stevenson rode home on Jockey; tired and cold but having removed one of the final barriers blocking the canal's progress at Westminster.[2]

On the final day of 1770 the committee met at the George in Worksop. The wording of the re-drafted petition to Parliament was accepted. A formal approach was to be made to the House of Commons for an Act to authorise the construction of the Chesterfield Canal.[3]

***

The major difficulty when trying to imagine the canal promoters at

Westminster is that the building they saw was almost completely destroyed by fire in 1834. But the chamber of the House of Commons to which some of them were summoned would look familiar to us; later designs having followed the traditional layout. Many of the systems and customs of today's Parliament are the same as they were in 1771 but political parties on modern lines did not exist. The MPs who were to vote on the Chesterfield Canal Act were a mixed group. About half of them were country gentlemen who formed their own opinions and had no political ambitions. For traditional or principled reasons many of them tended to support the Government Ministers appointed by the King. Many others voted with the Opposition, but nothing could be relied upon. The other half of the Commons consisted of men who were intent on making a career in politics. Each of them tended to give his allegiance to a leader, usually a titled grandee, who was probably responsible for the MP being in Parliament at all. A relevant example was the Duke of Newcastle who could influence the election of MPs in Retford, Newark and Nottingham. These men usually voted as their sponsor wished. When picturing the 18th century House of Commons it should be remembered that political organisation has changed greatly; the layout of the House hardly at all; and the behaviour of MPs . . .?

> "The Members of the House of Commons have nothing in particular in their dress; they even come into the House in their great coats, and with boots and spurs. It is not at all uncommon to see a member lying stretched out on one of the benches while others are debating. Some crack nuts, others eat oranges or whatever else is in season. There is no end to their going in and out."[4]

&a &a &a

On 23 January 1771 a second petition for an Act of Parliament was laid before the House of Commons.[5] As before the House referred the matter to a working Committee, again under the control of the Duke of Devonshire's uncles, Lord George and Lord John Cavendish. Unfortunately the great fire of 1834 not only destroyed the Houses of Parliament but also the records of this Committee, therefore the only details we know are those contained in the reports made to the Commons. The first of these was made by Lord

George when, on 2 February, he read out the Committee's findings from his place in the Commons. He told the House that the Committee had called James Brindley to give evidence, the eminent engineer saying that the proposed route was practicable and that there would be a sufficient supply of water. He had even gone so far as to say it would be as great a benefit as any navigation he had ever been concerned with. The cost of construction would be about £97,000 and the traffic carried would amply repay the expense. Anthony Lax had also been summoned to Westminster. He said that over £55,000 had already been promised by prospective shareholders and that he was in no doubt that sufficient funds would be forthcoming. When asked about the anticipated cargoes Lax mentioned coal, limestone, lime fertiliser, lead, timber, corn, manufactured goods.[6] At the end of the report Lord George walked down to the centre of the House and delivered the papers to the Clerk's Table just in front of the Speaker. From these facts the House of Commons ascertained that the canal project was feasible and gave permission for a Bill to be prepared, the first formal step towards an Act of Parliament.

Without the lost Committee records it is impossible to know every detail of the canal as planned at that stage. There is circumstantial evidence to suggest that the waterway was to be a wide canal, capable of taking boats such as those that used the River Trent. The very first plans had been for a narrow canal, only usable by boats less than 7ft wide, but the width of the canal was continually discussed during the years of construction and there were powerful advocates of each option.*

As most of the work had already been done on preparing a draft Act it was only nine days later that Lord George Cavendish again rose to his feet in the House of Commons. On 11 February he presented the Parliamentary Bill for its First Reading, seven days later the Second Reading was completed.[7] On the same day the canal's sponsors already at Westminster sent messages to a number of their colleagues at home calling them to strengthen their ranks.[8] This was because the next few weeks were to be crucial, the next formal move of the House being a call to all interested parties to make their views known to the Committee, both for and against

---

*   See Appendix C for details of canal width.

the canal. This the House did on 26 February, but the diligent Seth Ellis Stevenson was prepared. He had already been in London for five days, travelling as soon as he had received the summons from his associates.

His journey from Retford to London had taken three days, probably by coach as Seth Ellis had not travelled alone. The momentous events justified a family outing; wife Elizabeth, eldest son Billy, and the young son of another canal promoter, little Bobby Sutton. They all set off from Retford on 19 February. The weather had been severely cold for the past week, leaving the Great North Road solid and rutted.[9] They had three days of jolting, cold travel and if they used a public coach it may have been quite an experience. It was common for advertisements for stage-coaches to state the destinations served, the timetable usually finishing with the phrase "if God permit". This inspiring comment led to the stage-coaches generally becoming known as "God permits". A verse of the time describes the travelling conditions:

The impatient coachman warns us to prepare
and, long before sun-rise, mounts his daily care.
Scarcely awake, in dreaming mood I rise,
enter the coach, and open my wondering eyes . . . on two
old females of the Falstaff size:
No choice is left me, so between the two
on each side elbowed I am doomed to stew.
A nurse, a child, a soldier swelled with pride,
and a fat landlord filled the other side.
Day scarcely dawns before the rugged road
from this to that side jolts the motley load.
One dame coughs, the other scolds and stares,
the landlord snores, child pukes and soldier swears.
Of "God-permits", if these the comforts be,
my feet, thank heaven, can still carry me.[10]

Whatever the Stevenson's journey was like they were at Westminster until the middle of March, during which time crucial amendments were made to the Bill which were to have a major impact on the construction and use of the canal.

≈ ≈ ≈

The draft Bill was already a lengthy document with many varied clauses.[11] For example, the canal was to avoid certain houses and gardens, cattle watering places were to be provided if such had been disturbed by the works, owners of adjoining land were to be allowed to build private bridges and warehouses. Regulations were stipulated about tolls chargeable, boat traffic, hours of usage of locks, the cargo to be carried. Administratively there were dispute settlement procedures, the definition of shareholders rights, payment of damages, financial rules, and the Company books to be kept. And many, many more. Even so, interested parties still complained that every aspect had not been covered.*

On 4 March 1771 the House of Commons heard a petition raised on behalf of the powerful rival of the proposed Chesterfield Canal, the River Don Navigation Company.[12] The vexed subject of water supply now became a crucial political issue. The River Don received a large proportion of its water from the River Rother, a tributary flowing in at Rotherham. The Rother in its turn had gathered such water from various streams and brooks, including the Doe Lea near Chesterfield. It was the contention of the Don Navigation Company that the water of the Rother was vitally important to the River Don below Rotherham. They stated that if the proposed canal was allowed to take much of its supply from the Rother, as planned, then the Don would suffer a substantial water loss and their business would suffer. Whilst this was a reasonable fear on behalf on the Don Navigation Company it also served to make life difficult for a fledgling rival before it had even left the nest. The House of Commons ordered that the matter be heard by the Committee and an agreed solution submitted for the approval of the House in due course.

The Committee records for the next two weeks would have made interesting reading. The Bill already contained many clauses about the supply of water to the canal, indicative of many hours of discussion and compromise with landowners and millers. The canal, by crossing the natural watershed of the hills at Norwood, was to go through two distinct

---

*   Appendix D. List of clauses contained in the Act of Parliament.

water systems. To the west of the hills was the Rother and its tributaries, to the east the Rivers Ryton and Idle and their adjoining streams. So far the interested parties to the east had been the most successful in guarding their supplies. The canal's sponsors had already agreed not to use the water from the several springs that served the Duke of Norfolk's house, Worksop Manor. In addition such supplies were pumped to the Manor by a "water engine", the flow of the River Ryton turning some sort of machine. In this case the canal men agreed that if the canal's use of the Ryton lessened the river's ability to run the machine then, with twenty-one days written notice, the Duke could open any sluice or lock on the canal to take water for the pump.

The Duke of Leeds had also made his presence felt in protecting the water supply to his houses, Kiveton Hall and Thorpe Hall. Burwell Spring provided the most, its waters flowing through an extensive system of pipes to Kiveton Hall. It had already been agreed that the canal would not use the water from the spring but a further difficulty was that the construction work would disrupt the pipe system. This was solved by the Bill containing a clause to ensure that the pipes would be taken over the canal by "an aqueduct, framework and trough", the dimensions and materials of which were to be agreed by the Duke. Construction and repair costs were to be borne by the Canal Company.

In hindsight we know that the steam-age was just dawning, a faint glimmer of the future, but in 1771 water was still the country's major power-source as it had been for many generations, and as it would continue to be for some time. Water-powered mills worked on every usable stretch of river and such time-honoured practices were not to be ignored. Various streams and brooks were listed in the Bill, as were the mills powered by their waters, and damages were to be paid if, in the future, their supplies were reduced by the canal diverting water for its own use. Not a one-off payment, but every six months while the problem persisted. Such clauses were to be the source of many disagreements over the years. Without modern flow-meters it was almost impossible to agree on the level of damages that should be paid, or if any should be paid at all. Dealing with irate millers was to be an endless task for Anthony Lax and his assistants.

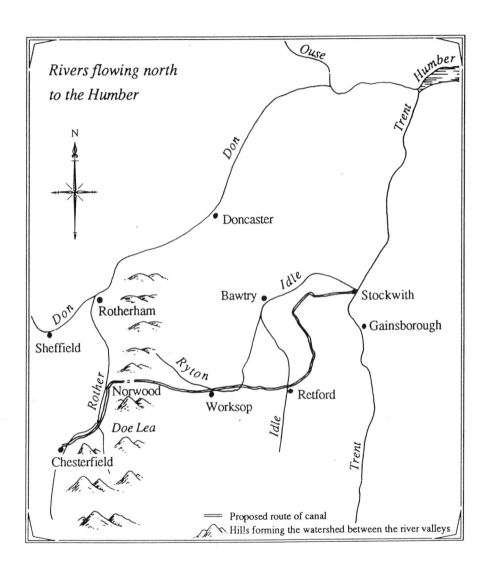

Rivers flowing north to the Humber

N

Ouse

Humber

Trent

Don

Doncaster

Idle

Bawtry

Stockwith

Rotherham

Gainsborough

Don

Sheffield

Ryton

Rother

Norwood

Retford

Worksop

Idle

Doe Lea

Trent

Chesterfield

Proposed route of canal

Hills forming the watershed between the river valleys

The Don Navigation's petition about the waters of the Rother was the first to focus attention on the western side of the watershed at Norwood. Lord George Cavendish reported to the House of Commons on 19 March that the Committee considered the grievance to be well founded and that a clause would be added to the Bill to protect the Don Navigation's interests. This would state that water from the Rother, or any of its tributaries, was not to be taken to the eastern side of the hill at Norwood, either via the proposed tunnel or via channels from the reservoirs. All water that would have naturally made its way down the western flank of the hills and into the valley of the Rother was to be retained there. The canal could use it on its passage but it was to be eventually discharged into the Rother. From there it would flow into the Don. This clause did not present too much of a problem for the canal's engineers or sponsors. It may have meant changes to the planned reservoirs, ensuring that water was collected at separate sites slightly to each side of the watershed. Some reservoirs serving the eastern Ryton and Idle valleys, others the western Rother valley. In addition, a stop-gate was planned at the mouth of the tunnel through Norwood hill, thereby stopping the water destined for the Rother from escaping through the tunnel. As previously planned, the flight of locks climbing up Norwood hill would still be served by the water flowing down from the tunnel mouth to the lowest section of the canal near Killamarsh.

The Rother/Don amendment to the Bill was agreed by the House but now, at this very late stage, two further clauses were offered for inclusion, one of which was to have a profound impact on the canal.[13] The first was probably the result of John Lister at Bawtry eventually giving up the fight against the canal by-passing his town. All he could obtain was damages if he could prove the canal had taken water from the River Idle to the detriment of his business. In fact it was to prove an almost useless amendment, for the canal very quickly took most of his trade, and the amount of water in the Idle at Bawtry then became irrelevant. The second extra clause was altogether more serious. The politics behind it are not known but at this late stage Lord George was not adverse to making apparent the influence of his Cavendish family. Mrs Elizabeth Cavendish was the owner of a furnace, forge and corn-mill, all on one site slightly up-

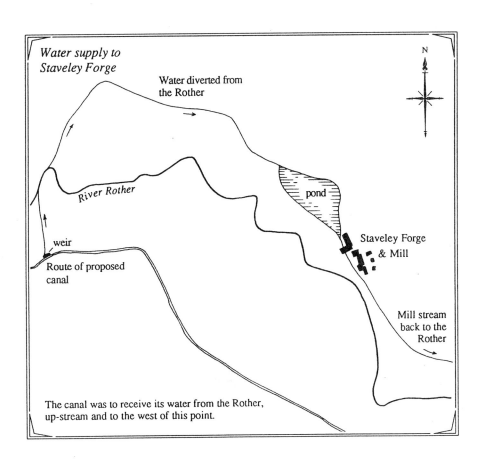

Water supply to Staveley Forge

N

Water diverted from the Rother

River Rother

pond

weir

Staveley Forge & Mill

Route of proposed canal

Mill stream back to the Rother

The canal was to receive its water from the Rother, up-stream and to the west of this point.

Cross-sections of the Canal Near Staveley

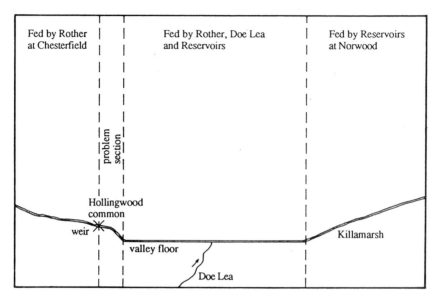

AS ORIGINALLY PLANNED

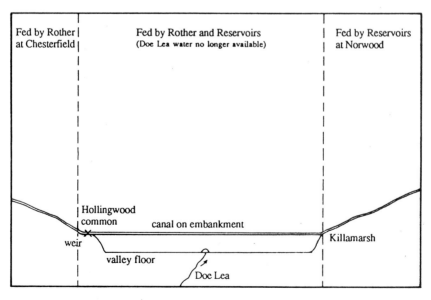

AS BUILT

river from Staveley. It was a very large undertaking and all the machinery was powered by water from the Rother. It seems inconceivable that a family so involved from an early stage did not foresee that if the canal was fed from the Rother then the river would have less water to power Staveley Forge. Certainly Varley's surveys had shown no sign of any special arrangements. Had the powerful Cavendish family been aware of the problem all along? Was the amendment purposely proposed late to avoid dissenting voices? Did it come via the Committee, or did Lord George simply take the clause direct to the House of Commons, its acceptance being the first most of the canal sponsors knew of the matter? The wording was quite simple. The water supply to Staveley Forge was to be maintained to the standard it had always enjoyed. This was to be done at the Canal Company's expense but was to include the provision of a weir on the edge of the canal which was to be four inches lower than any other on the section. This weir was to spill the canal's water back into the Rother just above Staveley Forge, from where it could flow into Mrs Cavendish's property. If, at any time, the Forge suffered from a lack of water the Canal Company was to pay the damages incurred.

The water for a canal was a basic requirement that was almost the first consideration of the surveyor. It was one thing to rule out certain supplies because they were already claimed for a distinct use, such as the mills. It was quite another to ruin the integrity of the canal by insisting on a low section in its bank which would allow large volumes of its lifeblood to flow away. There must have been some engineering input to the wording of the clause as the specific "four inches" reduction in the height of the weir must surely have been calculated. John Varley was at Westminster at the time, Brindley's attendance is uncertain. Was Varley aware of the amendment before it was proposed? If so, did he realise the implications? Did he make a crucial mistake? Opinions will vary. I believe in giving the benefit of the doubt if no damning evidence can be found. There would have been millwrights working for the Cavendish's who would have been experienced in water supply problems, indeed Brindley's career had started in such employment. It is just as likely that Varley knew of the proposals, disagreed with them, and that Cavendish millwrights made the calculations and Lord George looked after his family's interests by tabling the amendment. Brindley may have been able to stop such an influential family. Varley would have had no chance.

To understand the major impact of the Staveley Forge amendment it is important to remember the simple fact that water does not naturally run uphill. The canal could only obtain supplies in its sections that were lower than each water source. The site of the infamous weir was to be half way down the canal's descent to the Rother's valley floor. If, at that point, many gallons were escaping over the low weir then the stretch of canal completing the descent would be short of water. Once at its lowest point it was to have obtained a supply from the Doe Lea as that tributary flowed into the Rother, but that could not be made available further uphill. The water from the reservoirs in the hills at Norwood would flow westwards down to the canal's lowest point but would not flow up-hill to serve the starved section. The solution chosen was to stop the canal descending by raising the lowest section so that water from the reservoirs could flow along to the problem stretch, to create eight miles of level canal from Hollingwood Common to Killamarsh. To do this a large embankment would have to be built to carry the canal across the valley at its increased height.[*] Other small embankments would also be necessary as the level canal skirted the high points of land. The considerable cost of this construction was, of course, not included in Brindley's estimates and the canal's economics had already been agreed with the House of Commons. It is not known if the water supply problem was immediately apparent, and Brindley planned this solution, or if the dilemma only became clear as the canal was actually built in the Staveley area. But certainly it was the first major cause of the Canal Company's subsequent financial problems.

The Commons now ordered that the Bill be formally written out by the clerks of the House. This only took three days, the next Parliamentary action taking place on 22 March 1771. By this time many of the canal's sponsors had returned home, only Lax, other legal colleagues and Varley remained at Westminster. The Stevensons had left London on the Wednesday of that week, the 20th, reaching Newark the next day. Since

---

[*] Now known as Staveley Puddlebank.

there was safety in numbers – highwaymen were still prevalent on the roads going north from London – they travelled with the Wilkinsons, the financial members of the canal scheme from Chesterfield. Both families stayed at Newark for two days. Then, rested after a difficult journey, they left as soon as there was enough light, the Wilkinsons taking the road to Mansfield and Chesterfield, the Stevensons continuing up the Great North Road to Retford.[14] In Chesterfield, Retford and Worksop many people were now anxiously waiting for news from Westminster. Without an Act of Parliament nothing could be done; with such authority they could immediately begin the construction of the Chesterfield Canal.

During the formal Third Reading the House was told that "His Majesty's interest is concerned in the Bill".[15] This usually means that a proposed Act will affect a prerogative or interest of the Crown. If left until the Third Reading, as in this case, it indicates that the involvement is only small, perhaps some Crown land would have to be purchased. The Prime Minister, Lord North, told the Commons that His Majesty had been informed and that the Bill could proceed. This is still the procedure today and is referred to as the Queen's Consent, not to be confused with the Royal Assent which makes an Act a legal statute. The formally written out Bill now received its Third Reading and its official title became:

"An Act for making a Navigable Cut, or Canal, from Chesterfield, in the County of Derby, through or near Worksop and Retford, to join the River Trent at or near Stockwith, in the County of Nottingham."

Lord George Cavendish was then ordered to take the Bill to the House of Lords for their approval.

The Lords, as had the Commons, passed the matter to a Committee for a detailed investigation. This Committee sat less than one week later on 27 March; the Chairman was Lord Sandys. Anthony Lax was called and questioned about the various statements made in the Bill. He confirmed they were all correct and that general opinion was that the canal would be of great benefit to the local area. John Varley was then called in. He showed the Lords a plan of the intended route, the length of which he said would be almost forty-five miles. He explained that it was already marked out with stakes and that all the land required had been listed in the Field Book, which he also showed to their Lordships. The book contained the names of the landowners and tenants, together with the location and value of each plot. It was closely inspected, Lax and Varley being asked about the opinions of the landowners listed. Did they consent to their land being used thus? Had the valuations been agreed? Lax said that of the 215 owners involved, 147 had given their consent, 40 were doubtful and 28 did not agree. But he was also careful to stress that there was no general opposition to the Bill and that £56,000 had already been subscribed by prospective shareholders. Lax and Varley were told to leave the room, the two ambitious young men waiting in an ante-room for the Committee's decision. It was agreed to take the Bill to the House of Lords without amendment.[16]

The next day, Thursday 28 March 1771, the House of Commons was told of the approval of the Lords. Later in the afternoon the Royal Assent was given and the Bill became an Act of Parliament. All the legal hurdles had been cleared. The sponsors could now form a Company in which they could sell shares to the public, raise funds, purchase land, employ whom they thought fit, and build the Chesterfield Canal. The important matter now was to take the good news to those waiting at home, and without delay.

The speediest journeys were done by young men on horseback. Anthony Lax left London either on the evening of 28 March or early morning the next day. On Friday the 29th he rode along the Great North Road, his destination Chesterfield. With him was an unknown companion, who was to take the tidings to Retford, and at least two servants. The horses also carried saddle-bags heavy with food and clean clothing, necessary because of the bad state of the roads in winter. That night, cold and weary, they would have stopped at one of the large inns that catered for travellers. Muddy greatcoats, thick vests, boots and double gloves would have been removed, clean clothes donned and dinner taken. The servants' tasks were to see to the horses, unpack the bags, ensure the food was to their masters' liking, and to prepare the riding clothes, as best they could, for the next day. In the morning the party left to continue northwards. Somewhere near Newark the two gentlemen parted, each riding towards his own town with his servant. As always in the canal project neither Chesterfield nor

Retford was to be allowed an advantage over the other. The news would be received by both on the same day, Saturday 30 March 1771.

When Anthony Lax neared Chesterfield his approach was noticed and as he rode into town all the church bells were ringing. The rest of the afternoon was spent at the Corporation's favourite inn, the Angel, where Lax and the local canal sponsors enjoyed a celebratory banquet. In the evening it became apparent that the gentlemen who had left Westminster early had not been wasting their time back home. They had organised a tremendous firework display; it was even good enough to get them to leave their drinks to join the rest of the population in the Market Place.[17]

At the same time it was reported that Retford received the news with great rejoicing; the gentlemen of that town treating themselves to a dinner at the Crown. The Rev. Seth Ellis Stevenson was so pleased, or mellowed by the wine, that he arranged for the church bells to be rung for four days! A gesture that probably strained the hearing of the population as well as his pocket; he had to pay £1.11s.6d to the bell-ringers.[18]

1771

Horatio Nelson has joined his first ship as a twelve year old midshipman – Trade boom as American and Spanish disagreements temporarily resolved – Bad harvest follows a hard winter – Footpads and highwaymen near Nottingham – By November, war with Spain is again near.

To Be Sold

On Thursday the 6th of June, betwixt the hours of Three and Six in the Afternoon, at the House of Mrs Thacker, the Post-Office, Chesterfield;

One half Part of a Freehold Estate, situate in Whittington, near Chesterfield, consisting of a new built Stone House, with two arched Cellars, and twelve other good Rooms, three of them papered, and the House well finished. A Brewhouse, a neat Brick walled Garden, well planted with near thirty choice Fruit Trees. Also of fourteen Acres of exceeding good Land, adjoining to the House. This estate is very pleasantly situated, and being but two Miles from Chesterfield where there is a good Market, a Post and Stage Coach every Day, and as good a Hunt as most in England. Whittington has the Advantage of the London Road to Sheffield and Leeds through it, abounds with plenty of Game, fine large Coal at 3s a Ton; a good Church and a good Neighbourhood.

The above Estate is full of Coal, and not Half a Mile from the intended Navigation.

CHAPTER FIVE

Final Arrangements

The Act of Parliament gave the canal's sponsors all the legal rights they needed to build the waterway but it also laid down a strict rule; before construction could begin £100,000 must have been raised by selling shares to the public. Indeed, all the rights conferred by the Act would only come into force when the money had been raised. This was to be done by the sale of one thousand £100 shares with fifty as the maximum holding for any one person. In the 18th century £100 was a substantial amount of money and not many people could have paid in one lump sum so it was allowable for the shares to be sold with payments spread over four years. The first instalment, or Call, was for £4 and if a thousand shares could be sold on this basis the Act would consider that the £100,000 had been raised. Those with an early interest in the scheme had already paid towards the First Call, for instance as long as fourteen months before the Duke of Newcastle had paid £2 for each of the thirty shares he would eventually own.[1] It was these early investments that had paid for the route surveys, London visits, advertisements, maps and pamphlets. When Lax had told the House of Commons that £55,000 had already been collected he meant that five hundred and fifty £100 shares had been allocated and at least £2 paid on each.

A great number of the shares were sold locally. Not only were they considered a first class, blue-chip investment but the canal was also seen as a way to improve the area. Speculators and outside financiers had not yet become involved in great numbers; the early canals, such as the Chesterfield, having far more local subscribers than the later navigations built during the height of the canal boom. There were large shareholders, such as the Dukes of Devonshire and Newcastle, but the majority of investors were small local traders who bought only one or two shares. Indeed the average holding of the original sponsors, such men as Seth Ellis Stevenson, Lax and Heathcote, was to be only five.

The Act also stipulated that the Company was to organise two General Meetings of shareholders each year, one in May in Chesterfield, the other September in Retford. The studied even-handed treatment of the two towns was again evident in that neither was to gain the advantage of hosting the initial gathering, that was ordered to take place at the George in Worksop on 18 April 1771. Many gentlemen travelled to the historic meeting and by eleven o'clock in the morning fifty-three shareholders were present in addition to Anthony Lax and his clerks. They were a mixed group. Many were small traders who had had little or no involvement in the scheme but who had decided they could each afford £100 for one share, men such as Francis Atkinson, grocer; William Adney, butcher; John Smith, tanner. Those actively involved from the early days were also there in large numbers, Seth Ellis Stevenson, George Poplewell, Lindley Simpson, Richard Nall, Stephen Gamble, Joseph Storrs and all the others. Of course, the great men amongst the shareholders were not present – the Duke of Devonshire, Lord Scarsdale, the Duke of Newcastle – they were represented by their Agents, their business managers. The room started to fill and on arrival each man gave his name to a clerk and this was checked against the list of investors and noted for the Minutes. The voting powers were that a shareholder was to have one vote for each share owned, but to limit the influence of the rich and powerful thirty-five was the maximum votes per person, no matter how many shares were owned. Those present, and the great number of proxy votes, amounted to over 460 shares. At long last the Chesterfield Canal Company was in existence.

The General Meeting was convened and the first action taken by the fledgling Company was to appoint Anthony Lax as their "Clerk and Sollicitor", the chief administrative post. His salary was set at £100 a year, plus travel and postage expenses. Although legally the shareholding gentlemen ran the Company they all had outside interests and in practice were to rely on a small number of salaried professionals to do most of the work. Therefore, as a full-time employee Lax was expected to organise the paperwork and meetings, supervise the taking of Minutes, deal with land purchase and other legal matters, and generally to be responsible for everyday Company routine.

Next, the joint Treasurers were appointed, one from each town of course; Allwood Wilkinson of Chesterfield, and George Poplewell of Retford. As was usual in early Canal Companies they were not paid a salary, even though there was a reasonable amount of work involved. Financial historians think that in those early banking days it was considered acceptable for them to profit from lending out the large sums of Company money that passed through their hands.

The actual building of the canal was to be supervised by a Management Committee. As ordered by the Act this was to be elected at each General Meeting and was to consist of twenty-one members, all of whom must own at least three shares. They were to represent all the shareholders and the negotiations on their appointment must have involved lengthy discussions. The Committee was destined to be the major power-base of the Company, although they could be over-ruled by a General Meeting their control over the building of the canal would be widespread. As the Company's Engineer James Brindley would be expected to report to and receive directions from them even though dealing with Committees was never Brindley's strong point – his genius was not diplomacy. The Committee elected that day in Worksop reads like a roll-call of those who had been involved from the very start of the project. The majority were to serve on the Committee throughout the construction years and their names will become familiar as the story unfolds. Control was finely balanced with ten members from Chesterfield, nine from Retford (including the Chairman), and two from Worksop. The Committee's first meeting was to be on 25 June when, it was hoped, the rest of the required money would have been raised and building could commence.

In the meantime, Lax was to put notices in the newspapers of Derby, York, Nottingham and London advertising the sale of the remaining shares. Subscription books were opened in Chesterfield, Retford, Worksop and London and in addition Lax was also told to ensure that the First Call of £4 had been paid by all the current shareholders. It is worth considering here the difficulties Anthony Lax and the two Treasurers would have encountered in handling the Company's funds. Not only was there no national banking system but the basic currency, the coinage and notes, was scarce and of dubious value. The Canal Companies were the first to require large amounts of financial backing and, as with the roads, the methods that had coped before could not cater for the new industrial age. No national banking system meant that it was difficult to move funds, there were no cheques to replace cash and no secure storage. But these difficulties were as nothing to the state of the country's currency. Today it is taken for granted that the tokens we receive and call "money" are worth their face value, and that all coins of one denomination are equal to each other. This was not the case in 1771. For many years the Government had failed to ensure that the face value of coinage kept up with the value of the metal from which it was made. Therefore, it was more profitable to melt coins down or snip pieces off the edge and sell the metal. As a result complete coins were scarce, and as a result of that, counterfeits were rife. The Bank of England refused to issue a national paper currency, those notes they did issue in London were easily forged and, again, they were scarce. All this meant that most traders and industrialists had to find other ways to finance their businesses, Bills of Exchange and Promissory Notes were common but satisfactory only if both parties to the deal knew and trusted each other. Another problem was that workforces were larger than had ever been known before and this caused a scarcity of coinage for wages. As there was often no alternative Companies issued their own tokens to their employees, exchangeable in the shops of the local area. Again, this was only acceptable if the shopkeepers trusted the Company to give them the value of the tokens collected.[*] So Anthony Lax and the two Treasurers, Allwood Wilkinson and George Poplewell, had a rather more difficult role than their counterparts today.[2]

---

[*] Such tokens were to become infamous during the later years of the canal age. Some Companies would only pay their navvies in tokens and perhaps this could still be justified because of the currency problems. But the scandalous aspect was that such tokens were often only redeemable at the "tommy shops" owned by the Canal Company where prices were exorbitantly high.

1771

Borough of Derby,   13 Feb, 1771

WHEREAS a Hamper of Counterfeit HALFPENCE being seized on Monday last in the said Borough; and as large Quantities of the same Counterfeit Coin hath frequently been brought into the said Borough, and paid away as good Money, to the great Detriment of the Publick in general:

This is therefore to give Notice that whoever shall for the future be detected in paying and uttering such Counterfeit Coins, he or they shall be prosecuted as the Law in such Case directs.
HENRY FLINT, Mayor

Note. No Persons are obliged by Law to take, either in Wages or Change, more than Five-pence three-farthings.

A Dutch Merchant lately brought three Hundred pounds in silver to the Bank, amongst which were a Number of bad Half Crowns, made by the Dutch Jews, who, it is supposed, have manufactured a deal of the silver now pouring in upon us from the Continent. The receiving Clerk at the Bank weighed the Half Crowns, and returned to the Merchant the light ones.

It is said, that preparations is now making at the Tower for a silver coinage.

ια ια ια

Throughout May and most of June 1771 the shares of the Chesterfield Canal Company continued to be purchased, new investors making a £4 first payment to match the current shareholders. So it was in an atmosphere of success that the Management Committee met for the first time on Tuesday 25 June, at the Black Bull in Worksop. Two groups geographically divided, rather than one assembly, these men were to know each other better by the time the canal was completed. In the Chair was Robert Sutton, a senior member of Retford society and a man much respected over a wider area. The Rev. Seth Ellis Stevenson was one of his eight associates from the same town, the churchman having earned his place by his tireless efforts for the Company and knowledge of canals in general. Having already done so much there was no way he was going to be left out now that real progress was so close. The opposite of Stevenson was George Mason who had hardly any previous involvement but was the Duke of Newcastle's Agent in Nottinghamshire, that was all the qualification he needed. Lindley Simpson had a strong reason for inclusion as the canal was due to pass within a few yards of his home, Babworth Hall on the outskirts of Retford. The other five were all Bailiffs or Aldermen of Retford who had been involved in various ways; Edward Brown, William Kirke, Sampson Mosman, John Parker, John Taylor. As a group they could be described as landed gentleman farmers of a comfortable age, income and influence.

In those status conscious times it mattered that the Chesterfield representatives could not compare with their Nottinghamshire associates. They were mostly younger businessmen, sharp and ambitious but lacking in prestige. Nor did it help that inexplicably five of their ten members were missing from such a momentous meeting. Of the five that did make the journey John Frith and Joseph Storrs represented the important Derbyshire lead-mining industry; Samuel Towndrow was an ex-Mayor of Chesterfield but as a grocer lacked prestige; Richard Nall was a hosier. They did include one of the Treasurers but Allwood Wilkinson, even as a member of a powerful financial family, was only twenty-seven. There is no doubt that Retford achieved an early success in their powerful representation on the first Management Committee.

With a full Committee present the deciding votes could have rested with the two Worksop representatives, although as a small Nottinghamshire town Worksop was strongly influenced by Retford. Nevertheless in certain circumstances these two men could have achieved an important role on the Committee. Richard Roe's business was the tanning of hides into leather; Joseph Wilson was a woodman and timber supplier, a lucrative trade to be in considering the amount of wood the construction teams would need.

As would be the case at all future meetings the first Management Committee was supported by a number of officials. The second Treasurer, George Poplewell was there although not a Committee member, and the paperwork, room bookings and refreshments were looked after by the ever-present Anthony Lax and his clerks. They also took the Minutes at all Committee and General Meetings, probably using a form of shorthand, the clerks writing out the full text at the Company office in Chesterfield the next day. This would have been a laborious task especially as a copy had to be made for each Committee member as well as the master retained in the Company's books.

It will come as no surprise that the first six items on the Agenda covered the reimbursement of expenses that the gentlemen had incurred over the last months. The crucial Chesterfield law firm of Heathcote and Lax put in a bill for £380. Seth Ellis Stevenson claimed £20 for attending Parliament, his Worksop church colleague, John Peacock, wanted £82 for the same reason. Having settled these important matters they turned their minds to the salary they should pay James Brindley. Of course as his fame had spread the engineer's fees had increased; the rate depended on the complexity of the work he would have to do but £200 a year had been acceptable in the late 1760's. But a couple of years ago the Coventry Canal Company had agreed to pay him £250 and now the Chesterfield Canal agreed to pay Brindley £300 a year until the work was complete.

The frustrating fact was that the canal's construction could still not begin, all the shares had not yet been sold, the £100,000 had not been raised. Lax estimated that two more weeks would solve the problem and the Committee adjourned until 11 July, summoning Brindley to attend in the anticipation that he could actually be told to start work.

৯ ৯ ৯

The work of Lax and the two Treasurers continued over the next weeks; with subscriptions being accepted in four towns it was important to keep track of the funds being invested and to ensure the accuracy of the Company's books. After much postal communication with London, and messengers riding between Worksop, Retford and Chesterfield it became apparent that not only had they reached the £100,000 total, they had actually exceeded it. By the time the Committee next met the books showed that £1,100 of excess contributions had been made. So the gentlemen again made their way to Worksop; continuing their tour of the inns this time they met at the White Hart. Even the presence of the nationally famous James Brindley could not encourage all the Committee members from Chesterfield to attend the historic meeting. One who was there was Stephen Gamble, a ropemaker in Knifesmithgate, and he had been involved in the past wrangling about the canal's route. He reported that he had ended up holding the funds the gentlemen of Gainsborough had invested when they thought the canal was going to their town. Now, of course, they wanted their money back; what was he to do? Well, the Committee said they could not have it all back; funds had been spent on surveys and travel expenses and these costs would be deducted from their funds. Next item. Lax and the Treasurers were to ask for volunteer shareholders to reduce their investment as the Act would not allow the Company to keep the excess £1,100. A welcome problem after so many others but at this time all the obstacles appeared insubstantial. At long last the great moment had arrived. One thousand shares had been sold, the £100,000 as required by the Act had been promised, and on Thursday, 11 July 1771 the Committee of the Chesterfield Canal Company officially . . .

"Ordered that Mr Brindley do immediately begin to make the said Navigation at a place called Norwood . . ."

ILLUSTRATION OF COMPANY SEAL

Canal Companies authenticated their paperwork by affixing a seal, impressed into red wax, on the bottom of official documents. The design also acted as an 18th century "logo" and usually included some aspect of the canal or the area through which it would pass. The seal of the Chesterfield Canal Company simply included symbols for East Retford and Chesterfield.

For many years, before and after 1771, the symbol of Chesterfield was the pomegranate tree; the reason for this has been lost in the past but interestingly it is the only known use of such an emblem in the heraldic world. However, for a short period of time Chesterfield changed its emblem and in 1771 the centre of the town's arms was a diamond on a horizontal band, as in two quarters of the seal.

East Retford had no armorial bearings in 1771 but it did have a civic seal which even then was very ancient and showed two eagles facing each other, their wings behind their backs, and their feet raised between them, an exact description of the Retford quarters of the seal.

PART TWO

CANAL CONSTRUCTION

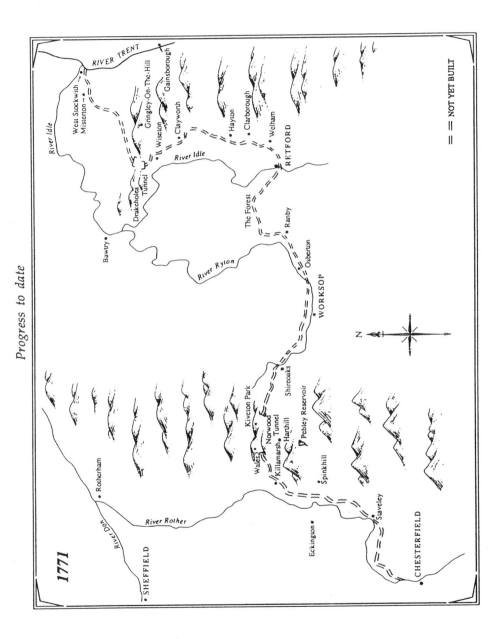

Progress to date

1771

== = NOT YET BUILT

RIVER TRENT
River Trent
River Idle
West Stockwith
Misterton
Gringley-On-The-Hill
Gainsborough
Wiseton
Clayworth
Drakeholes Tunnel
River Idle
Hayton
Clarborough
Welham
RETFORD
Bawtry
The Forest
Ranby
River Ryton
Osberton
WORKSOP
N

River Don
Rotherham
SHEFFIELD
River Rother
Kiveton Park
Wales
Norwood
Killamarsh
Tunnel
Harthill
Shireoaks
Pebley Reservoir
Spinkhill
Eckington
Staveley
CHESTERFIELD

100

CHAPTER SIX

Start at the Top

The construction of the Chesterfield Canal did not begin at one end and work along to the other, that would not have been sensible engineering. For two good reasons the canal building started half way along the intended route, at the tunnel through the hill at Norwood. First, this was the highest point the canal would reach, its summit pound, so water fed in here would flow down the completed sections making them usable.[*] Second, the tunnel was to be the major feature of the work involved on the whole canal; it would take years to complete so the sooner it was started the better. The problems were compounded by the fact that originally Norwood Tunnel was to be only 630 yards long, cutting through high on the hill, but by the time Brindley had been given permission to start work his plan was to go lower down with a considerable increase to just over 1400 yards.[1] A tunnel of over three-quarters of a mile would be a major challenge. From this base at Norwood the canal was to be extended in both directions as fast as possible and eventually the completed tunnel would form the missing link.

੨ⅆ ੨ⅆ ੨ⅆ

So far 1771 had proved to be a drier than average year. The farmers had suffered somewhat as their crops and animal fodder wilted but for canal engineering it was almost perfect. In July Brindley and John Varley were both well aware of the importance of achieving as much as possible before

---

[*] On a canal a "pound" is a level stretch of water between two locks, regardless of length. The "summit pound" is the highest above sea level and as a result the locks take the water down from both ends to the lower sections of the canal. Norwood Tunnel was to form a substantial part of the summit pound.

bad winter weather and short daylight hours hindered construction. They had no great banks of floodlights as seen on modern building sites; oil and candle lamps would throw enough light for the workmen inside the tunnel but outside tasks would be greatly restricted. It was also important to ensure that initial supplies of heavy construction materials were on-site before the winter roads made delivery impossible, or at least prohibitively expensive. So during the long summer days it was prudent to give priority to creating the immediate approaches to both ends of the tunnel, the setting up of initial workcamps, building access roads and clearing areas for storing the stocks of materials to see them through the winter. And although the tunnel was to be the first section of canal built it was not the only major site on Norwood hill, higher up was to be the reservoir to supply the water to the summit pound. This would also be a major undertaking, with progress on the dam also dependent on good weather and light.

Although the summer in many ways was a great advantage there was one disadvantage. The enormous amount of manpower needed to do the work could not be conjured up out of thin air, and there was no army of unemployed men just waiting to rush to Norwood. Neither, in those early years of the first canal age, were there large organised navvy gangs to be hired. Brindley could supply a small core of experienced men from his other projects but the bulk of the work, the digging, would have to be done by local recruits. Of course, the majority of the male population was used to working outdoors and on the land but they would still have to learn the techniques of digging a canal; that is if the men could be found. The area's greatest user of manpower was farming and during the summer harvest months large numbers of farmhands were needed. Even if the pay was better on the canal it did not do to annoy the farmer who may own your cottage and who would be your source of employment after the canal was finished. July, August and September were the main months for the hay and corn harvests in the extensive Nottinghamshire farmlands, a busy time not only for labourers but also horses, blacksmiths, carts and drivers; all of which were vital requirements for the Canal Company.[2]

So, bearing in mind all these facts and restrictions Brindley and Varley set out their schedule for the rest of the year. They had already formed a small workforce of experienced men, a nucleus for future expansion, and during July and August planned and made surveys for the accurate siting of the tunnel. Sometime during these investigations it became evident that their ideas would have to be radically changed. The details and the reasons are not known but on the 5th of September Brindley told a General Meeting of shareholders at the Crown in Retford that a "deviation is intended to be made in the tunnel at Norwood". The only two facts known are that Lax was ordered to purchase the required extra land and that the tunnel they built was double the length shown in earlier plans. The problem could have been with the tunnel itself, such as geological faults found when small bore holes were sunk, or it may have been outside influences. The tunnel would now pass through the hill at a much lower level so it may have been to lessen the number of locks needed to raise the canal. It could also have been a water supply problem in that the reservoir had to be a certain height above the level of the tunnel; perhaps it was found that this could not be achieved higher up the hill. It may have been to make the summit pound much longer, thereby holding a much larger volume of water to supply the locks at either end. Whatever the reason it must have been a crucial problem as the tunnel was now to be 2850 yards long, over one and half miles. At the time of its completion it would be the longest canal tunnel ever built in this country. Level tunnelling of this magnitude was at the limit of the available engineering skills, it was dangerous and, more to the point as far as the Company was concerned, it was expensive. Since the original estimate of £100,000 had been written into the Act of Parliament two major cost increases had arisen; the Staveley Puddlebank to protect the water supply to Staveley Forge and now Norwood Tunnel doubled in length. Financially this looked rather ominous. Nevertheless the gentlemen at the General Meeting voted that the interest earned on their investments should not be delayed and that the Company should make annual payments in March. Perhaps, in hindsight, a more prudent financial policy at that time may have prevented much future hand-wringing.

Whatever the financial ramifications there were also other matters to be resolved. The Company's small band of salaried professionals was increased by three more appointments. John Varley gained his reward for the substantial amount of work he had already undertaken; he was made Clerk of the Works with a salary of £100 a year, the same as Anthony Lax.[*] With Brindley being involved in so many other projects Varley was to look after the day-to-day organisation of the works. But Brindley would be accountable for major decisions, after all they were paying him three times as much as Varley, so his shoulders were expected to bear much of the ultimate responsibility for the canal's success. The Paymaster was to be the Reverend John Peacock of Worksop, the companion of Seth Ellis Stevenson on the promotional visit to the Archbishop of York. He was to somehow manage the problems of paying the workforce without adequate currency, the Treasurers passing to him whatever amount Varley considered necessary for the sub-contractors. For these duties Peacock was to receive £25 a year but he was also to give the Company a Bond of £300 which he would forfeit if any financial faults were found. Trying to keep track of all the payments would be the Company's new Examiner and Bookkeeper, Richard Dixon of Grove, near Retford. For a salary of £40 he was to maintain the central set of accounts and keep the Management Committee informed about the Company's situation. From this relatively junior post – compared with Lax and Varley – Richard Dixon was to progress to a more influential status over the coming years.[**] Again the symmetry between Chesterfield and Retford had been maintained. Varley was an outsider but the other three appointments were an exquisite balance of influence; Chesterfield had a crucial representative in Lax, and not much happened without him knowing about it. But Retford's man, Dixon, was watching the money and in Worksop, much under Retford's influence, the Reverend Peacock was responsible for paying the sub-contractors. Together with the two joint Treasurers, Allwood Wilkinson and George Poplewell, the management of the Company was now complete.

---

[*] Today's equivalent of Varley's title is Resident Engineer. He will now be referred to as such, to save confusion with a modern Clerk of the Works who is an unqualified person looking after an engineering site.

[**] There is no evidence that this Richard Dixon was involved with the Dixon glassworks near Chesterfield.

☙   ☙   ☙

By the middle of September the preparatory work was progressing smoothly although Brindley had probably left by now. For almost two months he had been on-site supervising the initial arrangements and now that the tunnel decisions had been made he gave Varley his instructions and left for one of his other projects. His absence was acceptable as the land for the tunnel approaches had been surveyed and set out and the first major order for construction materials had been placed. Timber was an extremely useful commodity and the first batch was for general use as scaffolding, props, hoists, dams, site buildings and tools; it was a mixture of softwoods from coniferous trees and it came in planks and roughly squared heavy beams. These would have been delivered by horse-drawn carts and stored for future use, the wood being taken to saw-pits for cutting when needed.

By the autumn good progress was being made and those involved were full of confidence. In October, at the end of the harvest months, Varley had amassed nearly three hundred men who were put to work excavating the two tunnel approaches.[3] Others would have been building the reservoir dam further up hill at Pebley. These large-scale workcamps were like a magnet to the gentlemen of the Committee, such overwhelming construction projects had never before been seen in the area. Seth Ellis Stevenson could not keep away; on the 10th of October he rode from Retford to see what was going on.[4] From his early tours of the canal sites in the north-west he must have had more knowledge than most of the visitors, and an appreciation of the skills involved. He was impressed enough to give two shillings to the navvies; a good day's wage for one man although how many were to share his largesse is not clear. With the lengthening nights one day was not enough to see everything so Stevenson stayed overnight at Harthill, a nearby village.

Situated between the tunnel and the reservoir, and less than a mile from both, unfortunate Harthill was to take the brunt of the navvy invasion. Prosperous and well-educated by the standards of the time, there were just over a hundred families. The Lord of the Manor was the 4th Duke of Leeds who lived at nearby Kiveton Hall and fifty of the children went to the local school, thirty of them paid for by the Duke. For hundreds of years the ancient village had been almost self-sufficient, everything but salt being available to them. The houses were built with timber from the woods, stone, lime and sand from the local quarries, and bricks made from clay. They could grow wheat, oats, barley, rye, flax, peas, hops and all types of vegetables. Most fruits thrived and before the days of cheap sugar the numerous smallholders, almost without exception, kept their straw-hived colonies of bees for honey. Even drink could be provided in variety, ale from native malt and hops, mead from honey, and wine from hedgerow and orchard fruits. Their clothes were made from cloth spun and woven in the village from the wool of their sheep and every house had a spinning wheel. They also had home-made linen tablecloths, napkins and sheets. Local timber, mostly oak, was used to make furniture for the houses; also carts and wagons; and sheds for the cattle and dogs. Barrels, churns, buckets, bowls and other farm and house utensils were made by the village coopers; cartwheel rims, axes and tools by blacksmiths; knives and sickles by cutlers. Other resident tradesmen were masons, tinkers, dressmakers, candle-makers, weavers, clockmakers, tailors and shoemakers. Leather for shoes and jerkins was made by taking oak bark from the woods and lime from local limestone to tan the hides of sheep and cattle. With the parson to care for the soul and run the school, an apothecary to care for the body, the church-wardens to administer local law, the village constable to enforce it, and the parish clerk to write things down, Harthill socially and industrially was a good example of the complete village community. Then along came the Chesterfield Canal Company, its construction workers bringing the Industrial Revolution to the quiet self-contained community.[5]

Strangers had been rare but now there were crowds of rough navvies wanting shelter for their wives and families. The village had little in the way of accommodation and this became a serious problem, as did entertainment, the few inns becoming crowded and rowdy. However, the major source of the villagers' complaints was not the navvies, but their families; at least the men were missing during the day but their wives were a continuous headache. Their petty thefts, belligerent behaviour, and fondness of drink disturbed and angered the residents and in an effort to calm the atmosphere the parson called a village meeting to discuss what could be done. They decided to report the problems to the Canal Company and as a result the Committee told Anthony Lax to put up handbills in the neighbourhood of Harthill stating that:-

---

CANAL NAVIGATION FROM CHESTERFIELD TO THE RIVER TRENT

Where the Works shall be carrying on for the future:

That if any wilful Mischief or Damage shall be done to any Person or Persons whatsoever by any of the Workmen employed in the Works of the said Navigation that such Workmen will be

IMMEDIATELY DISCHARGED

from the Works and that they will be

PROSECUTED FOR THE OFFENCE

by them committed at the Expence of the Company of Proprietors of the said Navigation.

These navvies were probably the core of experienced men brought from Brindley's other projects and that was why they had their families with them; they would have included blacksmiths, masons, tunnellers, carpenters and overseers for the actual digging. As with the senior posts the Company directly employed very few manual labourers, the majority of the work was done by sub-contractors who entered into an agreement to complete a set piece of work for a set payment. The sub-contractors were then responsible for employing and paying the men and finishing the task by the agreed date; the work could be a bridge, a number of locks, a section of canal between two agreed points, a number of yards of Norwood Tunnel. This way of working had the same advantages and disadvantages as it does today. On the plus side – the Company did not have to employ a huge work-force with all the problems of discipline, accommodation, food, and finding the coinage for wages; construction costs and completion dates were agreed in advance so management of the project was simplified. On the minus side – any contractor working for a fixed price is tempted to do the work as cheaply as possible, the smaller the outlay the larger the profit in his own pocket. To counter this Brindley set high standards for the work done on his projects and one of Varley's many responsibilities was to check the contractors' work to ensure the end products were satisfactory. Then, once a fortnight, two gentlemen of the Committee would visit the tunnel and reservoir sites to see for themselves and keep John Varley on his toes. Probably most of them did not know what they were looking at, but Varley accompanied them on their tour to explain the details. Generally Committee gentlemen were mainly interested in problems that would harm their investment. As long as the Resident Engineer said things were satisfactory they were content to leave matters to him. The result of this philosophy is that not many details have survived of work that went smoothly; the picture left in the Canal Company's minutes is one-sided and negative. If for no other reason but to be fair to John Varley, it is important to remember that most of his good work on the Chesterfield Canal was not written on paper; the canal itself is his main testimony.

ﾞ⬛ ﾞ⬛ ﾞ⬛

By the middle of November 1771 the work on the tunnel approaches was going very well. Morale was high and Company publicity stated that the whole canal would be finished within three years. Not only that but they had accidentally found two streams near the tunnel and these alone were said to be capable of supplying the summit pound with water, even without the reservoir.[6] As with their earlier estimates of goods that would be carried they were prone to overstatement when they were confident.

In this spirit the Committee met again on Boxing Day at the Castle Inn, Chesterfield. Unlike the other Retford gentlemen Seth Ellis Stevenson had not been able to travel the day before, as a churchman he could not leave on Christmas Day. So he had set out early the next morning, the dangers of a winter ride being alleviated by the attendance of two travelling companions, the bookkeeper Richard Dixon and Sampson Mosman.[7] For the first time the Chesterfield representatives were the majority but still the chairman was Lindley Simpson from Retford, indeed it was to be almost another two years before a Chesterfield gentleman was appointed chairman of the Committee. As usual, financial matters took up much of their time. In the three months since the Committee had last met the canal promoters in Gainsborough had made it clear that they wanted all their money back, not just the portion offered. The Company was loath to let money slip through their hands but retention was not going to be possible. The Treasurers were ordered to refund the full amount and at last the Gainsborough aspect of the canal's history was complete.

By now the Second Call or instalment was due and altogether £10 should have been paid for each share owned. Right from the start Anthony Lax had a continuous problem chasing these payments; every time a Call was due there were always some shareholders who neglected to pay as required. The Act did give the Company the power to deduct fines and, in the last resort, to order the forfeiture of shares but they were reluctant to do so. What they wanted was the money paid, not shares handed back to the Company. But it was important to set a good precedent at this early stage so Lax wrote to each defaulter stating the penalties that could be enforced if payment was not forthcoming. This had the desired effect but for three small shareholders whose stake in the Company only amounted to seven shares, all of which were taken back. In an ingratiating move five of these were offered to the Duke of Leeds; the tunnel was to be built mainly under his land and his home, Kiveton Hall, was near the eastern portal. So far he had shown no interest in the canal scheme and the Company probably wanted to tie him into a financial involvement. The move was not that successful, the Duke did take three shares but he gave the other two to his Agent; obviously the Duke of Leeds was immune to canal fever.

Those who did pay their Calls were given a receipt by one of the two Treasurers. At first these were hand written but by the end of 1771 Lax had installed rather more efficiency into the operation and pre-printed forms were available, looking rather like the small receipts commonly seen today.[8]

Canal Company Receipts

Rec.d 15 Jan.y 1771 of John Bright Esq. Ten Pounds being two P Cent.m upon his Subscrip.n for a navigable Canal from Chesterf.d to the Trent.   Geo Popplewell

£10:—

RECEIVED the 25.th Day of Dec.r . . . . 1773 of John Bright Esq.r . . . . . the Sum of Fifty . . . . Pounds, for a Call of Ten P. Pounds per Cent. on his Subscription of Five Hundred . . . . Pounds, towards the Expence of making a NAVIGABLE CANAL from CHESTERFIELD to the River TRENT.

Geo Popplewell
£.50:— TREASURER.

University of Nottingham Library

࿈   ࿈   ࿈

Norwood Tunnel, at its new length of 2850 yards, was to be the major challenge of the entire Chesterfield Canal. Compared to other construction work tunnelling was – and still is – difficult, dangerous, noisy and dark. The essential excavating knowledge was supplied by the skilled men who had been brought to the site, their mining background being the nearest available equivalent. The ancillary jobs, on the surface and in the tunnel, were done by the local men who made up the un-skilled majority of the hundreds involved. It took four years to finish Norwood Tunnel, four years of hard labour, four years of stress for John Varley.

It was pioneering work. Although mining tunnels had been dug for many years, and there were many similarities with the work at Norwood, there was one major difference; mining tunnels changed direction and level to follow the ore-bearing seams in the rock, no matter how much they had to twist and turn to do so. By contrast a canal tunnel had to be as straight as possible, maintain a standard headroom throughout and, of course, it had to be level. And level no matter what was encountered; hard rock, soft rock, coal, clay, sand, everything had to be dug or blasted out of the way, the level had been set by Brindley and Varley and was inviolate. There was no experience of doing this for over one and a half miles. The famous Harecastle Tunnel on the Trent & Mersey Canal was being built at the same time and was to be of a similar length but each project was learning its own lessons. And the high-profile Trent & Mersey had rather more of Brindley's time than the more remote Chesterfield. It was to be hoped that John Varley was up to the challenge.

The method of ensuring one level was to survey the line on the surface and then, at intervals, to dig vertical shafts down to the depth of the intended tunnel. The straight alignment of the shafts, and therefore the tunnel, was achieved by posts on the surface being placed in line of sight with a telescope. Depths were calculated by once again using the surveying method of markers on the posts giving height differences. Once the shafts had reached their assigned depths two plumb lines were dropped down each one, the top ends of which were aligned on the surface. At the bottom of each shaft the required heading was indicated by the two lines. At Norwood there were sixteen shafts spaced out along the route and their excavation was a major undertaking in itself; elliptical in shape, and brick-lined, they measured 7ft x 6ft and the deepest is thought to have gone down 97ft.[9] Men and materials were lowered down each one and from there they dug or blasted their way in both directions along the line of the tunnel. In this way they could have had thirty-four simultaneous workfaces, two at the bottom of each shaft and one at each tunnel entrance, but this is unlikely. Some of the shafts were near together, others further apart; at the deeper western end there were few, at the shallow eastern end more. A possible explanation is that sinking and lining a deep shaft involved a considerable amount of work so the minimum number were dug. Shallow shafts involved little investment for the benefit of extra workfaces. The shafts were also used to raise the rock and soil excavated to the surface, large baskets being filled and hoisted up by pulleys and winches above. Eventually the various workings extended far enough to meet with the neighbouring shaft and when they were all joined up the tunnel would be complete.

After the shafts had been sunk they probably worked night and day; there was no reason not to, as it was dark in the tunnel all the time. Tallow-oil lamps lit the scene, their flickering light casting huge shadows on the walls. The excavating gangs did the hard toil with pick-axes, shovels and gunpowder. The noise must have been deafening; the ring of iron tools on rock, the thunder of explosions, the hammering of props into place, the rumble of spoil being dragged to the foot of the shaft, the voices of the men bellowing above the clamour. Noise may be uncomfortable but there were also real dangers to contend with. Norwood hill was rich in coal and as the tunnel progressed through the seams methane was released which, when mixed with oxygen, formed the explosive and poisonous fire-damp. When the gas was found pipes were laid from the source to the bottom of the nearest shaft, there a stove was lit, the hot air rose and took the fire-damp with it up to the surface. Fresh air naturally flowed down an adjacent shaft to replace it and this meant that strong air currents, sometimes glacial in the winter, were also characteristic of working at Norwood. A further uncomfortable feature was water. In a controlled state it would be a valuable commodity when the canal was finished, but not when it was oozing or gushing out of the rock. Basic steam-driven pumps had been developed by the 1770s and these were used to remove the water. It is thought that those at Norwood were built by Francis Thompson of Ashover and were similar to his surviving engine in the Science Museum, London.

The excavating teams worked on. As they progressed they used the rough timber ordered by the Company as temporary props and stays to bear the pressure from above. A small bore was excavated first as this could be corrected more easily if an error in direction had been made. Once contact had been made with the workings from the adjacent shaft the small tunnel was enlarged to full size. Following the diggers the carpenters built a wooden arched lining to the tunnel to replace the props. Varley or one of his supervisors checked that the section was of the correct size and level, and then a further group of workmen arrived, the bricklayers. The whole tunnel was to be brick-lined, all one and a half miles of it. The bricks were laid over the wooden framework and then clay was rammed into the remaining gap between the brickwork and the tunnel surface. When the mortar had set the wooden framework was removed and if the correct angles had been achieved the arch of brickwork would remain.[*]

Timber supplies had been obtained before the winter set in, and now, in January 1772, it was necessary to think ahead to the following summer. The vast number of bricks required to line Norwood Tunnel would all have to be made on-site. This was an age of self-sufficiency, not because it was a trendy ecological philosophy but because it was necessary. Today a building contractor can simply contact the London Brick Company and order so many bricks, specify the size, colour, strength, delivery date and wait for them to arrive. John Varley's world was of a rather more basic nature. One of the major factors when planning the route of the canal was to ensure that as much construction material as possible could naturally be found in the surrounding area. For bricks they needed coal to fire the kilns and clay. The coal being dug out of the tunnel did not belong to the Canal

---

[*] Some lengths of Norwood Tunnel now have the bottom half lined with stone, with the top half of the walls and roof lined with brick. There is no mention of stone being used originally. It would have been difficult, but not impossible, to install it at a later date.

Company; the Act of Parliament stipulated that it was the property of the original landowner, in this case the Duke of Leeds. But the Company did have the right to use the tunnel coal for construction purposes, if they considered it politically expedient. Nevertheless, the area was so rich in coal that making a deal with a nearby supplier was a simple matter. Clay could also be found so all that was required was skilled brickmakers to carry out the work. Anthony Lax placed advertisements in newspapers throughout the area; anyone interested in making three million bricks during the coming summer was to contact John Varley at Harthill. The reason for waiting until the summer was that it was not easy to produce good bricks in the winter. The soft, moulded pieces of clay had to be piled in stacks until they were dry enough to go to the kilns to be burnt, and in this state they were highly vulnerable to rain and frost. Three million bricks, all to be made by hand, one at a time. Varley specified the size they were to be; the Company supplying moulds 10 inches long, 5 inches wide, 3 inches thick, although with the varying consistency of the clay the finished products would not have been all the same size.[10]

This lack of consistency in the construction materials and supplies is an important factor to bear in mind. Nothing was standardized, guaranteed or branded, no two manufactured articles could be relied on to be exactly alike. The design, workmanship, and materials used would not be known to the Canal Company; they had to rely on the trader's word as an expert. And if many traders were honest, probably as many again were not; the regulation of trade was at a minimum in that century and national laws to safeguard standards were unknown. So the majority of traders were simply more or less honest by the accepted standards of trading, and these gave them plenty of opportunities for sharp practice. Society, under its veneer of cultured elegance, was violent, crude and very tough and trade reflected these rough social conditions. It was an unregulated jungle in which, in spite of some fat pickings, the penalty for failure was often disaster and the debtors' prison. There was no limited liability for the trader to fall back on and on the other side there were virtually no laws to protect the consumer; so caution and trouble were needed on both sides all the time.

Another aspect of unstandardized supplies was the resultant engineering problems. In addition to the bricks the ironwork for making the tools and the sluice gear of the locks must have differed not only from one item to another but in the quality of the iron itself. Safety was also severely impaired. For example, the gunpowder supplied to the navvies, and more importantly the material for the fuses, could not be guaranteed to act the same way each time it was used. Also, the breaking strain of cordage when lifting heavy weights from the tunnel shafts or from the bottom of locks could not be relied upon.

Continuity of supply was also uncertain. Wisely or unwisely, Englishmen had chosen to use their land to produce grain and livestock rather than trees, the need for timber largely being met by imports from Norway and the Baltic coast. This trade was affected by the weather for the sailing ships and in times of war by enemy action. International relations with France and Spain were very strained during the early 1770s with invasion scares often sweeping coastal areas. English merchants held fairly large stocks of timber for these reasons but a prolonged interruption of the sea lanes by war always led to shortages. And the Canal Company needed many other supplies; in addition to coal, timber and bricks, they needed books, bedding, gunpowder, ironwork, lead, lime, nails, paper, pitch, tar, oil, posts, rails, ropes and stone. However, timber was the major material needed at this time, indeed such was the volume required that in addition to the imported supplies landowners were contacted to see if whole woods could be purchased near the line of the canal so that the trees could be used as required.

Tools could not be bought or hired and the great majority of them, as well as cranes, pumps and winches were made on-site. For example, a large number of wheelbarrows were needed to manhandle the vast amounts of excavated material. Constructed from iron and wood they were made by blacksmith John Barber and carpenter Thomas Sykes, self-employed craftsmen who supplied a service to the Canal Company.

ﻌ   ﻌ   ﻌ

The weather in early 1772 was very bad. It had started to snow heavily on the 8th of January; in low-lying Nottinghamshire it was still possible to travel, but only just, and hilly Derbyshire was brought to a standstill. Ten days later it was still impossible for the Chesterfield gentlemen to reach a Committee meeting in Worksop. The temperature stayed below freezing for weeks and the snow was still on the ground on the first night of February when conditions became worse. A fresh heavy fall of snow was blown into drifts by high winds and in Derbyshire there were reports of many travellers dying on the roads. Work at Norwood must have stopped during this period; with such low temperatures, short daylight hours, thick snow on the ground, and a biting frost, it is difficult to imagine what tasks could have been done.

Such a winter meant that most people stayed indoors for a considerable amount of time and it was a relief when an improvement in the weather meant that travel was again possible. John and Hannah Varley took their daughter, also Hannah, to be baptised at Harthill church.[11] Becoming the Company's Resident Engineer had enabled Varley to bring his family together again and he and Hannah lived at Harthill – but we will never know if she was one of the navvies wives who upset the villagers so much. The spring weather also saw Seth Ellis Stevenson travelling with his daughter. He and sixteen year-old Polly went from their home in Retford to Norwood to look at the canal works, probably the first time the Rev. Stevenson had seen them since the end of the previous year. A number of the general shareholders also seem to have been out and about and it become their habit to dine with the Committee whenever they met. This became so prevalent that the Company made a rule that such shareholders were, of course, welcome but that they should pay their own costs; one shilling for dinner and two shillings for a bottle of wine.

There was an atmosphere of great intensity about the canal construction at this time, everything had to be done "with the greatest expedition" and the pressure on the work-force was severe. It was important that the summer be used to substantially increase the progress of the initial phases; the excavation of Norwood Tunnel and the approach channels at each portal, the dam for the reservoir at Pebley, and the production of the three million bricks ordered the previous winter. With these matters in hand James Brindley was back in Harthill in June telling the Committee of his formidable plans for the second phase. Finishing Norwood Tunnel was to be a priority task and he estimated that it would be completed in two years time. Meanwhile, the next major objective was to extend the canal two and a half miles towards Retford, from the eastern end of Norwood Tunnel to the first lock which Brindley intended to be near Old Spring Wood (Thorpe Salvin); this was to be done as soon as possible.[*]

The priority given to this work highlights Brindley's sensible practice of making sections of a canal navigable so that the Company could benefit from water carriage for the heavy construction materials. If the whole point of building the canal was to move substantial loads more easily then it was common sense to arrange the work so that the Canal Company would be the first to benefit. Brindley's usual practice was also to have boats fitted out as floating carpenters and smiths workshops to enable the craftsmen to move along to where they were needed. Therefore, boat-building was undertaken at a very early stage and the first boats on the Chesterfield Canal were involved in such work. Brindley's plans for the summer of 1772 also included the accumulation of the abundant amounts of timber and stone needed to build the great flights of locks which were to descend from both ends of the summit pound; the Norwood flight going westwards towards Chesterfield and down to the Rother valley, and the Thorpe and Turnerwood locks going eastwards towards Retford and down into the valley of the River Ryton. The construction materials were to be acquired and moved during the summer, using boats on the canal and taking advantage of the dry roads, ready for the locks to be built during the next winter. An example of the lack of the concise engineering planning we would expect today was that Brindley thought these locks would be "about 40 in number". Nevertheless, the construction of these large flights of locks, simultaneously with Norwood Tunnel, was a tremendous engineering feat. At this early stage of the canal age it is indicative of Brindley's breadth of vision, his engineering knowledge, and his confidence, that he could embark upon such an undertaking in so little time. It also says much for his reputation that shareholders in the Company were willing to invest substantial sums to carry out his plans when nothing on this scale had been achieved before. In addition to this

---

[*]   Built as intended this is the top lock of the Thorpe Top Treble flight.

the configurations of the Norwood and Thorpe lock flights were bold and, at the time, breathtaking. The Thorpe flight contains two treble and two double staircases, the Norwood flight has one quadruple and three treble staircases and this has remained unique in this country.*

As Brindley had already stated, the rest of the summit pound to the top of the Thorpe locks was to be dug and filled with water so that it could be used, but the stretches of canal between the locks was to wait until all the locks and bridges were done. Brindley estimating that all the digging of these parts of the canal channel could be done in less than one year. As if that was not enough the schedule also included the banking for the approaches to the two aqueducts that would be needed to carry the canal over the River Ryton at Shireoaks and Worksop. Not a man to waste time, Brindley expected the whole canal to be completed in four years, that is by June 1776.

The Committee, having heard Brindley's presentation of the above schedule, ordered that "the same be proceeded upon and the works executed accordingly". A simple enough phrase for the gentlemen to utter but its interpretation into innumerable actions rested on John Varley's relatively inexperienced shoulders – but the towering presence of Brindley was behind him, a solace to both Varley and the gentlemen shareholders.

Brindley's presence at the canal workings also resolved, for the present time, the question of how wide the canal should be. Should it have narrow locks and tunnels that would restrict the boats to just under 7ft beam, or should wider boats be catered for? Retford had always favoured a wide canal, the influence of the Idle and Trent in their area showing that if large boats could use the canal they could also go out onto those rivers, whereas narrow canal boats would have to move their cargoes to river boats for onward shipping. The Retford gentlemen had raised the matter yet again at the last General Meeting because if the plans were changed Norwood Tunnel would have to be wider to take the larger craft. The matter was unresolved at that time as Brindley was not present but when he did return to Harthill his opinion was that the canal should be built to

---

* A "staircase" of locks is where two or more locks are linked without any intervening length of canal between them. The top gate of one lock being the bottom gate of the next.

the original plan, that is with narrow locks and tunnels.

Unusually for him Seth Ellis Stevenson was not present at this latest meeting with Brindley so had been unable to argue the case for a wide canal. Instead he was touring the Midlands, and probably various canal sites, with a party of friends and did not return until the end of June. And before that the poor man had spent five miserable days at home, in agony with a violent toothache and an abscess which burst after swelling the left side of his face. Dental treatment was available but it was very expensive; it rather sounds as if he was inclined to let the infection take its course and keep his money in his pocket.

ᘒ   ᘒ   ᘒ

Throughout the summer of 1772 the construction continued in accordance with Brindley's plans. The working methods and organisation at Norwood must have been similar to those described on other Brindley canals; he always used his own techniques, had set ideas, and John Varley had been trained the same way.

"Arriving at the head of the works we were struck with the excellent and spirited appearance of active business. Here is a very large timber-yard, well stowed with all sorts of wood and timbers for framed buildings, and building boats, barges, and all kinds of floating machines. The boat builders yard joins, and several boats, barges, etc are always on the stocks. Next to these is the stone mason's yard, where lie vast piles of stones, ready squared, for loading barges with, to convey to any part of the navigation where they may be wanted, either for building, or repairing of bridges, aqueducts, wharfs, warehouse, etc. Thus every part of the whole design acts in concert, and yields mutual assistance, which is the grand art of economical management."

Everywhere was buzzing with activity and John Varley had more than enough to do, his first post as Resident Engineer leaving him little time for rest. He rode again and again between the various work-camps; along the line of the tunnel, to the reservoir, and along the new canal to Thorpe Salvin. As a surveyor he checked that all the excavations were being made in the right place, as a manager he had to watch the actions of at least his supervisory staff, as a purchaser he had to inspect all the

Examples of the treatment Seth Ellis Stevenson could have purchased for his bad tooth.

DERBY
To the NOBILITY and GENTRY

ARRIVED here three Weeks since, from Birmingham, where she has met in her Profession as a DENTIST with an Encouragement far exceeding her Expectations, Mrs DE ST. RAYMOND, who practices the Art (in which she is acknowledged to excel) of scaling, cleaning, whitening, preserving, drawing, and transplanting TEETH. She takes away without causing any Pain, all Scurf fur and stone-like Substance, which evidently destroys both Gums and Teeth. She fastens those which are loose, fills up the hollow ones, prevents their farther Detriment, and such as are found from aching and decaying. She occasionally draws Teeth and Stumps, even the most difficult to be got out; and when the Skill of other Practitioners proves ineffectual, she makes and sets in artificial Teeth; also transplants natural ones from one Head into another. Which Operations she performs with a matchless Skill and Tenderness.
Her price for cleaning Teeth is 5s.3d but if extraordinary bad, or else if either a Tooth or Stump should be drawn, it is Half-a-Guinea, and the same for filling up a Tooth, or setting in an Artificial one. Her Terms for transplanting a Front Tooth is 6 Guineas, to be paid when the Tooth is strongly rooted into the Jaw and useful.

Mr Wooffendale, Surgeon-Dentist in Sheffield, performs all Operations on the TEETH; fixes in artificial Teeth, from one to whole Set; also whole and half Sets of artificial Teeth, with the enamel on every Tooth. Likewise fixes in natural Teeth, without Pain or inconvenience, so as to escape Discernment. He recommends to the Public, his ABSTERGENT LOTION for the Scurvy in the Gums, and DENTIFRICE for cleaning the Teeth. The Lotion 5s, Dentifrice 1s with Directions, and Brushes for the Teeth and Gums at 6d each.

supplies as they were delivered, as an official he had to write reports for the Committee on progress to date and the costs involved. Above all he had to solve all the day-to-day engineering problems that arose, only major strategic matters could warrant the delay of referring to Brindley.

As well as all these tasks Varley had to ensure that everyone knew that the need for bricks to line Norwood Tunnel was paramount, they must make as many as possible during the summer. But nevertheless the requirement, advertised during the previous winter, for the manufacture of three million bricks must have run into manpower problems. In July the Company admitted that "a number of understanding brick-makers are wanted immediately upon the works at Harthill . . . where they will meet with encouragement equal to their merit . . ."[12] Such was the magnitude of the task that there were many jobs involved with brick production; Overlookers of the Brickworks, Clerks of the Brickworks, Master Brickmakers and Clay Temperers amongst them. The pay varied for each grade but an Overlooker, such as George Blake, was paid twelve shillings a week.

Brickmaking had not changed for many years, it was only the volume required for canals that was new. Each Brickmaker sat at a table with a pile of clay by his side which had already been mixed and prepared by the Clay Temperer so that it was the right consistency. The Brickmaker then took a handful of the clay and threw it into a wooden mould, heaping up the material to ensure that all the corners were filled. Then he took a flat tool, which was kept soaking in water, and passed it over the top of the mould to remove the excess clay. He then slid the mould to the edge of the table where it was adroitly turned onto its side by the brickmaker's assistant, the Carrier. He then placed the clay and mould onto a board on which he carried a number of bricks outside. There, in a storage area, he placed the bricks flat on the ground and lifted the moulds to leave the soft clay. The Carrier then cleaned the moulds with sand and took them back to the Brickmaker, who had meanwhile filled some more. A good team, a Clay Temperer, Brickmaker and Carrier, could make two thousand bricks in a day; an exceptional team could make three thousand. A number of such teams would have been working near Norwood Tunnel for a considerable amount of time.

121

The soft bricks were left on the ground for a day for the clay to harden then stacked up to ten courses high and covered in straw. They were left like this for three or four weeks and then moved to the kiln. The kiln itself, of course, had to be built on the site and supplies of wood and coal obtained for fuel. The hardened bricks were then stacked in the kiln and a fire allowed to burn for two days. Then, after they had cooled, the bricks were ready for use. Because of the differences in the clay mixture and the degree of heat in various parts of the kiln the finished bricks varied in size and strength; yet another example of the non-standardisation that Varley had to deal with.

As well as the bricks the mortar for laying them also had to be made on-site. Again, in a pre-cement age, it was not a case of contacting the Blue Circle Cement Company and ordering a number of lorry loads of ready-mixed. Lime mortar had to be made by burning broken limestone in kilns for about five days and then mixing it with sand and water. It is one of the oldest building materials known; the Great Wall of China was largely laid with lime mortar and the Romans used it extensively for their military engineering. So as the canal progressed kilns for making bricks and lime-mortar were strategically set up, not necessarily at the nearest point to where the bricks were needed, but sometimes where the input materials were available. The logistics of obtaining and moving construction materials in the most cost effective manner was a crucial part of the Resident Engineer's responsibilities.

ï ï ï

During the busy construction months of the summer of 1772 it was obvious to any visitor the work involved for John Varley, but the paperwork making it all possible was continuing outside the glow of the limelight. Behind the scenes Anthony Lax was assiduously working in his office in Chesterfield; writing to shareholders who had still not paid the latest Call on their shares, arranging Committee and General meetings, dealing with any legal disputes about the contents of the Act of Parliament and, most importantly at this time, arranging for the purchase of the land required for the next stretch of canal. Because the Company's money was being raised by shares paid in instalments they did not have the money in hand to purchase all the land in advance. In addition to this cash flow problem it was not possible to make an accurate survey too far in advance as geological problems on the previous sections may have caused a detour there. So Varley worked ahead of the navvies, accurately surveying the next stretch and passing the details on to Anthony Lax.

Land purchase was a fundamental part of the canal's construction and it was crucial that it was done efficiently. Although the Act of Parliament gave compulsory purchase powers it did not stipulate the price to be paid. Of course, the landowners wanted the price as high possible, the Canal Company as low as possible and somehow Lax was to reconcile the two sides. As an employee of the Canal Company it would not have been acceptable for him to set the price so he used independent Land Valuers, some of whom were more "independent" than others. They took into consideration not only the use to which the land had previously been put, but also the inconvenience that would be caused by having a canal cut through a field and making access to the other side impossible. They also considered the status of the landowner; in a perfect world this would not make any difference, in the materialistic world of 1772 the distinction was clear. Dealing with the Agent of a great Duke was one matter; large tracts of land could be purchased by one agreement. Dealing with myriad small-holders, each the owner of a few yards, was altogether more time-consuming, albeit more economical in the price paid. Lax, as usual, dealt with these matters effectively; negotiations at a Ducal level warranted his personal attention, but contacts with lesser beings he delegated to his assistants.

It may sound as if writing in his office was an easy option for Anthony Lax compared to Varley's working conditions. It may have been comfortable, but not safe, as smallpox was in Chesterfield.[13] After the disappearance of the plague a hundred years before, smallpox remained the most feared of all diseases, killing one in seven of those infected. It was known that people did not catch smallpox twice so a form of treatment was available, if you could afford it, but it was to be another twenty-six years before Edward Jenner published his findings about inoculation with cowpox. In 1772 if Anthony Lax had visited Mr Sutton, the travelling surgeon who was in town, he would have been inoculated by having the actual smallpox virus introduced via a shallow scratch on his arm. If this resulted in a mild attack of smallpox the method worked, if a more severe attack was the result then he would have been unlucky! The occurrence of disease was a factor to be taken into account when travelling about the country and the introduction of such a virus into the navvy gangs on the canal would have been disastrous.

INOCULATION

MR SUTTON, Surgeon, formerly of Thurlby Hall, Newark, and Brother to Mr Sutton in London, informs the Public that he having engaged to inoculate a Party of Patients in Chesterfield, and the Small Pox prevailing there, has taken lodgings at Mr Wright's Jeweller, in Chesterfield, in order to inoculate Gentlemen's Families, or others in the Town and Neighbourhood thereof. Mr Sutton thinks it unnecessary to say any Thing in favour of a Practice so universally approv'd of, except that he has inoculated near Seven Thousand Patients in the Space of eight Years, without Loss of a single Patient

Chesterfield, July 27, 1772

John Varley was busy surveying near Worksop, and the area required his personal attention as much of the land belonged to the Duke of Norfolk. The canal would have to cross fertile areas currently growing grass, wheat, beans, oats; and Haggonfield and Worksop Commons were covered in valuable timber-producing trees.[14] The purchase of such land would not be easy or cheap and for the rest of the year Anthony Lax was to be busy dealing with the Duke's Agent, and the Duke himself when he was in residence at Worksop Manor.

ε❧ ε❧ ε❧

The summer of 1772 had been well used. By the autumn Norwood Tunnel was well underway, the approach works had been excavated and a great number of bricks produced, the reservoir high in the hills was progressing. The canal channel had been dug from the tunnel to the top of the first lock on the descent to Worksop. This stretch passed through the rock-producing area of Anston and clung to the rock face, its twisting course following the contour so that the canal could stay level and the summit pound be as long as possible. Much of it was wooded and many trees had to be cut down and the roots moved by ropes and winches. For much of this length the land on the south side of the canal rose above it, on the north side, beyond the towpath, the land immediately dropped away to fields and Lindrick Common. It had not been easy work. In accordance with Brindley's orders various supplies had been accumulated ready for building the first locks, those at Thorpe Salvin, during the winter; coal, oak and ash trees, posts and rails for fencing, ironwork from Messrs Walker & Co of Rotherham, bricks, lime, and large amounts of general timber – six tons of squared beams fifty feet long plus ten tons of various lengths between twenty five and forty feet, all to come from Riga on the Baltic coast. The two Treasurers and Richard Dixon the Bookkeeper were busy paying for such items and keeping the financial records. Varley was responsible for checking all the supplies before they were paid for, a rule brought in because some timber purchased earlier had not been satisfactory. At the same time a water supply had to be found to fill the new section to Thorpe Salvin so that the supplies could be moved to where they would be needed in the winter.

On the 2nd of September the gentlemen of the Committee met at one of the busy coaching inns in Retford, the White Hart on the corner of the Market Square. The meeting was brief, the main object being to wind up any outstanding items before the General Meeting to be held at the same inn the following day. Starting at three o'clock, there was plenty of time to finish their business before dining in the evening with their Engineer, the famous James Brindley. The next morning more shareholders arrived for the General Meeting at 11 o'clock. In an atmosphere of prosperity the gentlemen revelled in the glow of success and Brindley's presence. They heard that the Company's financial situation was so favourable that the next Call for paying for the shares was postponed until December, the Treasurers stating that the Company had enough money in hand to pay for any foreseeable expenses. Most of the Company officials now owned shares; Richard Dixon had two, Anthony Lax five, Godfrey Heathcote ten, the two Treasurers had also invested their money – Allwood Wilkinson in Chesterfield had fifteen, George Poplewell in Retford, sixteen. Seth Ellis Stevenson now had eight shares and his Retford friend, Lindley Simpson, fifteen. These were substantial investments for such gentlemen but everything was going so well and Brindley himself had shown his confidence by buying fifteen shares.

At the end of the General Meeting they dispersed, confident that their foresight in becoming involved in such a prominent project had secured their status as leaders of their local communities. Three weeks later James Brindley was dead.

CHAPTER SEVEN

The First Crises

On leaving Retford Brindley had ridden across the high Derbyshire hills to Staffordshire where the Management of the Trent & Mersey Canal, led by Josiah Wedgwood, wanted a survey made. A short branch canal from the main line at Stoke-on-Trent to Froghall was required, bringing access to valuable deposits of coal, iron-ore and limestone. In completing the final stages Brindley was soaked in a violent downpour of rain and caught a chill. He was taken to the inn at nearby Ipstone where his condition was worsened by his being put into a damp bed. He became seriously ill and was taken to his home at Turnhurst. Josiah Wedgwood called a friend, an eminent scientist and physician Dr Erasmus Darwin,[*] who visited Brindley and diagnosed the complaint that had troubled his patient for several years as diabetes. This, together with the chill that had turned to pneumonia, put Brindley beyond help. About noon on 27 September 1772 James Brindley died at his home. He left a young widow, Anne, and two daughters, thousands of worried canal investors, hundreds of distraught gentlemen on Management Committees, and a group of apprehensive Resident Engineers who suddenly had sole responsibility for major civil engineering projects.

The stunning news reached Chesterfield at the beginning of October. Anthony Lax immediately called the Committee together for an unscheduled meeting on the 6th of that month at the George in Worksop. The atmosphere was rather different to their last meeting there, just over two months ago when confidence and hopes were high. Now Seth Ellis Stevenson was saddened as well as worried, describing James Brindley as his "worthy and much respected friend". But no matter how disheartened

---

[*]   Grandfather of Charles Darwin.

they were the Company had to respond to this sudden crisis. Who could replace the irreplaceable Brindley? No one. What options were there? Cancel the project – no, it was far too advanced for that. Call a special General Meeting to allow the shareholders to decide – no, that was politically unsound, better to keep the power for such crucial decisions in the Committee's hands. Carry on as they were – almost every other Canal Company is in the same predicament – all very well, but was John Varley good enough? The vital question. Was John Varley good enough?

Luckily Brindley had been on-site just a month ago and had given Varley his instructions for the schedule laid down earlier in the year. This work alone would fill the winter and spring months so there was no immediate engineering dilemma. As long as the major shareholders could be calmed it was possible to wait a little longer before officially appointing a new Principal Engineer. Poor John Varley, everything had been progressing so well on his first major project, and now everything was again uncertain. Was this a great opportunity for promotion or the death knoll of his career? Would the Company appoint someone else who would bring in his own man to replace him? Looking at the situation from beyond a two hundred year safety barrier it is easy to see that Varley would have been unwise to worry. There were not that many canal engineers in the country and almost all were engaged on projects of their own, on Brindley schemes. If the Company did not promote Varley, the shareholders would only accept an experienced outside candidate and they were going to be much sought after by all the Canal Companies in the same situation. Varley's main advantage was that he had been involved in the Chesterfield Canal right from the original surveys, his knowledge of the project was unsurpassable. An outside appointee would need to retain him as Resident Engineer, there was really no alternative. Even so, it was an uncertain time.

Varley was called before the Committee and "carefully examined" about his ability to carry out the plans laid down by Brindley, at least in the short term. He was certain that he could but the gentlemen had to consider that there had already been one or two minor problems with his paperwork and management skills. Were these unimportant or were they indicative of fundamental lapses? A bill for a large amount of timber had been presented by a Mrs Wilson, widow of one of the members of the first Committee, Joseph Wilson of Worksop. He had been a woodman and now his widow was carrying on the business. The timber did not appear in Varley's records and he could not explain to the Committee why this should be so. He was told to go and investigate and if the bill was correct he was to sign it before passing it on to Treasurer George Poplewell for payment. As a result of this lapse Varley was ordered to check all supplies as they were delivered, to keep a record of the value of each item, and to present the bills at the next Committee meeting for payment authorisation. Two further rules were made to put additional curbs on Varley's financial actions; he was not allowed to decide from whom supply purchases were to be made, and he was not to deal direct with landowners who had timber to sell, instead the Company appointed two Timber Valuers who were to conduct the negotiations. Varley was told to keep a record of all financial obligations so that the Bookkeeper could include the figures in the Company accounts. This Varley had been doing for the last few months but the figure he advised to Richard Dixon for "debts owing for materials" was another of his suspiciously round figures, £300 exactly.

With whatever misgivings they may have had the Committee really had no alternative but to allow Varley to carry on. No faults had been found with his surveying or engineering, it was only his administrative skills that were less effective. For the meantime John Varley was "ordered to continue to carry on and execute the work pursuant to the Plan and Directions given him by the said Mr Brindley until further orders". The meeting finished and the gentlemen dispersed to consider their options. The next General Meeting was scheduled for May and by that time a new Principal Engineer must have been approached and terms agreed, the shareholders only having to vote on his appointment.

As the most knowledgeable of the Committee on canal matters it was natural that Seth Ellis Stevenson should play a crucial role in the selection of Brindley's successor. Three weeks later he went from Retford to Harthill, riding his old horse Jockey and accompanied by a servant, to carry out a detailed investigation of the current state of the canal workings.[1] Stevenson not only formed an opinion on the engineering but on the Engineer as well, lodging in the same village as Varley for ten days. The Committee was next scheduled to meet in Retford at the end of November, the venue and the winter month meant that few Chesterfield representatives would be present – with some pre-meeting canvassing it would be easy for Stevenson to obtain a vote in favour of his views. In the event, only two of Chesterfield's ten eligible members attended at the White Hart – even though the two gentlemen were of some stature in the Company. Charles Kinder, a hosier, had attended Parliament as a witness and Joseph Storrs, an iron and lead merchant, had also been involved in the canal project from the very earliest days. They both attended the majority of meetings, no matter when or where they were held, and it may be surmised that if the rest of Chesterfield's representatives on the Committee had been as diligent many crucial decisions may have been reversed. On paper the influence in the Company was split evenly between Retford and Chesterfield – in practice Retford was all-powerful, at least during these early years of the canal's construction. Seth Ellis Stevenson's recommendation to the Committee was that a new Principal Engineer should be appointed and that for the sake of continuity of working methods he should be one of the men trained by Brindley, but rather more experienced than John Varley. Seth Ellis Stevenson's choice was Hugh Henshall.

The appointment would have to be on the same basis of attendance as had been accepted with Brindley, an overall responsibility and inspection visits made as appropriate. More time would not be available as Henshall was the Resident Engineer of the most illustrious canal project of the day, the Trent & Mersey Canal being built on the other side of the Pennines. His father, John Henshall, was a surveyor who had been a colleague of Brindley in the early days of the great man's career. Brindley often visited their home to discuss business, at the same time taking a liking to the young daughter of the household, Anne, whom he married and was now his widow. Being Brindley's brother-in-law and involved with the Trent & Mersey Hugh Henshall had been groomed to succeed.

The Committee accepted the proposal and Anthony Lax was told to write to Hugh Henshall asking him if he would inspect the work being undertaken on the Chesterfield Canal and give guidance to Varley. If this was acceptable would he also be agreeable to his name being submitted to the General Meeting in May for appointment as the Company's Principal Engineer. In the meantime, the gentlemen of the Committee would take it upon themselves to increase their own surveillance of the canal. Instead of officially visiting the work-sites once a fortnight, they would now bother Varley every week; two representatives from Chesterfield covering alternate weeks with two from Retford.

Henshall did agree to the Committee's proposals and he was asked to make a complete survey and inspection of the work done so far and to report his findings. This he did but by the General Meeting a subtle change of mind had taken place, not by Henshall but by Stevenson. The reports on the canal work must have been complimentary to Varley because the Committee now saw a way of saving some money. Seth Ellis Stevenson addressed the General Meeting and proposed that Henshall be appointed to a new post, Inspector of the Works; for a contracted number of surveys and reports he could be paid a lower salary than as Principal Engineer. The shareholders unanimously accepted the proposal. At subsequent negotiations agreement was reached on the responsibilities of the new Inspector of the Works. Such had been Brindley's status Companies had been unable to set a minimum attendance stipulation on his salary. Hugh Henshall did not have the same prestige. Therefore, the Committee took the opportunity to increase their overall control of the project, especially the finances. One inspection every quarter would be required with Henshall presenting his findings, in person, at the following General or Committee Meeting. Annually he was to spend at least fifty-six days on this task. If he found any faults he was to give written and signed directions to Varley who would show them to the Committee for approval to carry out the corrections. The first survey was to include a valuation of the work done to date, broken down into separate operations and including the supplies purchased and still not used. For these duties the Company would pay Hugh Henshall an annual salary of 130 guineas.

ða   ða   ða

Such administrative matters, important though they were to the

131

Committee and the shareholders, were low in the navvies list of priorities. Men were dying in Norwood Tunnel.

Living in a later century it is difficult to imagine the impact that pain, disfigurement and death made on the everyday life of the whole population. Slight wounds became infected and festered for weeks. Fractured bones set badly; minor irritations such as headache and toothache became, as with Seth Ellis Stevenson, major problems paralysing ordinary activity. To combat pain there was only opium or alcohol, in the volumes necessary to be effective they were hardly helpful in maintaining a normal lifestyle. Gastric upsets from eating bad food and septic problems from rotten teeth were universal. The medical "profession" could not offer much in the way of treatment; a survey of northern England showed that of 266 practitioners only 68 had received any form of medical training. They had no thermometers or antiseptics. Surgery was not always available, with no anaesthetics perhaps some patients were thankful; its impact was devastating and the outcome incalculable. Patent medicines for every ailment were widely advertised in newspapers, together with letters from satisfied customers – what effect they had on their unsatisfied customers is not known. Currently at the Three Cranes in Chesterfield "a Practitioner in Physick" was claiming to cure "dropsy, the King's Evil, cancers, ulcers (with cutting), ruptures and bearings down, thick necks in men and women, stone and gravel, rheumatism, surfeits, fits, hypocondriack, over flowing of the gall . . . and many other disorders too tedious to mention".[2]

Toiling as a navvy on a canal increased even this high level of suffering. The men were used to manual labour but for them the work was still hard; the muscular exertion a source of frequent injuries and ruptures leading to premature ageing and physical breakdown. For some the price was higher.

John Hutchinson was one of the local men who had been tempted by the rewards of working on the canal. The expansive work-camps of Norwood Tunnel were just over a mile from where he lived in the village of Wales, together with his wife and a considerable family of small children. He died in an accident as he was being lowered down one of the shafts to a tunnel work-face. In contradiction of the modern uncaring image of Canal

Companies the Committee authorised John Peacock, as Paymaster, to give Hutchinson's widow five guineas to help with the upkeep of the fatherless children. The shafts from the surface to the tunnel floor were dangerous places. Not long afterwards Edward Bunting was severely injured; standing at the bottom of a shaft he was hit by a large basket of rocks which, being hauled to the surface, broke free and crashed down on to him. He was taken to Harthill and put to bed at one of the inns. They called for medical attention but the surgery and drugs applied by George Frith were to no avail. Edward Bunting died and was buried in Harthill's parish churchyard. Again the Committee showed a caring face, after his death paying the bills outstanding for his accommodation and medical treatment.

The navvies were now quite an army, the size and distribution of which was making management difficult – but equally problematical was the transient nature of the workforce. It was not easy to keep track of them all and John Best was paid twelve shillings a week to count the men employed at the works as often as twice a day. The Company also made a new rule:

> ". . . that if any workmen shall run away and shall be brought back by Mr Varley, or any other person employed by him, that the expences incurred thereby be deducted out of such workmens wages."

But it should not be imagined that the workforce was untrustworthy without reason. Their wages were not paid as regularly as they should have been and another rule was passed to the effect that John Varley was to pay the sub-contractors, and therefore the workmen, at least once a month. However, the terms of employment were strict. If work was not carried out "in a compleat or proper manner" or not according to John Varley's directions then the cost of the damage was stopped out of the offending workman's wages. The offender was also dismissed and Varley was "never to employ them afterwards at any of the works of the said navigation". Most of the work was done via sub-contractors and they were also subject to strict management. One of their number was Charles Jones from Preston-on-the-Hill near Warrington, on the route of the Trent & Mersey Canal. He had left his son to carry on the work in Norwood Tunnel and this had not been satisfactorily carried out. Jones was told to attend a Committee meeting

> ". . . and give an Account of the Tunnel under his care and that if he does not attend and give such Account his Son will be discharged from the Service of the Company".

All these aspects made control of the project difficult and Richard Dixon, the Bookkeeper, was ordered to make a complete survey of the works once a fortnight and to allocate two days to the task. Immediately afterwards his findings were to be written in a report and sent to the Committee members in Chesterfield and Retford. It really does appear that it must have been quite busy along the new towpath – John Varley was continually riding up and down checking progress, John Best was along twice a day counting the navvies, Richard Dixon was surveying the works and the supplies not used once a fortnight, two Committee gentlemen were looking at whatever they looked at once a week, and Hugh Henshall was inspecting everything once every three months.

ਕ ਕ ਕ

In judging Norwood Tunnel the major feature of the canal, it should not be overlooked that the great flights of locks at either end of the summit pound were also outstanding examples of early civil engineering. At the eastern end the canal was to be taken down into the valley of the River Ryton, twenty-two locks to be built in one mile. The first fifteen, now known as the Thorpe flight, was to include two treble and two double staircases; below them the Turnerwood flight of seven locks was to drop the canal to Shireoaks on the outskirts of Worksop. As Norwood is often missing from a modern "roll of honour" listing canal tunnels so the Thorpe/Turnerwood flight is usually overlooked when lauding Brindley's work. Publicity creates fame, and fame creates publicity; as proven by the tabloid press the process sometimes has little to do with merit. But such errors and omissions are the faults of a later age and do not lessen the significance of what was achieved on the Chesterfield Canal. Certainly the local population in 1773 was fully aware of the magnitude of the works and the locks were looked on with wonderment; they were christened the "The Giant's Staircase" and they became the destination of many family outings.

The schedule that Brindley had defined stated that construction of the locks should start during the winter of 1772-3, together with bridges as required. The materials needed had been amassed during the summer – as planned the first section of canal, from the tunnel to the site of the first lock, had been finished so that boats could carry the heavy supplies. In accordance with Brindley's philosophy Varley built locks from whatever materials were most convenient, bricks or stone, but the majority of the work was hidden – the massive foundations and piling needed to cope with the immense pressure of the water that would be captured each time the lock was used.

Twenty-two locks in a mile was to be a tremendous challenge. The excavation of each lock chamber needed vast amounts of earth to be moved, the surveyor defining the depth and the navvies digging out the area including extra width for the foundation piles. The use of foundation piles for lock construction seems to have been such a well accepted practice that little attention was paid to it by writers of the time; as a result much of this pioneering work is poorly documented and it was not until a much later date that useful data on canal construction was recorded. One early writer did show timber piles under a lock in his drawings but dismissed them with the sole comment that they should be "12ft or 15ft long according as the ground is hard or soft".[3] When the foundations were in place the bricklayers or stonemasons used timber scaffolding to enable them to line the lock chamber with walls of strong masonry on each side and at the bottom; building up row by row until reaching ground level. Sometimes wood was used but there is no evidence of this on the Chesterfield Canal, not surprisingly as stone, and clay for bricks, was abundant. Sluices were also dug at each end of the lock so that the water flow could be controlled to empty and fill the lock when in use. The iron gear for working the sluices was cast and the carpenters constructed the massive timber lock-gates. To set the gates in place needed pulleys and cranes to take the immense weight, lowering them down to be fixed on their hinges. When a lock is in use the gates are strained in proportion to the depth of water they have to support; in the 1770s gate design was still basic and no more than twelve or thirteen feet of water could be supported, more than one lock becoming a necessity if a greater drop was required. One last important item was the excavation of a by-wash; as each lock would effectively form a dam across the canal it was always necessary to dig a channel for any excess water to by-pass a lock. For instance, heavy rain would increase the water-level in a canal if such escape channels were not available.

In one mile all this work had to be done twenty-two times, one mile that must surely be John Varley's greatest memorial. Norwood Tunnel was started under Brindley's eagle eye and finished under Henshall's; but the Thorpe and Turnerwood locks were built after Brindley's death and before Henshall had made his presence felt. The surveying challenge was as onerous as the construction engineering, with such a concentration of locks the level of the canal before and after each fall had to be very accurate. In his calculations Varley also had to allow for practical features such as the wharfs and bridges that had to be built on the short level stretches between the locks. Nothing of the magnitude of that one mile of canal had previously been attempted in this country and John Varley's reputation should surely reflect the enormity of the achievement.

છ્ટ છ્ટ છ્ટ

Construction of the Thorpe/Turnerwood locks, however demanding, was not allowed to fill Varley's time and the Resident Engineer had also surveyed ahead of the current work sites and designated the route from Shireoaks, at the bottom of the great lock flights, to Worksop. In a distance of three miles the canal would cross the River Ryton on an aqueduct and make a gradual descent, via nine more locks, to the outskirts of Worksop.[*] There was no reason to suppose that this section would cause any problems and for engineer John Varley this proved to be correct, but for administrator Anthony Lax it was to be anything but straightforward. Starting at Shireoaks, Lax entered into his usual negotiations with the landowner, this time John Hewitt of Shireoaks Hall. A cantankerous,

---

[*]   Worksop has grown in the last two hundred years and now the canal runs through the centre. In 1773 the town was rather smaller, not extending far beyond the market square which was just under half a mile from the new canal.

Progress to date

disorganised old man, Hewitt was very sensitive about his status as a landowner; always feeling the pressure of the surrounding estates of the various Dukes who over-shadowed him in local esteem. Nevertheless, Lax managed to agree a price for the parcels of land required, a substantial part of which was Haggonfield Common. As commonland this was not "owned" as such by anyone but the rights were held by the Lord of the Manor, a title John Hewitt said was his. A contract was signed and armed with this paperwork the Canal Company pegged out the route across the Common and, quite innocently, ran into a land-ownership dispute that had been going on for at least thirty years. The Company soon found out that the rights to Haggonfield Common were claimed not only by John Hewitt but also by the resident of Worksop Manor, the Duke of Norfolk.[4] To add to the confusion there was no obvious boundary where Haggonfield Common and the neighbouring Gateford Common met. This dispute, which up to now had only been a matter of local interest, now became a legal headache for Lax and the Canal Company. So far they had not had to negotiate for commonland and even Lax, as a man of the law, was uncertain of the legalities involved – the compulsory purchase powers conferred by the Act of Parliament being a new and controversial concept. During January 1773 Henry Howard, a distant relative and the Chief Agent of the Duke of Norfolk, heard about the Canal Company's plans and was not pleased. Only the previous week the Company had earned his disapproval by asking to discuss the purchase of some of the Duke's land, arranging a meeting between the land-valuers representing both parties, and then cancelling at the last minute with no reason given. Now Henry Howard heard that the canal was to cross Haggonfield Common and that the Company saw no reason to discuss the matter with him. From Howard's point of view the Duke of Norfolk was Lord of the Manor and therefore the Company's attitude was a gross insult and unacceptably high-handed.

Although Anthony Lax had already dealt with the Agents of the Dukes of Devonshire and Leeds his usual business acumen was to be insufficient this time. The young administrator was not astute enough to realise that although the other Agents adequately represented their master's interests they did not have the passionate loyalty of Henry

Howard to his Duke; a loyalty forged in years when fortunes had been low. When his wine business had failed Howard would have been bankrupt and destitute had not the current Duke of Norfolk kindly rescued him. The Duke paid off all his debts, appointed him Agent of his northern estates and gave him a house in Sheffield.[*]

Powerful aristocratic landowners are not to be treated lightly. The Duke's attorney, John Mander, took legal advice from London which was to make clear to John Hewitt and the Canal Company – and everyone else – the Duke's right to the soil and timber of Haggonfield Common, timber which was valued at nearly £1,500, so the dispute was not just a matter of pride. It was suggested that this be done by making a physical statement of ownership – cut down, and remove, trees from the intended line of the canal. The important point was to be the removal of the timber to Worksop Manor, a practical declaration that it was the Duke's property and he could take, and dispose of it, however he wished. And if no one stopped his men in this task, or disagreed with the right to do so, then by default they would have agreed to the Duke's right of ownership. So, on Wednesday the 3rd of February the Duke's officials went with workmen and carriages to Haggonfield Common and, along the intended line of the canal, cut down about forty trees and took the timber to the woodyard of Worksop Manor. They met with "no disturbance or molestation in the least" and at noon, when they had finished felling, a letter was sent to John Hewitt telling him what had been done and why. Hewitt was stung into writing back the same day. No doubt he was displeased but you have to be careful what you write to a representative of the Duke of Norfolk, especially when the Duke lives next door, so his letter was full of "profussions of peace and friendship". However, John Hewitt's stubborn and crotchety reputation was well deserved and that was not the end of the matter as far as he was concerned.

As the dispute worsened Anthony Lax thought it prudent to call a special Committee meeting in Worksop. For once Chesterfield managed to

---

[*]   The current holder of the title was the 9th Duke of Norfolk who had no children. Henry Howard would have been amazed if he had known that as a result of consecutive Dukes failing to produce offspring his eldest son was to become the 12th Duke.

amass as many as five representatives, the diligent Charles Kinder and Joseph Storrs having brought along Stephen Gamble, a ropemaker in Knifesmithgate; Richard Nall, a hosiery manufacturer; and Samuel Towndrow, the grocer who was still littering Glumangate with casks, stone and dung. They may have wished they had stayed in Chesterfield; three of the Duke's representative's invaded the private meeting. They ensured there would be no further misunderstandings by formally reading to the Committee the Duke's claim to the land and declared in the name of his Grace "that the Company must not enter Haggonfield without first contracting with the Duke of Norfolk" and then left the meeting. So the canal's further progress towards Worksop was effectively stopped, a disagreement with the Most Noble Edward, Duke of Norfolk, Hereditary Earl Marshal of England being a thankless task for which the Committee would gain scant support from the shareholders. The Committee decided that taking the side of Hewitt against the Duke was not a wise move. They resolved to ask the old man to drop his claim to the common, thus clearing themselves to make a new contract with the Duke. Hewitt refused. He was Lord of the Manor and no one was going to forget it.

From now on the Canal Company became relegated to the side-lines as the Agents of the two landowners sought to settle the dispute; what was certain was that the canal was going nowhere until the matter was resolved. In the afternoon of the next day, Thursday the 4th of February, Hewitt decided that what was good for the Duke was good for him – he sent his men to Haggonfield Common to cut down and remove six or seven trees, thereby using the same tactic as the Duke to stress ownership of the timber. The Agents had many meetings, letters went backwards and forwards to London for legal advice, the Domesday Book was scoured for evidence, and Henry Howard decided to cut down some more trees so that Hewitt was not "the last cutter" and the Duke's claim was again stated. If this went on much longer the Company would have the canal's route cleared for them!

Henry Howard considered that he would have to go to Lincoln's Inn in an effort to bring about a conclusion, no matter how bad the winter weather. He left his home in Sheffield on the 8th of February 1773, even though he was feeling ill, and went to Worksop Manor to check on the latest situation. At 6am the next day, after morning prayers, he set out in the dark for London. It had started to snow heavily before he left so the journey would have been cold, uncomfortable, long and dangerous. By this time there was very little trust or liking for John Hewitt, the fact that Howard was having to make such a journey can only have withered the relationship further. Howard told Mander and Eyre to stay at Worksop Manor "to watch the motions of the enemy until I return". Later that day Mander said nothing was happening "unless Mr Hewitt begins again, in which case we fall to again in ernest". There was quite a feud going on between the two estates and the Canal Company was caught in the middle of it.

Eventually the dispute was resolved in favour of the Duke of Norfolk, not surprising considering the legal weight that his representatives brought to bear on the case. His adversary, on the otherhand, was very wary about getting involved in law suits and finally backed down from the argument. At the beginning of April John Mander wrote to Lax saying they wanted a contract signed with the Company as soon as possible. Lax agreed and a meeting was arranged for Saturday the 10th of April at Henry Howard's home in Sheffield. There Howard, Mander and Lax agreed terms on the land required for the canal at Worksop, and its value, and drew up an agreement for the sale of such land.[5] It lists thirty one parcels of land through which the canal was to be built and almost at the end is Haggonfield Common and, for good measure, the neighbouring Gateford Common which had also been claimed by John Hewitt. So it was game, set and match to the Duke of Norfolk and at long last the Canal Company were again able to extend the line of the canal eastwards beyond Shireoaks.

&ε   &ε   &ε

The administrators may have been involved with the Worksop land dispute but John Varley had more than enough work to do while waiting for a resolution.

Throughout the winter he and his navvies toiled in the snow and the short daylight hours. Norwood Tunnel continued to expand at the bottom of the work shafts, the great Thorpe and Turnerwood lock flights neared completion and, away from the centre of attention, work continued on an often forgotten, but essential, part of canal construction; the dam forming the reservoir for water storage. Although dams had been built in this country since the 12th century the early examples were only a few feet high as they were generally designed to provide a supply for water-wheels. The formation of large reservoirs to supply millions of gallons to the early canals was the first time that dams of a major size had been needed. Design in the 1770s was still crude, merely using the material from the immediate locality to form a substantial bank, the earth piled up and lined on the face towards the water with clay. The inefficiency of this method was revealed in a very short time when slips occurred if the water level in the reservoir was lowered and then refilled, the differing pressures on the wall causing instability. The clay lining was also liable to crack if it was left uncovered in this way and as a result leaking and internal erosion of the dam occurred on subsequent refilling.[6] This is very likely to have been a major problem with the Company's reservoir near Pebley as this often had its water level lowered in hot weather by the miller who also used the water to power his mill. This could have been one of the major causes of the water shortages which soon became apparent after the canal was completed. Generally, the clay lining was abandoned by the 1790s in favour of a clay core inside the earth wall of the dam, thereby being protected from excessive drying by the material enclosing it.

Other crucial parts of the water supply system were the feeder channels carrying the water not only from the reservoir but direct from rivers into the canal. The feeder from the reservoir at Pebley was to wind down, cross over the top of Norwood Tunnel, and discharge its water into the summit pound of the canal just beyond the eastern portal at Kiveton Park. Each time a lock is used it takes thousands of gallons from the level above it and empties them into its lower level. Therefore, the summit pound, with locks at either end of it has to be constantly topped up from whatever supply is available. Massive lock flights such as those down to Shireoaks move a prodigious amount of water down a canal. Varley foresaw that the lower locks could be starved of water and built the Brancliffe feeder from the River Ryton, near Lindrick, which emptied a welcome supply of water into the canal halfway down the Turnerwood flight. Often forgotten, such feeders were a surveying art in their own right, the gradient had to be just right – too flat and the flow would be insufficient to supply the canal, too steep would be wasteful of a valuable commodity, the fast flow taking too much from the river, more than the canal could efficiently manage. The accuracy involved is still admired by today's waterways engineers, for example the Brancliffe feeder falls a precise 1ft 3in in just over one and a quarter miles. Virtually little canals themselves, nearly all feeders had control gear installed, especially at the reservoir or river end, usually wooden slats that could be wound down or up to control the supply as appropriate.[*]

☚   ☚   ☚

So Varley had more than enough to keep him busy during the snowy February of 1773 – waiting for Anthony Lax to solve the problems at Worksop and for the spring weather to bring longer working hours. By then the construction work had been going on for eighteen months and the mundane, but essential, matters of supplies and advertising for sub-contractors had slipped into a routine. Financially the first signs of cash-flow problems were starting to become apparent. So far the shareholders had been asked to pay five £5 instalments, or Calls, on their shares but these funds had been severely depleted by the substantial purchases of land and supplies that were now necessary. The outgoings were considerable and the canal was not earning any income – the completed section only being used to convey the Company's own materials as it did not yet reach any area useful to the public. Still the bills from suppliers flooded in to the Treasurers – nails, bricks, ropes, ironwork, coal, timber, timber and more timber. The Committee tried to alleviate the situation in various ways; making rules to limit the expenses claimed by officials, asking Messrs Walkers of Rotherham for a detailed bill of the ironwork they had supplied, changing the date of interest payment on the money invested to reward prompt payment of Calls.

---

[*]   Both feeders are still in use.

Newspaper advertisement – notification of payment of the sixth Call and the next General Meeting.

CANAL NAVIGATION
From Chesterfield to the River Trent

In Pursuance of an Order of the Committee of Proprietors of the said Navigation, held at Worksop, in the County of Nottingham, the 8th Day of April 1773; all and every the said Proprietors are required to pay to Mr George Poplewell in Retford, or Mr Allwood Wilkinson in Chesterfield, the Treasurers to the said Navigation, or to Messrs Smith, Wright and Gray, Bankers in Lombard Street, London, on or before the 25th Day of June next, the Sum of Eight Pounds for every Share they respectively stand possessed of in the said Navigation, being the sixth Call under the Act.
N.B. A Penalty of £5 per Share is by the Act inflicted upon every Person who shall neglect to Pay the Call on the Day appointed for that Purpose.

The next General Meeting of the Company of Proprietors of the said Navigation is appointed to be held at Mr Cowley's, the Angel Inn in Chesterfield, in the County of Derby, on Thursday the thirteenth Day of May next, at Eleven in the Morning, and the Committee will meet at the same Place on Wednesday the 12th Day of the same May, at two in the Afternoon, for the Dispatch of Business.

ANTH. LAX
Clerk to the said Company

A convenient and cost-effective method of obtaining general timber was to agree with owners of land near the canal that the Company could fell and pay for trees as required, but experience had taught some lessons. In the past the financial savings the Company had gained from this convenient supply had sometimes been swallowed up by the time and expense of removing the wood from difficult locations. Now landowners making such a deal were required to lodge a sum of money with Anthony Lax which would be forfeited if undue costs were incurred by the Company. Expenses were restricted; if Varley sent any of his staff on duties that required an overnight stay he was to pay only a daily rate, the Company was not going to pay for lodgings, food or stabling. Anthony Lax wrote to all the shareholders still defaulting on their Call payments; if they did not pay their arrears within the next ten days they would have an extra £5 per share added to their debt as a penalty. Furthermore the next Call, scheduled for June, was to be £8 per share rather than the usual £5.

Despite the tightening financial restraints the Committee still thought it necessary to send Richard Dixon on an errand to Leicestershire. Lime was urgently needed, presumably for mortar, and for some reason the local supply was not adequate. So in March, just one month after prolonged snow falls, the poor man was sent to Barrow to purchase six wagon loads of lime which were to be transported "by land in the most convenient manner". With the basic roads of the time still showing the dire effects of the winter weather it is hard to see what "convenient manner" was possible. Both he and the Paymaster, the Rev. John Peacock, applied for – and were granted – salary increases, but apart from these the stricter financial regime was implemented. Part of this philosophy was to always obtain heavy supplies as cheaply as possible. A fact that must have been a prominent thought in the minds of Brindley and Varley, when they were planning the route of the canal, was that a vast quantity of lock-building rock was available in the area from the eastern end of Norwood Tunnel to Shireoaks. The commodity was famous even then so all the supplies were in private hands, and would have to be paid for at a commercial rate, but at least transport delays and costs would be negligible. Unfortunately, the main source at the convenient location of Shireoaks was a quarry owned by John Hewitt, the infamous loser of the commonland dispute at Worksop.

Dealing with his Agent was straightforward but whenever the crotchety old man interfered there was trouble. And it always had to be remembered that the Act of Parliament contained a clause that canal buildings were not to be raised within one thousand yards of Shireoaks Hall – no wharfs, warehouses, cranes – and that the towpath was to be on the opposite bank, the common boatmen and their horses were to be kept at a distance. If the Company forgot John Hewitt would soon remind them. Nevertheless, Anthony Lax managed to get an agreement for the Company to extract rock from an area near the bottom of the Turnerwood flight. Near as it was to the canal it would be more efficient if a side-arm or cut could be dug to the quarry so that boats could be loaded near to where the rock was dug. Varley surveyed the land, planning the side-cut to join the canal just above the bottom two locks, and within a month Lax had agreed terms for the extra land and sub-contractors were hired to dig the channel.

Varley had also been busy setting out the line to the far side of Worksop, taking the canal four miles eastwards; included in this section would be a 1700 yard feeder from the River Ryton, two aqueducts to cross the river and the feeder, and a further two locks. Back along the line the navvies were toiling. The majority of the work was the "common cutting", the term for the digging of the miles of canal channel. It was hard, continuous work but not very skilled; certainly there were techniques to learn but these only increased the rate of a man's work. Basically it was dig it out, put it in a wheelbarrow, move it somewhere else, empty the wheelbarrow, go back, dig some more. On these early canals the usual price a labourer could earn for his efforts was 2½d for digging a cubic yard, and in a day he would be expected to maintain an average of three cubic yards. The more time-consuming job was lining the canal to make it watertight, "puddling" as it was, and still is, called. James Brindley perfected the practice and it has never been bettered. Clay was dug from a nearby area and at the workings it was mixed with water until it was semi-fluid. Not one but many layers of this mixture were applied to the bottom and sides of the canal, each one pressed and pummelled until a thick water-tight lining was created. Some idea of the effort involved may be obtained by considering the words of a writer of the time who said the puddle-clay should be "well tempered and rammed every 6 inches."[7]

They had 46 miles to do. Each layer was left for a few days before the next was applied, but the puddle-clay was never allowed to dry before the next layer was applied. After this the water was let into the section and it was important to have a sufficient supply immediately available – if the puddle dried out it would crack and leak and become useless. Then the towpath was finished, a post-and-rail fence and gates were erected between the towpath and the adjacent land – and then on to the next length to be dug.

&a   &a   &a

While all this was going on the gentlemen of the Committee continued much as before. In Chesterfield Anthony Lax was busy, not only with canal business but the general running of the law practice. His senior partner, Godfrey Heathcote, had been ill for quite some time and had gone to Bath to take the waters; it was thought he may not last the year. Allwood Wilkinson was also in ill-health even though he was only twenty-nine. He retained his post as Treasurer but travelling to meetings was too much effort and from now on his relative, Isaac Wilkinson, would be elected to the Committee to oversee the family's interests. The doom and gloom currently pervading Chesterfield's canal men extended to Adam Slater, apothecary and surgeon; his wife had recently died of consumption and he was inconsolable. His house in Lordsmill Street was now to be let, set as it was in five acres of grounds with an orchard, gardens, stables, summerhouse and a fish pond. He had been on the Committee but from now on he lapsed and was eventually de-selected. He still kept his shares but he had no heart to continue any active involvement in the canal. It was fortunate that thirty-one year old Anthony Lax was still fit and energetically, if somewhat pompously, dealing with all the administrative affairs of the Company.

In Retford other human problems had occurred. William Kirke had been involved from the start of the canal project and had been the chairman of two of the first three Committee meetings, but since then his attendance had been sparse and he had been de-selected. His estate at East Markham was substantial but he had often borrowed loans from

George Poplewell, the town's unofficial banker as well as the Company's Treasurer, and on the 25th of May Kirke was found drowned in the River Idle; the official verdict being succinctly reported as "an act of lunacy". His son John inherited twenty shares and became quite actively involved in the canal, accompanying Seth Ellis Stevenson on visits and promoting Retford's interests whenever he could.[8] One of the most prominent citizens in Retford involved in the canal was John Bright – visitor to the Duke of Newcastle, Alderman, Bailiff, solicitor; lately he had gained the illustrious title of the town's Commissioner for Sewers. His wife Ann was the sister of William Kirke and was, of course, upset about her brother's death. Thomas Brumby, Bailiff and Alderman, still had his "manufactury" at Retford and was advertising for weavers to make various types of cloth; the promised fruits of canal investments could not be relied upon to put the food on the table.

But Seth Ellis Stevenson still carried on as headmaster of Retford's Grammar School as well as being a churchman. It was a family tradition – his father, Henry, had been headmaster before him and it had been assumed that Seth's elder brother would succeed him, but he turned out to be rather a disappointment to the family. So when old Henry was dying in 1748 he called for Seth and asked him to take over at the Grammar School. This he agreed to do but it was a great sacrifice; he was only twenty-four, had recently entered Cambridge University, and his ambitions had soared wider than Retford's boundaries. Nevertheless, he was made a curate the same day and ever since had loyally carried on with the role allocated to him in a small Nottinghamshire town. In the spring of 1773 Seth Ellis Stevenson was busy with an interest that had filled most of his life – gardening. He grew most of the food for his household and they ate well; asparagus, potatoes, cucumbers, runner beans, celery, carrots, onions, lettuce, cauliflowers, mustard, peas, radishes. He also bought in hops and malt from which to brew ale, some of which was drunk, some sold or bartered. On another small patch of land he bred pigs and cattle for food and horses for trade. Life was comfortable; Stevenson's church and school duties did not take up too much of his time, he was a well-respected figure in the town and his family was growing up. His eldest son Billy was now twenty-two and preferred to be called William,

Polly was quite the young lady now she was eighteen, little Catherine (Kitty) was only eleven but as she had almost died of smallpox when she was two it was a miracle she was alive. Young Seth and Elizabeth made up the Stevenson household, a fine family for their father who was by now forty-nine and his second wife, Elizabeth, who was forty-seven.

৯৯   ৯৯   ৯৯

John Varley's workload continued to expand. Early in the summer of 1773 he was told to survey and mark out a further section of the canal; this time the nine miles from Worksop to the western edge of Retford. On leaving Worksop the canal was to run parallel with the River Ryton and wind round to the grounds of Osberton Hall which, much to the Company's chagrin, was yet another mansion of the irritating John Hewitt. Again he had ensured that Osberton Hall was covered by the same clause in the Act of Parliament that had protected Shireoaks Hall. The rule that the towpath must be on the opposite side was of no consequence at Shireoaks as the path had crossed to the north bank just beyond Norwood Tunnel, but the line now laid out by Varley put Osberton Hall on the favoured north side – the towpath would have to move. So as the canal entered Hewitt's land Varley allowed for a bridge over which the boat-horses could cross to the opposite side for the passage past Osberton Hall. A little further along another lock was required as well as a bridge to carry the road to the estate village of Scofton; Varley planned to use this bridge to take the towpath back to the favoured north bank. Then along to Ranby where the river and the canal both turned to go due north, the canal eventually turning eastwards again to cross into the valley of the River Idle, dropping down four more locks through an area known as The Forest, now mainly open fields but in 1773 still a part of Sherwood Forest. Varley's line ran on, his accurately surveyed route reaching the outskirts of Retford, one more lock in West Retford leading the canal on to an aqueduct to cross the River Idle. Of course this was only Varley and his assistants working far ahead of the main work gangs and Lax had yet to be advised of the land to be purchased. Much of it, especially that at The Forest, belonged to Robert Rogers who happened to be one of the Company's official Land Valuers – freelance land experts who negotiated between the Canal Company and the landowners. Rogers had been involved in the project from an early date – making the trip to London to give evidence at Westminster – but had never bought any shares, nor did he have any other financial involvement. He lived at Brancliffe Grange, back along the canal at Turnerwood, halfway down the "Giant's Staircase" of locks. Rogers was the Land Valuer who had been drawn in to the dispute between John Hewitt and the Duke of Norfolk, meeting the Duke's Agent before the altercation got out of hand. He had put his early knowledge of the canal to good use, like John Hewitt ensuring that the Act of Parliament protected his interests – the towpath was to go along the north bank through his land at The Forest. But Varley had taken this into account and the towpath was already on the correct side since crossing back from the south after Osberton. Who valued Robert Roger's land when it was to be purchased is not known!

On the outskirts of Retford John Varley was fifteen miles away from where much of the construction work was still being done, Norwood Tunnel. Between there and the end of his surveyed line the canal was in various stages of completion, even so Varley was responsible for everything along the whole length. He could not deny that he was answerable, the Company being quite straightforward in their language – the rule being that if Varley could not blame anyone else for bad workmanship or neglect, then it was his fault and he would be accountable. This is an interesting management technique and one that must have led to much argument and dissatisfaction, because it may be imagined that with the volume and pressure of the work at that time many mistakes did happen and Varley would not have been interested in taking the blame for them all, or perhaps any of them. And once the blame had been apportioned Varley was to calculate the cost of the damage done and arrange for this amount to be stopped out of the guilty party's wages and, in addition, to discharge them immediately and never employ them again. Injustices must have occurred in some cases as Varley did not have the time to investigate each incident, and in an age before employment regulations it was distressingly easy to take the easy option and blame someone else. Not that there is any evidence of Varley having done so but such were the anxieties of his own position that perhaps only a paragon could have resisted such a temptation.

The irony is that during the summer of 1773, when John Varley was having to spend much of his time far ahead of the work gangs, it was not itinerant workmen who were adding to his problems back at Norwood Tunnel, it was his own family – problems that have blackened the name of Varley ever since.

1773

Warehouses full of tea, no market because of the American crisis – Parliamentary moves to stop duelling – Prisoner in the pillory at Mansfield – December, the Boston Tea Party.

Monday the first Instant, at Six in the Evening, the Cricket Match, eleven on a Side, between the Sheffield Club, and the Nottinghamshire Sherwood Youths, was finally determined at Sheffield, in favour of the former. The Nottinghamshire Party laboured under great Disadvantages; fatigued with their Journey, they went in first on a very wet Piece of Ground, and played in such a slippery Soil that they could neither run, strike or catch without Danger of falling, by which unlucky Situation they gained only fourteen Notches on their first Inning. Their Adversaries, who coming in fresh and in top Spirits, gained near seventy Notches, which gave them such a Superiority as could not be recovered. But here it is to be observed that, before the Sheffield Club went in, they ordered a large Quantity of Coal Slack to be laid on the Ground, and thereby secured their Running etc.

We hear from Nottinghamshire that a little old man, known by the name of Old Robin Hood, having on Monday night a Quarrel with his termagent Wife, went into a Garden and hung himself upon an Apple tree, but being timely discovered by a little Girl, the Neighbours ran and let him down – to the great Disappointment of his Wife, who was extremely angry with them for their Officiousness, as she called it, in saving the poor Fellow's Life.

THOMAS STEWARDSON
Taylor and Cloaths Cleaner

Begs Leave to inform the Public that he cleans all Sorts of Mens' and Womens' Apparel, in the best Manner; and restores such as are faded to their former Colour; Cleans and dies Scarlet Cloaks; also cleans Bed-Hangings and Turkey Carpets.

1773

Eloped from his Master at Chesterfield in Derbyshire, on Tuesday 14th Sept last, SAMUEL SUTTON, an indented Apprentice, about 17 Years of Age, with light-coloured lank Hair, fair Complexion, about 5 Feet 4 Inches high; went off dressed either in a dirty Fustian Coat and Waistcoat, or in a dark Brown Livery Coat and Waistcoat, turn'd up with Green. Is supposed to have taken a Silver Table Spoon, mark'd with a Hawk on the back of it, one Pair of Silver Buckles, and some other things being missed immediately after his Departure, besides his own Clothes.
Who ever will secure him, and acquaint Mr Avery Jebb of Chesterfield aforesaid therewith, shall have all Charges paid and reasonable Satisfaction for their Trouble.

TO BE SOLD or LET
And entered upon immediately
On the island of ST. JOHNS, in the Gulph of St. Lawrence,
NORTH AMERICA

Several exceeding good FARMS, on very low Terms, and are very Advantageously situated. It is extraordinary good Land either for Grain or Grazing, and in a fine Climate, much the same as England. For further Particulars enquire at the Talbot, in Hilton, where all Letters (Post-paid) will be duly answered.

* This St. John's is not St. John's Newfoundland, and may be run from London in 20 days.

Thursday, James Knight, convicted at the last Quarter Sessions of the Peace at Nottingham of a Misdemeanour, was set in the Pillory at Mansfield about twelve at Noon, and continued in it one hour. There was a prodigious Concourse of Spectators assembled on the Occasion, but the Delinquent was treated with more Humanity than he expected, or perhaps deserved. Rotton Eggs, Dirt, and Sludge being the only Articles with which the Mob pelted him, so that his Cloaths received more Injury than his Person. In the Evening the Prisoner was reconducted to the County Gaol.

CHAPTER EIGHT

Norwood and Retford

In the past the financial situation of the Canal Company had reflected the prosperous and booming national outlook but since then the country had entered a period of serious recession. There were various economic problems; many builders and contractors faced bankruptcy, a banking crisis stifled business – but the most serious cause for concern was the situation in the American colonies. This had looked more settled and the crisis had seemed to be over until a warship of the Royal Navy had gone aground on the American coast and was attacked and burned by a band of colonists. No Government could ignore such an act. It was widely known in the colonies who the perpetrators were but such was the dislike of the Government that no one would help in their capture. The problems between the colonies and Britain were now becoming intractable; in America every action of the King and Government was seen as tyranny, in Britain each protest by the colonies was seen as disloyalty or treason. The impact on a trading nation such as Britain was severe – the warehouses remained full of goods the Americans would not purchase and as trade suffered so less money was available for investment and prices rose.

The Chesterfield Canal Company could not remain aloof from such forces. Hugh Henshall visited the canal in July 1773, attending a Committee meeting in Worksop where he was told that his survey of the works was to include a financial assessment of the work done and the supplies in hand. Having done so Henshall recommended various practical and organisational changes. Now that the works covered such a wide geographical area he suggested that it would help accountability if the canal was divided into four districts, the costs incurred in each to be recorded in its own set of books and accounts. District One was from Chesterfield to the western end of Norwood Tunnel; District Two, the tunnel itself; District Three, from the eastern end of the tunnel to the aqueduct over the River Idle at Retford – District Four the remaining stretch to the River Trent at West Stockwith. The Committee agreed and it was arranged that the Chesterfield gentlemen would be responsible for the day to day running of Districts One and Two, the Retford gentlemen for Districts Three and Four. The full Committee, of course, would still bear official responsibility for the whole canal.

Henshall also reported that to save more costs brick production for lining Norwood Tunnel should be suspended, there already being enough bricks to last until next summer. So the fifteen kilns along the line of the tunnel were closed down and the tools that had been allocated to the brickmakers were collected up, all breakages being assiduously charged to the culprits. Further savings could be made in the methods used to build the boats needed to carry the construction materials; Henshall said that on Shireoaks Common it would be more efficient if a shed was put up with the end towards the canal so that the boats could float out when completed.

Even with such savings money was becoming scarce and the Committee found themselves in a dilemma; they had to raise more cash even though their investors might find it difficult. One move was to increase the seventh Call on the shareholders from £7 to £10 per share, even though the default rate would probably keep Anthony Lax busy. But this money was not due to be received until the middle of September, funds were already low and substantial bills were being held over until the autumn; Messrs. Booth & Walker were owed £403 for ironwork alone. The Committee decided to alleviate their cash-flow problems by the old, and sometimes dangerous, expedient of borrowing money to be paid back out of the next income. They raised a loan of £1000 at 5% interest, three of the Committee securing the money by giving a personal assurance of repayment. It was to be the thin end of the wedge; spending the money raised by the Calls before it was received. It was only a year since they had been so confident that a Call was actually deferred because they already had enough money in hand. In that twelve months their illustrious Chief Engineer had died and the financial climate, both nationally and locally, had deteriorated beyond all expectations. It was in this troubled atmosphere that John Varley became embroiled in a crisis that has haunted his name ever since; a sorry tale of bad workmanship and contractual misdemeanours.

ટ8. ટ8. ટ8.

During his survey Hugh Henshall inspected the work being done inside Norwood Tunnel and found that thirty-one yards of brickwork were below standard. As with the rest of the canal sections of work were let out to various sub-contractors – in the tunnel it was a number of yards as specified in each contract, the price paid for the work depending on the geological difficulties in each section. In practice a number of the contracts had been awarded to members of the Varley family; John's father and eldest brother, both named Francis, and a second brother, Thomas. The reasons for these appointments are not known, nor John Varley's part in their provision, but the faulty brickwork had been done by his brother Thomas. Furthermore, the preparatory work had been done by Francis Varley and Samuel Knock. Henshall estimated that it would cost £1.16s a yard to take the brickwork down and rebuild it; the Committee, weighed down with their financial worries, did not want any additional expense and ordered that the three culprits were each to contribute a third of the cost. Later Samuel Knock managed to extricate himself from most of the guilt and the blame fell squarely on the shoulders of the two Varleys.

This example of bad workmanship proved to be only the tip of the iceberg, the contractual aspects of the work in Norwood Tunnel proving to be as murky as the working conditions. Preliminary investigations pointed to excessive payments being agreed for the work, as a result the Committee halted the granting of new contracts until Henshall could inspect the site and define the maximum price to be paid for the work; the sections already in progress were finished at the payment rate previously agreed. If contractors wished to carry on with further sections it was made plain to them that they could do so only on the understanding that they would be paid in accordance with the value placed on the work in the future. This edict caused a cessation of work on the tunnel and Anthony Lax wrote to Hugh Henshall to make an urgent visit to the canal to offer his judgement on the situation. Although very busy with the Trent & Mersey Canal Henshall did manage to ride over to Norwood without much delay. He inspected what parts there were of the tunnel, defined a payment rate of £3.2s a yard, and went back to the Trent & Mersey; but even then the problems were not solved.

With the new division of the canal into four administrative areas the whole of the tunnel came under the direct control of Chesterfield. When, by the end of 1773, work had still not resumed at Norwood the gentlemen of Retford became rather agitated about the delay. Their prime concern was not simply that they wanted the canal finished as soon as possible – their motivation owed more to self-interest. The canal was progressing towards Retford at a very satisfactory rate and, with adequate water supplied, it would soon be able to bring goods to the town from Yorkshire. But the commodity they really wanted was coal from Derbyshire, the other side of Norwood hill. If the coal had to be taken over the hill by road before loading onto boats then the price would not be much reduced from its present level. What they wanted was Norwood Tunnel finished so that boats could reach Derbyshire and return to Retford laden with coal – cheap coal. But those characters in Chesterfield did not seem to care about the delays – after all it made little difference to their town if the tunnel was finished or not, it would give no benefit to them until the canal progressed in their direction, and there was little sign of that at the moment. The Retford gentlemen decided to do something about it.

They ascertained the latest situation from John Varley who told them that none of the contractors would take the work on for Henshall's flat rate. Instead they wanted £3.5s at which price they would supply their own gunpowder, the Company to provide the carpentry work for the wooden framework for the initial support of the bricks. Or, if they had to do the carpentry themselves, £3.8s a yard. The gentlemen pondered, and eventually proposed a compromise; agree to the rate asked but only allocate two short lengths – twelve yards at the western end, which geologically was the most difficult section of the tunnel, and six yards at the eastern end. That way some work would be going on while Varley contacted Henshall to advise him of the quandary. If Henshall replied that he disapproved and thought the rate too high then he should be told

The reason Hugh Henshall could not spend more time on the Chesterfield Canal was the huge workload he had taken on as Brindley's successor – especially on the Trent & Mersey Canal.

16 April 1773

By an Account lately delivered in at a General Assembly of the Proprietors of the inland Navigation from the Trent to the Mersey, it appears 66 Miles of this Navigation are now entirely finished, that the Canal from the River Trent near Wilden Ferry in this County, to Stoke-upon-Trent in Staffordshire, being in Length 56 Miles, hath for some Time been navigable; and that many Vessels have accordingly been employed thereon. It appears also, from the Estimates, that 40 locks, 114 cart-bridges, 9 foot-bridges and 120 culverts or aqueducts, including those magnificent ones over the Rivers Dove and Trent, were compleated. Also that 2151 Yards of the subterraneous Passage at Harecastle (the Whole being 2500) and 770 of that at Preston-on-the-Hill, were compleated; and that the Whole of this great and useful Undertaking was carrying on with the utmost Success.

to supply his own men to do the work at the price he proposed. Richard Dixon, as Retford's senior Company official, was told to write to the indolent gentlemen in Chesterfield with this proposal; that should wake them up and get some tunnelling done. Chesterfield did not agree, and more to the point they had no intention of allowing the Retford interests to revert to their previous leading role. Recently there had even been a full Committee meeting held in Retford but with a Chesterfield chairman, the first time in the Company's history that that had occurred. Samuel Jebb had been elected to the Committee earlier in the year, his lead-mining background and status, and his fifteen shares, adding welcome power to Chesterfield's presence. Since then he had attended every meeting except one and had recently inspected the full set of Company accounts. This was no time to allow any Nottinghamshire brow-beating – the proposal was rejected and work at Norwood remained at a standstill.

The gentlemen in Retford were incensed. Under the leadership of Sir Cecil Wray – shareholder, wealthy Lincolnshire Baronet and MP for Retford – they invoked the clause of the Act of Parliament that allowed for a special General Meeting to be convened if fifteen shareholders so wished.

It is noteworthy that Seth Ellis Stevenson did not support the move, even though, politically, he was a supporter of Sir Cecil Wray; in his usual way Stevenson preferred to make up his own mind. The weather was bitterly cold – for the last month, since just before Christmas, there had been a severe frost every day and moderate falls of snow. Nevertheless, Stevenson set out to visit the work sites to see the state of the tunnel for himself. He took a servant with him for security and to arrange his overnight accommodation, but his faithful companion of numerous journeys was missing. Jockey, his old horse, had died three months ago; nineteen years old, he had taken his inquisitive master all over the country for the last fourteen years, and in all weathers. He was sadly missed. Stevenson returned home from his visit of inspection and distanced himself from the most vociferous Retford clique; perhaps deeming their case weaker than others thought. Meanwhile, the Chesterfield representatives were not idle. They knew that their lead-mining connections gave them access to expert opinion on tunnelling through rock; even if their tunnels were not level or brick-lined. They arranged for a party of Derbyshire miners from Hell Carr Sough to inspect the tunnel and report to them and, if their findings were acceptable, to the special General Meeting. Charles Potter and his colleagues spent nine days inspecting and working in Norwood Tunnel and they made their own estimate of the cost per yard of the outstanding work.

Both camps were busy sounding out the opinion of other shareholders and, if sharing their views, securing a proxy vote for use at the meeting. This took some negotiating as the Retford gentlemen planned to take the opportunity to right more than one wrong; their main proposal was that the work at Norwood Tunnel should recommence immediately. Secondly, that work on an aqueduct near Osberton should be progressed. Also that another reservoir should be built in the hills at Norwood, and that a new Committee be elected to supersede the lack-lustre present incumbents. So on Monday, 24th of January, at 11.00am, the gentlemen gathered again in Worksop at the George. Both sides presented their case; the leader of the Derbyshire miners making his report, the Retford interests stating John Varley's latest assertion that no one would do the work for the price defined by Henshall. When the votes were counted on the various resolutions Retford had won the day on the crucial Norwood Tunnel issue, plus the progression of the work on the aqueduct near Osberton. But the proposal that another reservoir should be built was defeated by 484 votes to 407. In hindsight this was a wrong decision. The move to oust the Committee was also unsuccessful, the same group of twenty-one being re-elected; ten from Chesterfield, ten from Retford and one from Worksop.

This special General Meeting brought matters to a head and the head which very nearly fell was John Varley's. After most of the gentlemen had dispersed the Chesterfield members of the Committee held a meeting of their own at the same venue; still smarting from the audacity of the Retford moves they called Varley before them to investigate matters further. Retford had taken Varley's word for the refusal of the contractors to do the work at the rate stipulated by Henshall – Chesterfield, under the chairmanship of the capable Samuel Jebb, was less trusting. Who were these contractors, name them? Varley said that he had not dealt with the matter personally, he had delegated the matter to Samuel Knock, a contractor himself, and told him to advise all his colleagues that £3.2s a yard was to be the going rate. Therefore, he could not name those who had refused the work. Samuel Knock was then called into the room and, in Varley's presence, vehemently denied that he had received any such instruction from the Resident Engineer. Varley was then asked if he could name anyone else to whom he had offered the work at the said rate and who had refused it. He had to admit that his brother was the only other person he could name, he had not spoken directly to anyone else. A further disclosure was even more serious. The ten Chesterfield inquisitors discovered that some sections of the tunnel had been "let" to three contractors; 230 yards to Charles Jones, 170 yards to Thomas Varley and 40 yards to Samuel Fletcher, but this was only on paper, no work had actually been done. It was also found that the contracts for these sections had been made imprudently and in a collusive manner and at prices far exceeding their true value. These admissions condemned Varley, but of what was he guilty? Looking back over two hundred years it is impossible to be certain; the most serious charge is collusion with other members of his family to inveigle the Company into paying higher rates for the work than necessary, the extra to be diverted into their pockets. Or was it simply careless management – was he so busy that he lost touch with what was going on in the tunnel, did his family take advantage of his laxity? Or was it naivety – trusting others beyond sensible judgement? Knowing how bad the picture would look, did he attempt to cover-up the family connection by involving Samuel Knock?[*] Certainly his father and brothers were not making his life any easier, they had yet to pay the cost of the defective work as ordered four months ago in August. Also outstanding was half the cost of sinking the shafts in their section of the tunnel as agreed in their contract.

As the shareholders had ordered a resumption of work in the tunnel it was incumbent upon the Chesterfield group to agree a price with some contractors so that progress could be made. They called John Handbury into

---

[*]   Although he was originally accused of involvement with the Varleys in bad workmanship Samuel Knock must have cleared his name as he went on to be a paid official of the Company. First as Overseer of the Brickworks; later he was appointed Overseer of the Locks (Norwood flight and Killamarsh).

the meeting, a tunnel contractor who was untarnished by the revelations, and asked him the lowest price at which he would do the sections specified by Retford; the twelve yards at the western end and the six yards by the eastern portal. Retford had suggested paying the high rate Varley had told them had been demanded – to Varley's shame Handbury did not simply match Henshall's stipulated price, he quoted an even lower rate. The western twelve yards, which everyone agreed was the worst work, he offered to do for £3 a yard and the six yards at £2.5s.6d a yard, the Company supplying all materials except gunpowder. To sweeten the offer even more he said he would do 220 yards in the middle of the tunnel for £2.13s a yard if he was given the other work; all to be completed within six months. Not surprisingly the Committee agreed and John Handbury signed the contract there and then.

Where did this leave John Varley? Certainly not in a good light with the gentlemen of Retford who had taken his word for the situation at Norwood Tunnel and who now looked rather gullible, even though their action in calling a special General Meeting had forced the issue. And Chesterfield could not have been impressed by his performance at their meeting, the revelations that had come to light and their having to do his work in dealing with contractors. And no one was pleased with two months wasted tunnelling time. We shall never know what was said to Varley at the meeting as it was not recorded. We do know that his accounting and work control methods were investigated and made the subject of a string of orders from the Committee. He was ordered to close his present set of record books and to take the advice and assistance of bookkeeper Richard Dixon in opening and maintaining a new set. He was also to cease making payments for any work done or items purchased unless it was in accordance with strictly priced contracts based on a measured format.

For all his management failings there is no evidence of fault being found with Varley's surveying work and, at the same time as all these reorganisations, he was told to extend the line of the canal by setting out the route from Retford to the open fields on the approach to Misterton. But when money was involved he now had to work with Richard Dixon. For instance, Varley was told to offer contracts for digging the easy stretch of the canal in the Forest area but the financial details were not left to his discretion. The Committee ordered that the price was to be a maximum £200 per mile with allowances being made for extra depth wherever necessary. The contractors were to supply their own wheelbarrows and tools although the Company would supply the planks for shoring up the workings, the towpath and the banks were to be finished off before the contract was complete and payment was only to be made after Richard Dixon had measured and agreed the work done. Varley's only financial freedom was that he could sell any of the Company's wheelbarrows to the contractors at "a fair price"!

Modern opinion of John Varley's actions has generally been harsh; that he was involved, with his family and others, in collusion to defraud the Company. When, in the following summer, his relatives were eventually dismissed it is judged that he retained his post as Resident Engineer only because at that early stage of the canal age there were very few men who could do the work, most of whom were employed elsewhere. But perhaps more understanding is called for in assessing the situation. The Chesterfield Canal was being built outside the main canal construction area and visits from Brindley and Henshall may have been fewer than perhaps necessary. Also Varley's troubles were mainly at the early stages of Norwood Tunnel and this was to be, at the time of its completion, the longest canal tunnel in the country; it was a mammoth responsibility and using untried methods. Men skilled in such work were almost non-existent and the demand for them was great, the powerful Trent & Mersey Canal attracting most of them to dig Harecastle Tunnel. It is easy to see that John Varley may not have had the support he needed at Norwood and that perhaps the only contractors willing to miss Harecastle Tunnel were his own family, even if their motives may have been selfish. Obviously with young John as Resident Engineer senior members of the family may have expected fat contracts to come their way, which they did, but in the circumstances does this make John Varley dishonest or gullible? Perhaps a young man, he was still only 33, in charge of his first large project, with immense pressure from his employers to finish work that was at the frontier of engineering knowledge, and with a lack of skilled men to help him, could be forgiven for falling into the trap of giving work to his own family as an easy option. No one had found fault with his surveying or engineering, his failings were in his administrative work; keeping account books and maintaining an overall control of the project.

Perhaps at this distance in time it would be fairer to judge John Varley bearing in mind the words of John Smeaton, a great civil engineer of the same era. He described a Resident Engineer's problems as follows:-

> "To fit a man fully for this employment, requires so great a number of qualifications, that I look upon it as impracticable to find them united in one person. I therefore take it for granted, that he will, of course, be materially deficient in something; and as such, there is the greatest difficulty in the world to preserve good understanding between the resident Engineer and the Committee who directs him."

𝕰 𝕰 𝕰

During this infamous period of John Varley's career there was at least one brighter aspect to working for the Chesterfield Canal Company. At last his family was to have a home of its own. His wife and baby daughter, his two Hannahs, had been in lodgings in Harthill since moving to the area at the start of the project, but the previous summer Varley had persuaded the Committee to allow his workmen to build a house for his own use. It was to be at Pennyholme, just a few yards beyond the eastern end of Norwood Tunnel, and was to incorporate an office for the clerks who would eventually be needed to check the tonnage carried by the boats as they waited to enter the tunnel. It was to be a sizable, solid, brick-built residence and the remains of the cellar and foundations can still be seen today; in later times it was divided up into separate accommodation for four families. John Varley lived at Pennyholme for the rest of his life, his family staying there while he was away working on other projects when the Chesterfield Canal was finished.

In Chesterfield, during the final days of 1773, Anthony Lax was taking on more duties; Godfrey Heathcote, his 72 year old senior partner, had died at Bath after a long and painful illness.[1] The old man had been one of Chesterfield's most distinguished residents, his handsome fortune having been earned by years of steady application to the laborious business of the law. He had practiced as an attorney, solicitor and conveyancer for fifty years, including twenty years as Chief Steward and Auditor to three successive Dukes of Devonshire and fourteen years as Clerk of the Peace for Derbyshire. As befitted such an eminent citizen his body made the long journey from Bath in a horse-drawn hearse, an elegant mourning coach following behind. By the 8th of December the procession had reached Derby, resting overnight at the George Inn before setting off for Chesterfield as soon as it was light the next morning. Godfrey Heathcote's funeral service was held at St. Mary's church, under the famous crooked spire, his memorial stone bearing an inscription he had written himself some years before. His patriarchal, but prudent, attitude to his fellow citizens was reflected in his will – he specified that £60 was to be made available to Chesterfield's "inferior tradesmen", not as a gift but as loans at 2.5% interest. The residue was to be used for intellectual improvement; an annual lecture in the church on the evening of Christmas Day, the money paying for the organist, candles, chandeliers, etc for the occasion.

Anthony Lax must have been carrying out the duties of Clerk of the Peace during his partner's long illness, now the county lost no time in appointing him to the office. All the administrative work of Derbyshire was now his responsibility – organising and recording the Quarter Sessions, communicating with the operators of the turnpike roads, summoning the militia for training, and countless other tasks. All this in addition to his duties for the Canal Company, duties that did not look to lessen for a few years yet. He had done well for a man of 31, even though humility and a sense of humour had yet to be included in his achievements.

ໄ   ໄ   ໄ

The discovery of suspicious contracts and slack management did have one positive result; it acted as a catalyst and the changes made led to steady progress during the rest of 1774. A further development was that the balance of power in the Canal Company was tipped the other way; the Chesterfield gentlemen had a new-found confidence and Samuel Jebb and his colleagues were the majority of attendants at Committee meetings for the next eight months. For once they had thrown off Retford's smothering blanket of influence and prestige. The representatives of the

Nottinghamshire town had badly misread the Norwood Tunnel dispute and their self-assurance was left battered and torn, the astute Seth Ellis Stevenson being the only one of their number to have distanced himself from the campaign. Although many of his Committee companions deserted him, bruised egos being tenderly pampered at home, Stevenson remained as determined as ever to preserve the progress towards Retford; not only to benefit his town but also to generate income for the Canal Company, every boat paying a toll on the cargo carried to the new market.

In hindsight Stevenson's judgement may have been at fault on one point. He had formed a good relationship with John Varley and had thought the young surveyor able to manage the immense task left to him as a result of Brindley's unexpected death. Again in hindsight it was easy to see that Henshall's appointment to the purely supervisory role of Inspector of the Works had been a false saving; without a doubt recent events had shown that Varley needed stronger management from a more experienced engineer. Very little time was wasted in offering Hugh Henshall the post of Chief Engineer of the Chesterfield Canal Company, his annual salary to increase from 130 guineas to £250. By the beginning of March travel was again possible – the severe frost and snow of the last two months having cleared – and Henshall made his way to Worksop to receive his promotion. Because of his many responsibilities on other canals he was not expected to be permanently on-site, like Brindley he was to take the ultimate responsibility for the construction of the canal and to delegate the day-to-day work to Varley.

The new Chief Engineer wasted no time in making his presence felt, new brooms swept as clean in the 18th century as they tend to do in our own. Henshall knew the canal was usable from the eastern end of Norwood Tunnel to the aqueduct at Shireoaks although such fripperies as bridges, wharfs and fences had been left until a later date, a quite acceptable practice. Such items were low in the list of priorities, precedence being given to extending the functional section of the canal. The actual digging of the next length had already been started with progress hampered by the bad winter weather, now as the spring months approached plans were made for the construction of the locks between Shireoaks and Worksop. Henshall immediately provided the contractors with a plentiful amount of work. One such was the splendidly named Fortunatus Lawrence, a mason who was to supply and work the stone for four of the locks. Lawrence was lucky in that the usable part of the canal meant that, unlike previous years, the heavy stone did not have to be obtained and moved during the summer, now there was a little more flexibility. His agreement with the Canal Company stated that he was to use stone from the Pennyholme and Anston areas, the quarries of which were not far from the eastern end of the tunnel. This was very good quality stone and for some purposes it was worth bringing it down the canal rather than using the nearer supplies at Shireoaks. Boats were available to move the stone, the Company very quickly building their own on Shireoaks Common, and Fortunatus Lawrence had the Committee's approval to use such vessels. He was to arrange for crews to take them up the great Turnerwood and Thorpe lock-flights to the summit pound, at Pennyholme loading the stone for the payment of one penny per foot. This was probably done by the stone being pulled to the canalside on horse-drawn low carts, a simple crane swinging the load off and into the boats where it was arranged to form an evenly distributed cargo. The boats, low in the water, demonstrated the advantages of water transport as their horses pulled them back to Shireoaks. From the end of the finished canal the stone would have been hoisted out of the boats and onto carts for the last few yards to the four lock-sites; there Lawrence used his skill to cut and set the stone as required by the main contractor for each lock, this more estimable work attracting the payment of 3½d per foot.

Other contractors found that Henshall's presence meant higher standards and more action. Four months ago Varley had told Henry Ibbotson that the stone lock he had built was defective and that it would have to be repaired, but nothing had been done. This was an important matter as one lock uncompleted or unworkable meant that the whole section was closed, as far as the passage of boats was concerned a dam might as well have been built across the canal. The new Chief Engineer went to inspect the site of the faulty lock and told Ibbotson in no uncertain terms that his workmanship was as inadequate as his lock. Using all the status conferred on him by the Committee Henshall told Ibbotson that unlike Varley's earlier unspecified orders he expected action to be taken at once, four months shilly-shallying was not acceptable. No one, especially not Ibbotson, was left in any doubt that the builder had one month to dismantle the whole structure; then, in a further seven weeks, he was to build another lock at the same site, this time rigidly adhering to the specifications now in force. If Ibbotson did not carry out these instructions within the time constraints he was told the Company would do the work and then sue him for the costs and his breach of contract. This threat of legal action was put in to the hands of the ever-efficient Anthony Lax who wrote out the order and presented it to the contractor – control of the project had improved beyond measure.

Although at the moment he had to work with the present incumbents Henshall did not approve of using different small contractors, such as Ibbotson or Lawrence, for each lock, bridge, building, wharf. These were still the formative years of the first canal boom and improvements in the control of the various schemes were being made all the time. It was an advantage that Henshall had over Varley, indeed over all Resident Engineers, in that he was involved in different projects and was forever increasing his knowledge from lessons learnt elsewhere. Such lessons had shown the advantage of giving substantial contracts to a few well-trusted men who would ensure that a standard was maintained throughout their work, thereby taking much of the onerous inspection workload off John Varley's shoulders. Two other vital advantages were also achieved; one, financial control became much easier for the Company when large lengths of canal were priced in one contract at one rate; and two, completion dates could be specified and rigidly enforced. As a result cash-flow could be accurately forecast, both in volume and date, and therefore the Committee could determine the Company's financial viability. Henshall's first move in changing to the system he preferred was to write to James Bough and ask him to attend a Committee meeting with his proposals for the stonework for a large section of canal. This obviously went well as two months later the Company signed a contract with Bough, and his partner William Noake, for all the stonework between the aqueduct at Worksop and the aqueduct at Retford, a distance of seven miles with seven locks and many bridges. In a classic example of the new order it was agreed that the stonework of the locks would be done for 4d per foot, the edging of the towpath where necessary at 1s.8d per yard, the coping on the bridges for

1s.10d per yard, and the stonework of the aqueducts for 3d per foot. The work was to be undertaken throughout the summer and was to be finished by the end of October. How many men the two contractors used to complete the task and how much they were paid were of no concern to the Committee; prices and deadlines had been set and accepted. The only aspect for which the Company was responsible was the delivery of a constant supply of stone although the viability of this task rested on the canal being usable beyond Shireoaks. Delivery costs could only be restrained if the boats could go from the quarries at Shireoaks, Anston and Pennyholme and deliver the stone as near as possible to where it was needed.

Having organised the stonework Henshall used the same method to award the contract for the woodwork of the locks. Since work on the canal had started late in 1771 the bulk of the Company's purchases had been timber, a useful all-purpose material without which canals such as the Chesterfield could not have been built. Much of the vast quantity was for short-term use – as shoring for the sides of the canal channel as it was dug, scaffolding in locks and under bridges, temporary dams to control water access, supports for the brickwork in Norwood Tunnel. General timber was used for such tasks, the specialist types being reserved for permanent structures, the most impressive of which were the massive gates needed at both ends of each lock. John Allin was the carpenter who won the contract to make the gates for ten locks, as well as any other woodwork that may be needed, all to be completed within six months. Having made the cumbersome gates, each weighing about one ton, it was not the least of tasks to hang them in position; lifted via hoists and pulleys on the lockside they were slowly inched into place and attached to the hinges. For all this John Allin was paid £12.8s.6d for each lock.

Although completing Norwood Tunnel was an on-going task the current top priority was to make the canal usable to Retford and when contracts were issued this emphasis dictated the order of the work done – locks, aqueducts, the towpath, the canal channel itself were foremost; bridges and buildings were only included at this time if they were essential, the majority would be added later as demand dictated. One bridge that was built was at Worksop, difficult to omit as it carried the small town's north-bound route to the nearby Sheffield road. This location was the first time the canal had passed close to an important highway and it was an opportunity to improve the accessibility for cargoes as well as supplies, the first link with the existing transport network – not that the outrageous roads could justify such an exalted description. Nevertheless, it was deemed prudent for the Company to build its own road to run the 100 yards from the canal bridge to the Sheffield road and, as with everything else, the road was to be finished as soon as possible. Thomas Seddon won the contract, agreeing to do the work for 9s per rood, although by modern standards not much would have been done – it was not until the beginning of the 19th century that Thomas Telford's and John McAdam's methods produced soundly engineered roads.

All this activity, and the rapid expansion of the work areas, meant that the manufacture and distribution of construction materials had to be continuously reviewed. The distance between the work-sites and the stone quarries grew, very soon it would be prudent to use bricks instead, the stone being reserved for the special purposes already agreed with James Bough and William Noake. This point was reached at the Forest, the four locks there scheduled to be made of brick, only the coping to be of stone. As with other activities Henshall's credo had been applied and most of the brickmaking had now been concentrated on one supplier, in this case the partnership of Edward Lewis and John Day.[*] At the Forest, the most advanced site along the route, the two men had been attempting to make the bricks for the four locks, but early surveys had been misleading and there was not enough clay in the area, the little they could find being unsuitable for the job. Rather than struggle on – wasting time and money and producing sub-standard bricks – they advised that it would be more efficient to go back to Shireoaks Common where the clay was abundant and reliable; it would increase the transport costs but the boats would soon be able to carry the bricks most of the way to the Forest and it would be cheaper in the long term. The Company agreed and Lewis and Day returned to Shireoaks and started to make one million bricks for a

---

[*]   Edward Lewis had been involved in the project from the earliest times, a Master Brickmaker at Norwood Tunnel.

maximum price of 12s.6d per thousand. The supply of ironwork was also reorganised. Up until now many blacksmiths had been separately employed along the line of the canal, the Company purchasing the iron and the smiths working it into the shapes and sizes defined on-site. Controls had recently been placed on the amount of iron taken from the Company store by each blacksmith but Henshall was still not satisfied. Now one contract was made to cover the whole system, Thomas Gillott being responsible for supplying the iron for the entire canal and for working it as required. Good news though this was for Gillott the self-employed blacksmiths were not so happy, although their past conduct in wasting the iron stocks left them with little sympathy from others. All the smiths were dismissed with very little warning and their implements, tools and iron stocks were collected, valued for the Company's books and locked away. Of course, Thomas Gillott may have employed some of them as he needed a workforce of his own, or he may have brought in men of his own. He planned to use one main base for the majority of the work and as part of the agreement he was allowed to use the Company's smithy at Shireoaks, for which he was to pay a set fee. Again this arrangement greatly simplified Varley's inspection responsibilities, now he had only to check that the quantity of iron supplied matched the invoice; for the rest of the work the onus was on Gillott.

ε& ε& ε&

The 10th of February 1774 saw the last of the severe frosts and snowfalls that had hampered travel, canal construction and much of everyday life for the last six weeks.[2] Many were struggling from their homes for the first time that year but not Seth Ellis Stevenson, he was miserably confined indoors for a further eight days, an inflamed neck causing him violent pain.[3] In an age of patent medicines, untrained doctors and self-reliance most people had favourite cures they mixed themselves, general cure-alls handed down in their family or recommended by acquaintances who looked reasonably healthy. The Rev. Stevenson had a favourite remedy, taken for various ailments it was an "infusion" that he mixed when needed: take half a pound of fresh Water Dock Root, cut it into thin slices, put it in a stone jar, cover it up and let it stand for a day, then put the

171

whole into a pan and boil it about eight minutes, let it stand until quite cold, then strain it off without squeezing. Half a pint of this medication was taken twice a day and, together with moderate exercise and the avoidance of high seasoned foods, was well trusted to cure most disorders suffered by the Stevenson family.

The new house at Pennyholme for John and Hannah Varley should have been finished by now. No definite evidence exists, but it was the previous summer that permission had been given for the building and any Resident Engineer worth his salt would ensure his new home was finished before the winter, even one under as much pressure as Varley. What is known is that in March the family travelled the few miles to Harthill and gathered in the church for the baptism of another daughter, Nelly. The following month another church service was held, this time in Retford for the funeral of the Rev. Thomas Cockshutt; involved with the canal for the last two years he was a member of the present Committee, and of high enough status in the past days of Retford domination to have been Chairman five times.[4] The aged churchman was Rector of Ordsall, near Retford, as well as the holder of various other church offices in the area, his contacts within the establishment had made him a valuable participant in the canal's affairs.

After he had recovered from his inflamed neck Seth Ellis Stevenson rode with his servant to Chesterfield for an afternoon Committee meeting at the Castle Inn. Planning ahead the gentlemen agreed that making bricks as far back along the canal as Shireoaks was necessary in some degree but if production could be moved eastward it would make commercial sense. Lewis and Day, the Company's major brickmakers, were busy at Shireoaks so Seth Ellis Stevenson suggested that as he had past experience of dealing with the brickmakers of Retford – he was often changing the walls and buildings in his garden and small farm – he would see on what terms they would produce a sizable order for the Canal Company; 200,000 bricks to build the lock at Retford Town End. The rest of the business that day was agreeing their stance for the General Meeting to be held the next day at the same inn, business that once again was to put Varley in the spotlight. When they had finished the gentlemen from Worksop and Retford stayed overnight, dining in the evening with their

Chesterfield colleagues and the shareholders who had already arrived –
no doubt discussing what the next day may bring.

This was the first scheduled General Meeting since the discovery of the
Varley family's disreputable involvement in the tunnel contracts – now
the gathered shareholders were told of further transgressions. In the
intervening four months John Varley's account books and papers had been
scrutinised by Company representatives and more dubious entries had been
found, transactions which the engineer could not explain. On Varley's
authority several sums of money had been drawn from the Paymaster and
the two Treasurers, the declared reason being the settlement of payments
due to various workmen and contractors. But on checking the account books
of the contractors the discrepancies were obvious; the sum drawn to pay a
Mr. Summers was £75 more than was due to him, on another occasion the
money drawn for a Mr. Seddon exceeded that due to him by £47. Where
had the extra money gone? Once again members of Varley's family were
found to be involved in these iniquitous dealings; twelve guineas of
Company money had been paid to his brother but Thomas Varley's books
contained no record of the payment. John Handbury was owed £19.16s for
his work in Norwood Tunnel; this sum had been drawn from the Company's
funds and it had been paid, but not to Handbury – it went to Thomas
Varley. These and other sums could not be recovered from Varley's father
and two brothers as they had already left the works so the Resident
Engineer was deemed to be responsible for the debts. John Varley was
ordered to sign a £500 bond, the value of which he would have to pay if he
did not settle the debts; it was also to hang over his head as long as he
worked on the Chesterfield Canal, the bond was the Company's insurance
if his future behaviour and demeanour again fell below an acceptable
standard. The charges announced at the General Meeting were very serious
and it is harder to defend Varley against them than the earlier
disclosures. It is still possible that he was duped by men who took
advantage of the distractions caused by his heavy workload, his
inattentive accounting allowing them to claim money to which they were
not entitled. It must be agreed that Varley may have been guilty of
criminal practice, at the very least it was criminal negligence. Francis
Varley senior, Thomas Varley and Francis Varley junior were all

immediately, and officially, discharged from the Company and the works, but the damage to their family name, and possibly John's career, was done.

At the end of this disagreeable matter the General Meeting moved on to discuss a financial item which was still to be resolved – the fifteen shares originally owned by James Brindley. It was beyond question that the exalted engineer had achieved many things in his lifetime but writing a will had not been one of them. Although other shareholders were assiduously chased for payment of their Calls a tactful silence had been maintained on the fact that Brindley had not paid one penny for his shares. Before he died he was £15 in arrears, since then the deficit had risen to £60 on each share, leaving the Company £900 out of pocket. Fortunately Brindley's estate was being administered by his brother-in-law Hugh Henshall who was acting on behalf of his widowed sister Ann. Henshall could not afford to take all fifteen shares but he did agree to ten being transferred into his ownership and to paying the outstanding £600, a substantial and welcome addition to beleaguered funds.

Financial management and cashflow problems still plagued the Canal Company; they had made significant changes to put their own house in order, but outside influences could not be ignored. The trade recession had increased the number of shareholders who could not, or would not, pay the Calls on their shares; the task of chasing such payments still taking up much of Anthony Lax's time. Threats of war with America, France or Spain – or all three – held up supplies and raised prices. And these national complications had arisen at a very awkward time; the works had expanded to major proportions and included the tunnel, a reservoir and soaring lock-flights – but still no income had been generated. The vital fact was that cargoes would only be forthcoming when the canal reached a population centre, a market place for traders. So this was the crucial year; Chesterfield and the Derbyshire villages were unreachable on the wrong side of the unfinished Norwood Tunnel, the Company's salvation could only be found in the east. It was imperative that Retford be reached by the end of 1774. If the Company had to go into the next year still bearing such crippling costs with no income to alleviate the strain then matters would be critical.

With their Nottinghamshire goal firmly fixed in mind, and the crucial timescale equally clear, the diverse personnel of the Canal Company scheduled their work for 1774. During the late spring more and more contracts were signed, more and more supplies purchased; nails, rails, posts, cordage, iron, lead, tar, lamplighters. For once balk timber was not on the list, especially ash as too much had been purchased in the past and all except twenty or thirty trees was now being resold to earn some money. There was also a substantial amount of planks and sawed wood lying about along the line of the canal, abandoned by the contractors as they raced to complete their work. The Company, in its new frugal mood, ordered that these items be collected, sorted, numbered and locked away for future use. The canal continues to project a littered image – the stark newly-formed towpath festooned with building materials, a minimal track past the heaps and mixtures being kept clear for the horses, some pulling boats, others carrying Varley and his associates on interminable treks of inspection and Committee-ordered duties. As well as picking their way past the timber they had to skirt piles of tools and ironwork, stone and coal, the latter in considerable quantities – wastefully left unused it had deteriorated during the winter and was now fit only for firing lime-kilns. In Retford Thomas Morton, had already agreed terms with Seth Ellis Stevenson for 150,000 bricks, now they were discussing the production of another 50,000 – probably the first time that such a large order had been made in the town. On Shireoaks Common a second order for one million bricks was placed with Edward Lewis and John Day, to cope with the demand they had to build an extra kiln and extend two older ones.

All these supplies were needed as the number of work contracts continued to increase. It was vital during the summer months that the progress towards Retford was accelerated and to maintain the schedule completion dates were written into agreements, the latest being the middle of November.

Meanwhile, Norwood Tunnel was not forgotten. The previous year Henshall had judged the stock of bricks there too high and had closed down the kilns. Those stocks were now near exhaustion and Lewis and Day received another contract to make 200,000 bricks near the tunnel shafts for 10s.6d per thousand, the navvies wheeling their own bricks from the kilns.

The arduous work in the tunnel continued unabated; often ear-splittingly noisy, sometimes stiflingly hot or chillingly cold, always dangerous. It needed only a modicum of sense to know that next year, when the pressure to reach Retford had ceased, the Committee's beady eyes would focus on Norwood Tunnel; seeing it as a money-eating barrier between Derbyshire and the modern era. Jonathan Ballington was doing his best to progress further into the hillside; he had made a bid for sections 11, 12, and 13, altogether measuring almost two hundred yards of "the most difficult work in the whole tunnel". Because of the problems it was agreed that £3.3s would be paid but Ballington would have to supply his own gunpowder. The same price was paid to John Handbury for sections 2 and 3; the easier 4 and 5 only earning Charles Jones £3 a yard – easier perhaps but such was the extent of the underground water that Charles Jones was allowed to exceed the November completion date if he could prove the water was responsible. And hopefully the final remains of the Varley scandal were laid to rest when it was agreed that Samuel Fletcher would be paid £2.10s a yard to finish the parts started by Thomas Varley, uncompleted since his dismissal from the canal.

≈ ≈ ≈

The Chesterfield Canal was even now a disruptive gash across the countryside, few bridges alleviating the severance of land never before divided. The motives for those that were built were seldom altruistic; sometimes the Company thought it profitable or convenient for its own purposes, others were a political ploy to placate an influential landowner. Even when there was a legal requirement for a bridge the Company was not exactly diligent in conforming with the law. For instance, the Act of Parliament stipulated that the Company must build and maintain bridges at various designated locations, six of them in Worksop, and all wide enough for a carriage to cross. In blatant contravention of the Act three of the Worksop bridges were never built, and as the Company did not receive a complaint until fifty years later it must be agreed that the gentlemen of the time were successful in conserving the Company's sparse funds.[5] Those they did deign to build would have conformed to Brindley's standard design, now a familiar sight on many canals, but originated by the great engineer on the Bridgewater Canal. The many remaining examples in the country please the eye not only because of their weathered appearance but also because of the lack of straight lines, their curved angles being remarkable examples of engineering and bricklaying. But their beauty is only providential. Their function was to be convenient, not only to the road users crossing them but also to the boatmen passing underneath; the span allowing for the towpath and the headroom needed for the boat-horses as well as the width of the canal. Thought also had to be given to the approaches; boats perhaps seventy feet long could not make too tight a turn into a narrow bridge, plus the towpath had to be correctly angled so that horse and towline could pass under without hindrance. How few of these structures were currently spanning the Chesterfield Canal can be surmised from the fact that it was only now, nearly three years after construction work had started, that the Committee defined the dimensions for the bridges on their waterway. Those that were to carry a "capital road" had to be not less than 21ft wide within the walls, the walls themselves and the battlements being not less than 5ft 3ins high from the crown of the arch. Bridges for "bye roads" were to be a minimum 15ft wide within the walls; bridges "of communication" not less than 12ft wide. Both of the last two types were to have battlements not less than 4ft 9ins high from the crown of the arch. The few already built were to be altered to conform with these standards.

The canal was forging ahead but in its wake it left the same resentment that local residents now feel when new roads cut through their neighbourhood, especially when there are few bridges by which they can safely reach the other side. Individuals who had not gained any benefit from the new phenomenon – which so far was most of the local population – considered it intrusive, inconvenient, noisy, ugly; it cut across their fields so that they had to walk miles to the nearest bridge, it ruined the natural drainage of many acres, their cattle and horses were fearful, their environment was disfigured. As in all other centuries there were some who decided to do something about this disruptive product of "a new age". William Downes lived near Worksop and he and his servants, together with Robert Arthur, rode over to the canal and damaged the banks to such an extent that the water began to leak away – a most serious haemorrhage as without water the canal became no more than a wide muddy groove. When the vandalism was reported to the Committee the gentlemen donned their most officious manner and determined to "prosecute the offenders with the greatest severity", and severe they could be; the Act of Parliament stated that damaging the Chesterfield Canal was a felony and authorised the courts to sentence those found guilty to seven years in the American colonies, or lesser punishments as thought fit.[*] John Varley carried out an investigation and found that William Downes was a tenant of the Company's old adversary, John Hewitt of Shireoaks Hall – in no way could the old man be considered a calming influence, probably the exact opposite. Whether or not this made any difference to the Company's subsequent reactions is not known but when a penitent Downes presented himself at the next Committee meeting he was treated quite leniently; the damage was estimated at £3 and if he would pay such a sum to the Paymaster they would not prosecute, their judgement being that it was his first offence and he had willingly gone before them.

In an effort to eradicate future violations the Committee wasted no time in publicly stating that compassion should not be considered their permanent sentiment. To deter those tempted to emulate William Downes the penalties that could be inflicted were written out by Anthony Lax – to tempt others £5 was offered to anyone giving information about damage done to the canal, the reward to be paid on the conviction of the offender. This strident information was printed on handbills and posted up all along the canal. However, not all the damage suffered was a result of human activity and the handbills had little effect in deterring a formidable group of activists - the local mole population was making quite a nuisance of itself. The rival "navvies" were making their own tunnels but unfortunately they were through the banks of the canal, actions not conducive to good water retention. It became such a problem that Edward Moody was hired to patrol the towpath to catch the culprits. He charged 10s.6d a mile so it was not a cheap solution for the Company but the

---

[*] The more famous transportation to Australia was a later option. In 1774 Captain Cook was still on the second of his three voyages of discovery in the southern oceans, the American colonies being used by the courts until the War of Independence forced Britain to look for a new penal colony.

Moodys had plenty of experience in such work, their services also being used by such eminent landowners as the Duke of Norfolk and Seth Ellis Stevenson. But no matter how much damage the moles did they were not in the same nuisance league as their human rivals. To understand the next problem suffered by the Canal Company it must be appreciated that for as long as anyone could remember almost all the implements used around a house, on a farm or for trade had had to be made by the user or a local craftsman. Because of the effort involved and the fact that they did not change much over the years such items were made to last, a disposable culture it most certainly was not. Now another era had arrived, blatantly flaunting new values and aims. The massive constructions cutting across the land were awe-inspiring but on a practical level the amount of tools and implements used by the navvies was almost beyond belief; not only being used but also strewn along the workings. The temptation was too great, soon large numbers of the tools began to disappear, "borrowed" by the local inhabitants. It was not difficult to spot those wielding such treasures but when caught by Canal Company officials they simply claimed that the tools had been lent to them by the navvies and that they would be returned when a special job had been finished, or they could take them back now. This farce became widespread; because of the volumes involved it disrupted the work but it was difficult to disprove, the culprits always pleading ignorance of the rules. So the handbill display along the canal, and in the nearby towns and villages, was augmented by further notices stating that if any unofficial person was caught in possession of the Company's tools they would be prosecuted, no matter how ingenious their excuse. With only a small number of working people being able to read it was probably word-of-mouth that eventually spread the message.

At a more exalted level other residents were brooding over the damage done to their land and they were familiar names to the Company's administrators. At Worksop the Agents of the Duke of Norfolk were quietly gathering information on the effect of the workings on the ducal estate; next door John Hewitt was starting to make a fuss about his quarry at Shireoaks. In the spring of the previous year Hewitt and the Canal Company had agreed the value of the stone required for the canal and the land from which it was to be extracted; now, in August 1774, his grievance was that surrounding areas had been damaged or scattered with debris. Their old adversary's claims were discounted by the Committee, they considered the value he was now placing on the stone and the extra acres was excessive. They pointed out that much of the rock-bearing land had been underwater and that their side-cut from the canal to the quarry was not only for boat-loading, it also acted as a drain to dry the area. But nonetheless the Company was keen to reach an agreement with Hewitt – knowing it was prudent to placate such landowners if at all possible.

After lengthy diplomacy, it was agreed that one hundred guineas would be offered, a one-off payment for all the damage done in the past and in the future – perhaps this would settle the matter for all time. John Hewitt agreed that it would.

Meanwhile the Duke of Norfolk's representatives were quietly monitoring the actions of the Company in the Worksop area, quietly carrying out surveys and measuring the land taken for each canal structure.

❧ ❧ ❧

As the year drew to a close, the major construction work was still towards Retford, the canal lengthening as the autumn days shortened – before the onset of winter they had to be at their target, the lock on the outskirts of West Retford. Very soon the roads would deteriorate along with the weather, the price of coal increasing as the mud deepened around the wheels of the struggling wagons. Most winters the supply of coal ceased altogether, just when demand was at its height. The coal-starved Nottinghamshire towns and villages were a ready market, if only the canal could reach them in time to satisfy the winter need. But even when West Retford lock was achieved the boats would need some cargo to carry, to date the canal had not passed through a coal-bearing locality – unfinished Norwood Tunnel was still the barrier between the head of navigation and the mineral-rich areas of Yorkshire and Derbyshire. The Company's main source of supply was Mr. Norborne's pit near Killamarsh, three hilly miles away from the present end of the canal. During the late summer the Company began to organise the transportation of substantial coal stocks from the pit to Dog Kennel bridge at Kiveton Park, the nearest road access to the canal. Accurately weighing such large amounts of coal was a problem, another manifestation of how the new industrial age was continually requiring ingenuity from its participants. Martin Worstenholme had proved to be a versatile servant of the Company; judging the value of timber in local woods for subsequent purchase, capturing the offender when the canal had been damaged – now he had designed a machine to weigh the Company's coal as it was loaded onto wagons at Mr. Norborne's pit. After consulting Henshall the machine was made, although it proved to be more of a task than Worstenholme first thought; by August he had still not completed the task and the Committee pointedly reminded him that the coal had to be moved before the roads degenerated to a semi-liquid mire. Eventually the coal was moved and carefully stacked by the canal ready for collection by the Company's boats – ready for Retford customers.

For ten days in mid-September it did nothing but rain; in Derbyshire the deluge caused the River Derwent to flood, trade suffered in Chesterfield as the cheese fair was reduced to a shadow of its usual eminence. In Nottinghamshire, especially around Retford, the roads became so bad that normal life could not carry on; the fields had to be prepared for next months wheat-seed sowing but the farm wagons could not move.[6] The local courts ruled that in the circumstances they would permit an extra horse to be used on each wagon, but only for the next month – an extra horse to try to pull the loads through the clinging mud.[*] But no matter how bad the weather the Company's suppliers still struggled through to the canal sites with timber, tar, lead and gunpowder. At least it was possible to move heavy loads by water. Shireoaks was still the source of the majority of basic materials – stone from John Hewitt's quarry, bricks made by Edward Lewis and John Day, ironwork from Thomas Gillott's smithy – and these products, together with the lime-mortar from Joseph Holmes' kilns at Haggonfield, were carried in the Company's boats

---

[*] Laws such as the one temporarily set aside were an effort to control the damage done to the roads by regulating the traffic; limiting the number of horses that could pull a given weight and governing the design of vehicles, especially the wheels, to protect the road surfaces. The idea that perhaps the roads should be made to suit the traffic is a contentious concept of later years.

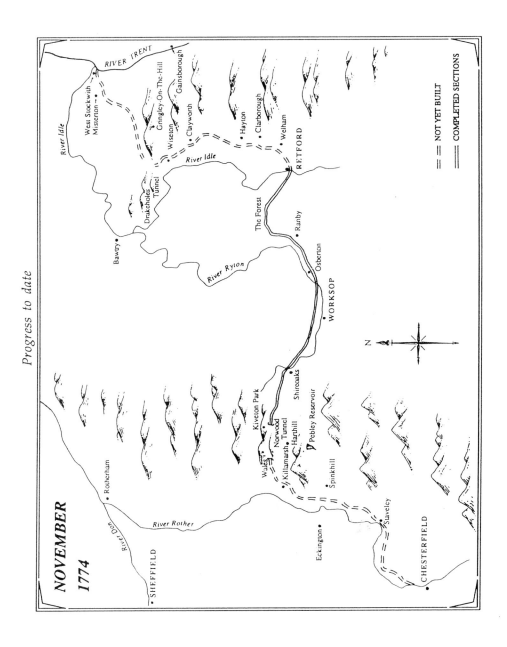

Progress to date

NOVEMBER 1774

== == NOT YET BUILT

=== COMPLETED SECTIONS

182

by John Nock. The bricks had been stacked on the canal bank by Lewis and Day so Nock's men had to load them themselves, the stone and the lime being shovelled and wheelbarrowed into the boats by the Company's men. As soon as the destination was reachable Nock was to take the materials down the canal to build West Retford lock; the pay was 2s for a thousand bricks, 10s for a ton of stone or lime.

Slowly but surely the canal progressed towards its winter goal, little money and effort being expended on structures that were not vital to the passage of boats. One exception to the rule was a bridge near the top of the four Forest locks, the canal having cut across the old London Road leaving it unpassable. This old route was still used by the enormous herds of animals going down to the London markets and if they could not get through on the old road, they would use the new London Road – straight through the centre of Retford. Not surprisingly the work was quickly allocated; John Read, a bricklayer from Worksop, being given six weeks to build a substantial bridge and receiving eleven guineas for his trouble.

At long last, on the very edge of winter, the canal reached Retford. On the 1st of November 1774 the first boat carrying a commercial cargo reached West Retford lock – coal for who else but Seth Ellis Stevenson.[7] There were celebrations in the town, the canal promoters meeting together, dining and deciding to involve the rest of the population. A hogshead of ale was purchased and the contents distributed around the town to whoever wished to join them in toasting the new canal.[*] It was not until the next day that John Bright wrote to the Duke of Newcastle and told him the astute gentlemen had taken the liberty of actually charging the cost of the ale to his Grace, and the town thanked him for it.[8]

---

[*]   A hogshead of beer is traditionally 54 gallons.

1774

The day-to-day problem of knowing the value of the coins in Canal Company or private hands was still very complicated.

	dwts	grs
COIN allowed current after the 15th of July 1774.		
Guineas coined SINCE 1771 that weigh		58
Half ditto ditto	2	16
Guineas coined BEFORE 1771 ditto		56
Half ditto ditto	2	14
All Quarter Guineas that weigh		17

COIN that will be exchanged from the 15th of July to the 21st of August.
Guineas coined before the Reign of George III which weigh 5dwts 3grs, and do not weigh 5dwts 6grs.
Half Guineas coined before the Reign of George III which weigh 2dwts 13grs, and do not weigh 2dwts 14grs.

The following being unpassable must be cut and sold as Bullion.

	dwts	grs
Guineas coined since 1771 that do not weigh		58
Half ditto ditto	2	16
Guineas coined during the Reign of George III and before 1772, that do not weigh		56
Half ditto ditto	2	14
Guineas coined prior to the Reign of George III		53
Half Guineas ditto	2	13
All Quarter Guineas ditto		17

STANDARD WEIGHTS
For WEIGHING GOLD COIN
Agreeable to the King's late Proclamation, assayed and marked at the Office in London, may be had at BARKER'S Toy and Perfume Shop, in the Corn Market, Derby – Where also may be had, neat SCALES accurately adjusted for weighing as above.

1775

April; first shots fired in the American War of Independence – Trade suffers because of the American war – Capt. Cook has been on his second voyage of discovery since 1772; searching for a great southern continent, further charting New Zealand and numerous Pacific islands, leaving in November 1774 to return home.

By authentic Intelligence from the Cape of Good Hope, where one of the Ships are arrived which sailed with Capt. Cook to the South Seas, we are informed that they explored in vain to the Southward in search of a Continent, and therefore bore up for New Zealand where they had landed but lost a Lieutenant and two Men who, by venturing too far into the Country, had been cut off by the Cannibals, and devoured. In consequence of this Loss they had dispatched a second Boat, and the whole Crew were massacred, roasted and eat by the Savages; the next Boat having only a miserable Spectacle of their Bones after the Inhuman repast. From thence they sailed to the Cape of Good Hope, and speedily will pursue their Voyage Home. No very material Circumstances further passed in the Course of their Expedition.

Last night there was a numerous Meeting of Seamen at a Public-House near Rotherhithe, when the brave Tars came to a Resolution not to serve on board any Ship of War destined for America, and at the same Time declared that if Press Warrants should be issued out, sooner than be forced like Slaves to fight against the Americans they would die on the Spot.

At the Quarter Sessions of the Peace for Derby Borough, John Hall, a Stockiner of Nottingham, was found guilty of stealing a Common Prayer Book and was ordered to be whipped round the Market at the Cat's Tail, next Friday.

CHAPTER NINE

Through Norwood Hill

By the final days of 1774 an onlookers perception of the canal's progress would have differed if viewed from Chesterfield or Retford. It was almost four years since Anthony Lax had ridden into Chesterfield's Market Place with the news from Westminster – the excitement engendered then had long since faded, together with the memory of fireworks and banquets. In the intervening years very little evidence of a canal had appeared, in fact if anyone wanted to see anything of the marvellous construction it was necessary to ride quite a distance to see an unfinished tunnel.

On the otherhand Retford's canal proprietors could show evidence of their business acumen – there were boats floating where once there had only been trees and grass. The canal age had reached the outskirts of the town and was there for everyone to see, a great boost to the morale of the gentlemen involved. As in Chesterfield the end of the year saw everyday life continuing much as before, but here it was alongside the construction of a marvellous waterway, and some aspects of the canal became interlinked with other events. For instance on the evening of the 28th of December the navvies were involved in a disturbance; not as instigators but as peace-makers. Two opposing groups involved in the forthcoming Parliamentary election had clashed at The Crown; windows had been broken and a sizeable crowd threatened to pull the building down. Two of the Duke of Newcastle's sons were trapped inside, their decision to call the navvies to their aid a result of their father's major shareholding in the Canal Company. The navvies appeared to need little encouragement as they soon arrived outside The Crown and "fell upon the mob, and after a bloody contest drove them off". Peace was restored but some of the navvies had been injured. One called Williams had a serious head wound and was not expected to survive, another had a broken leg. Many of the mob were also badly hurt. A few months later in February there was more rioting; this time it was even more serious, the rabble breaking all the windows, frames and shutters on the front of the building and forcing their way inside where they broke and destroyed the furniture in five rooms. Many people were injured but luckily no one was killed, the material damage being estimated at £250. Eventually six of the ringleaders were caught and sent to prison in Nottingham, and by the end of the month two troops of Elliott's Light Dragoons had been quartered in Retford to forestall any more disturbances.*

❧ ❧ ❧

The boats could now carry cargoes between Kiveton, Shireoaks, Worksop and Retford – not yet a great market but full of potential. This was the start of a new chapter in the creation of the Chesterfield Canal and it is a typical example of the changing problems faced by the early Canal Companies. As is often found today it takes entrepreneurial spirit to conceive a new project, to promote its aims, to engender enthusiasm and to overcome all obstacles; a spirit which is often bored by the mundane everyday duties needed to run the business created. The very fact that they had become deeply involved in building the canal had shown the Committee gentlemen to be pioneers not settlers – but from now until the construction work was finished they would have to manage as well as build the canal. By the very nature of such men the situation evolved along predictable lines; the Committee spent most of its time directing the high-profile construction work, the commercial management gradually being delegated to methodical creatures who thrived in a different environment, Anthony Lax and Richard Dixon being two prime examples. Below the Chief Clerk and the Bookkeeper were other salaried officials with varied responsibilities. The number of these employees would grow with the canal as more boats and cargoes needed regulating – eventually there would be lock-keepers, toll-collectors, maintenance men, clerical

---

* It may be indicative of life in Retford in 1775 that when ten Dragoons were needed to serve in America eighteen volunteered to fight the colonists rather than stay where they were.

staff and wharfingers. Each major town along the canal would become the location of a Company-owned wharf and warehouse, a busy centre where the public could deliver and collect cargoes. In charge of each of these sites would be a Wharfinger, a Company official responsible for all the goods handled, the weighing of cargoes, the loading of items onto the correct boats and the calculation of the cost to each customer. He would also be the Company's representative at each location, acting as an agent and promoting canal transport whenever he could. The first of these officials was the newly-appointed Wharfinger at Retford, John Best. Having worked for the Company for the last three years – counting the navvies in the workforce had been one of his duties – Best had more than earned his promotion. When things became a little more organised, that is when the Company had actually built the canal past the town instead of just reaching the outskirts, he would have porters, checkers, warehousemen and clerks working for him. At the moment Best hardly had a wharf, let alone a warehouse, but nevertheless his was the crucial job of generating as much cargo, traffic and income as he could for the infant canal.

Whatever else he lacked, Best had been supplied with rules and regulations; governing the conduct of the staff and the basis of the service offered to the public, they had been printed and posted up in the wharf office. The Act of Parliament stipulated what charges could be made by the Canal Company; in general they could levy various payments per ton on cargoes carried by boats on their canal, and they could also charge for goods left for more than twenty-four hours on their wharfs or in their warehouses. The shareholders could set the tolls at whatever they thought fit to maintain the canal and make a profit but only within the maximums stated in the Act. Numerous objections and petitions had also resulted in Parliament agreeing to various exemptions from toll payments. As a result a toll-collector's job was not easy. No more than one penny per ton per mile could be charged for lime but coal, lead, timber, stone, and other goods could be as much as one and a half pence per ton. But the "other goods" were not to include soap, ashes, salt, salt scrow, foul salt, grey salt, soot, bone dust, pigeons dung, rape or cole seed dust, rags, or tanners bark to be used for manuring the lands of any person whose land has been cut by the canal. Such items could be charged at no more than a halfpenny per ton per mile. The legal exemptions did not make life any easier. Hay or corn was toll-free as long as it had not been sold but was being taken for storage by its owner. This also applied to gravel and sand to be used for making or repairing roads (not Turnpikes) in the towns and villages through which the canal passed, so long as such cargoes did not go more than five miles on the canal. And there was even the complication that these and other exemptions did not apply when the water supply in the canal was low as measured by a gauge on the locks. The only help was that the carriers of such cargoes were to give the nearest toll-collector at least six hours notice of their intention to pass through any lock.

In an effort to simplify the poor toll-collector's lot the Act also stated that the boats must be "gauged", that is a scale was to be marked on the outside of the hull which would show the number of tons carried as the boat sank lower in the water. To our eyes this may seem a simple and accurate way of measuring a cargo but in the 1770s weights and measures were in the same confused state as the currency. We take for granted that any stated weight is an official amount, but it was not until 1797 that Parliament attempted to end conflicting local laws and customs by stipulating standard measures, including the testing of them by Examiners of weights and balances. But it was one thing to pass a law, it was another to enforce it against time-honoured local practice. It was to be many years before a national standard could be achieved, the measurement of cargoes on the Chesterfield Canal staying unbelievably complicated into the next century. For instance, the unit of weight for lead was traditionally the fodder and at the Derbyshire smelting houses a fodder was equal to 2820 pounds. But when the lead reached West Stockwith it was transhipped and recorded in fodders of 2408 pounds, the Custom House duties being payable by the ton, 2240 pounds. From West Stockwith the lead was taken by larger craft to Hull where it was sold in fodders of 2340 pounds, eventually reaching London where it was sold by the fodder of 2184 pounds.[1] Such discrepancies could be explained by the traditions maintained in various parts of the country but there were also local differences. Although the Canal Company made their rules for the wharfingers it did not stop different interpretations of the weights carried in the boats; lime was measured in quarters and at many wharfs this was equal to eight level bushels, at other wharfs it was eight heaped bushels. And these examples could be multiplied many times, almost every commodity being carried and sold in different units; liquor and dry goods in hogsheads, brooms and reeds in bunches, hoops and spades in bundles, millstones measured in hands, pots and glass in crates, iron, salt, cheese, ox horns and rags in tons, soap in chests, rabbit skins in packs, gunpowder in barrels.

The early Canal Companies operated in an environment that was not ready for the industrial revolution they were heralding. As with the currency, weights and measures had not yet evolved into a system capable of use on a national scale – but until then Richard Dixon was caught between two worlds, trying to record Canal Company transactions that defied accuracy.

ಶ ಶ ಶ

Ever since he had first heard of the canal scheme the Rev. Seth Ellis Stevenson had been convinced that Retford should be served by a wide canal. Several campaigns had been fought in the past but the extra expense of building the canal to such dimensions had always been considered prohibitive by the shareholders in general. But the Rev. Stevenson was a practical man who was not easily discouraged. If he could not have the whole canal built to take wide craft there was no reason why the section between the River Trent and his town should not be built to do so. After all, the main reason behind his campaign was to aid Retford's trade by allowing the keels sailing the Trent and the Humber to come right up to the town. If Chesterfield and the rest of the villages further to the west were content with a narrow canal then so be it, but Stevenson was determined that Retford should not suffer for their lack of vision.

Narrow canals were a compromise between construction costs and commercially viable cargo loads. Early in this first canal age it had been calculated that each boat should be able to carry at least 20 tons if a canal was to be a successful business venture. Additional considerations were that the boats be handleable by a crew of two and light enough to be pulled by one horse. Bearing these items in mind the dimensions of a canal were designed to allow for such boats while reducing the amount of soil to be moved to a minimum, thereby holding down building costs. Of the three relevant dimensions the length of the canal was set by the locations it was to link, but savings could be made in restraining the width and depth. The result of all these studies was the standard narrow canal designed to take almost flat-bottomed boats, just under 7ft wide and 70ft long. The very first boats were probably double-ended in that the tiller and rudder could be moved to either end, thus saving the building of wide turning places.

Of course such calculations did not take into account the circumstances of a canal linking with a river where larger craft were already trading. This threw into the ring the business costs involved in trans-shipping cargoes from the narrow canal boats to the larger river craft – would it be cost effective to make the canal wider so that the river vessels could use it? This question had never been fully resolved amongst the proprietors of the Chesterfield Canal Company. The original Brindley plans for the Bawtry route were for a narrow canal but that was before Retford became involved in the scheme.[2] The Nottinghamshire parties must have raised the subject at an early point, certainly Seth Ellis Stevenson's first ideas were for boats carrying at least 30 tons. The Act of Parliament was written to allow the canal to carry "wide burthen" vessels but at some unknown time, and for unknown reasons, the decision was made to make the dimensions narrow. Was it as the planned Norwood Tunnel extended from 630 yards to 2850 yards? Or did the Staveley Forge amendment to the Act of Parliament mean that a water supply for a wide canal could not be achieved? Was the cost of Staveley Puddlebank saved by making it a narrow canal instead?

Whatever the reasons the Rev. Seth Ellis Stevenson was not going to let the matter rest. Having achieved the first priority of linking Retford to the coal-rich inland areas he now turned his thoughts and energy to the completion of the rest of the route, giving his town access to the commercially important River Trent. During the first days of 1775 he started canvassing his local colleagues and Corporation members about the prospect of building the section from Retford to the Trent as a wide canal. As usual he had done his homework well. Visits to West Stockwith and conversations with captains of keels on the River Trent had convinced him that it would be possible to bring large craft to Retford, the commercial benefits justifying the extra costs. Obviously the original subscription made by the shareholders could not be expected to finance the whole of the enlargement of the canal, especially when the Nottinghamshire area would gain more than most. But extra traffic on the canal would mean increased toll income for all shareholders so it was deemed reasonable that the Company should be expected to bear a proportion of the costs, the rest being donated by Retford. Such a proposition was drawn up by Retford's leading citizens and on that basis Stevenson proceeded to investigate the details of what would be involved. He had timed his activities well; the bulk of the canal construction was now taking place at Retford and during the dark days of that January there were many contractors, Company officials, suppliers and John Varley himself easily available for consultations. Varley immediately pointed out that the major problem was not the excavation of more soil but the fact that a wider and deeper canal would need more water to fill it. The plans would have to include a way of obtaining the extra supply.

The River Idle was the obvious source of extra water and the Act of Parliament did not rule this out, although the exact meaning could be argued. Throughout its short history the Chesterfield Canal Company had often shown a haughty disregard for the niceties of the legal constraints upon them – not surprising as Anthony Lax was not a man to use his legal training to inhibit his employers. He saw his role as ensuring the Company gain maximum benefit from the law when it suited, but without being held up by inconvenient clauses that could be blithely ignored, or at least given a generous interpretation. Taking water from the River Idle was another example of such cavalier attitudes. There was a trifling clause in the Act about damaging the business of the River Idle Navigation at Bawtry by taking water from further upstream but that could be ignored unless someone complained. Even then the legal arguments could be made to last for years. The more important part was the authority to take water from the river – the Act simply stating that supplies could be obtained "out of such brooks, streams and watercourses as are or shall be found within the distance of one thousand yards" of the canal. In future years this was to be interpreted by senior legal representatives in London

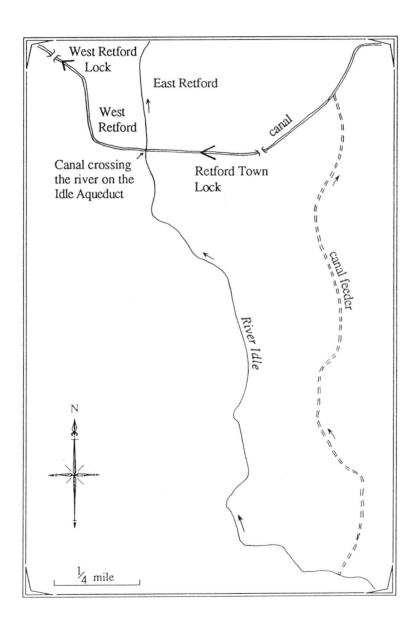

West Retford
Lock

East Retford

West
Retford

canal

Canal crossing
the river on the
Idle Aqueduct

Retford Town
Lock

River Idle

canal feeder

N

¼ mile

as meaning the Company could take water from the Idle at any point less than 1000 yards from the canal. In 1775 the same words were read by Lax and conveniently taken to mean that as long as the Idle passed within 1000 yards of the canal, which it obviously did as the canal passed over the river on an aqueduct, then water could be taken from any point the Company wished, no matter how far away.[3]

The reason for such an interpretation of the Act was that the canal was obviously higher than the river because it crossed over it. Just as obviously water did not run uphill so careful surveying was needed to find a point where the river was higher than the canal, thereby allowing water to be diverted along a slight down-slope to the canal. If you want to find a higher point along a river you go further up-stream, a lower point on a canal is found beyond a lock. Bearing such simple facts in mind John Varley did the surveying during February and March, he and his men often accompanied by Seth Ellis Stevenson. It was not pleasant work as bitterly cold north-easterly winds blew nearly every day in March, bringing sharp frosts and numbingly cold temperatures. But eventually the course of the feeder was marked out and it became evident that the water would be extracted more than 1000 yards from the canal – there was no alternative so a liberal reading of the Act was required, and achieved. The purchase of the land was no problem; the gentlemen of the neighbourhood were so keen to see large craft in Retford that they donated it free of charge, the major portion coming from Lindley Simpson, a stalwart Committee member. They even said that if any of their mills on the River Idle suffered from lack of water as a result of it being diverted to the canal they would not claim any damages from the Canal Company.*

The other important consideration was the cost of the work involved; building the feeder, and digging a wide channel spanned by wide bridges, controlled by wide locks. Behind the scenes it was agreed that £500 would be paid by the Retford proprietors, one lump sum to be in the Company's hands by September. By the time of the General Meeting in May the whole scheme had been devised, surveyed, costed and started. Hugh Henshall was at The Angel in Chesterfield on that day and gave his seal

---

* The feeder is now disused, but the route can still be traced through Retford.

of approval to the assembled shareholders. Nine of Retford's august gentlemen gave their word that the £500 would be paid as specified and signed their names to the agreement; Lindley Simpson, Seth Ellis Stevenson, George Poplewell, Thomas Brumby, John Parker, Edward Brown, John Taylor, Henry Bonsor and John Kirk. They had given personal bonds that the money would be forthcoming but that did not mean it would be out of their pockets, such was not their style They simply borrowed it in the name of the Corporation and passed it on to the Canal Company.

Such was the rush to complete the scheme before the General Meeting, and such were the private agreements which made it all possible that few records were kept. In later years, when disputes arose about the legality of the canal's use of the water from the River Idle, there proved to be very little evidence of the land donations or the acceptance of reduced water supplies to mills.[4] What is known is that the £500 paid by the astute Retford proprietors only went a small way towards the eventual cost of widening the canal; in 1807 the Canal Company said that the additional expense was "computed to amount to upwards of £6,000".[5]

❴ ❴ ❴

The great flight of locks at Norwood was to take the canal from its summit pound down into the valley of the River Rother. The top lock would be a few yards from the western portal of the tunnel, its location still the site of camps and storage areas for the work going on in the unfinished tunnel. But if the locks themselves could not be completed because of their proximity to other workings there was no reason to ignore the sections that could be built further to the west. In the first half of 1775 the Committee had to strike a fine balance between the Retford interests who wanted priority to be given to going east to the River Trent, and Chesterfield who wanted Norwood Tunnel finished and the canal to go west to their town. Reaching the Trent nearly always held sway because it was rightly stated that a junction with such a major waterway would generate more traffic on the canal and badly needed income for the Company. But the gentlemen of Chesterfield knew that when the Trent was reached their Retford colleagues would show less interest in completing the Chesterfield end of the canal. Not that they would leave it unfinished, but human nature usually generates less enthusiasm, initiative and energy once one's own targets are achieved. The compromise seems to have been that most of the actual digging would still be from Retford to the Trent, especially as they had now sorted out the width it was to be, but Yorkshire and Derbyshire would not be ignored. Land purchase would continue, some construction work would go on and contracts would be signed for brick production. It was also symbolically agreed that in future Committee meetings would be in Retford and Chesterfield alternatively, and not in Worksop as was the usual case until now. But the unfinished Norwood Tunnel always lessened Chesterfield's influence, and it would continue to do so while it remained a barrier between Derbyshire and the rest of the canal. Because of this John Varley was ordered to finish Norwood Tunnel as soon as possible; the contractors were to be hurried along, no time was to be wasted, if any delays were foreseen then extra men were to be transferred to the work. At one time the Company even supplied liquor to the navvies in the tunnel, what effect this had on the workrate is not recorded.

With the Company's main brick contractors still busy at Shireoaks and Norwood it was an opportunity for others to obtain the work on the Derbyshire section. There would only be small amounts of stone available as the canal progressed – the incomplete Norwood Tunnel barring the transport of supplies from Anston and Pennyholme – so bricks would be the main construction material. They could be made and stored, ready for use as the worksites progressed westward, and as the summer months were the best time for brickmaking early contracts were signed. John Toft did very well for himself. He agreed to make 50,000 bricks at Renishaw, and the same number again at The Hague, at each site building a kiln for which he was paid £2.10s. In addition he was to make 300,000 bricks at Doe Lea on the outskirts of Staveley; for those numbers a more substantial kiln would have to be built, valued at £7 of effort. In some places stone was specified. One such was the building of a bridge at Killamarsh, however the Company was careful to delegate the supply of the materials. John Story and John Holmes had to find and transport the stone, the Company only agreeing to find lime and sand for the mortar. It is noticeable that a few months later when the tunnel was finished the Company suddenly found it convenient to supply the stone for a further two bridges at Eckington. Norwood locks were still not operational but at least boats could bring the stone from the other side of the hill, it was downhill to Eckington after that. As a result Robert Mettam had the luxury of stone, sand and lime delivered where he wanted it, but only in exchange for a tight completion date – two months for two bridges. More preparatory work was the construction of a good standard road between the main coal supply source, still Mr Norborne's pit at Killamarsh, and the canal. As soon as Norwood Tunnel and locks were finished they would be ready to supply cheap coal to Nottinghamshire at all times of the year.

An important site of which we know very little is the reservoir at Pebley, high in the hills near Harthill. At this time it was the only supply of water to the usable part of the summit pound and as boats had been using that section for about eighteen months millions of gallons had gone down the fifteen locks of the Thorpe flight. The first hint of the water shortage that was to plague the summit pound was when Henshall and Varley were told to investigate and report back to the Committee. It may have been a lack of capacity in the reservoir, it may have been leakage through the dam – either way the Chesterfield Canal's bad luck with the weather struck again. During the past three years rain and snow had often hampered the construction work, the transportation of supplies, and the mere process of travelling for meetings and inspections. Now – after they had striven to reach Retford, making the first lengths commercially viable - their vital water supplies were hit by an unusually dry spring. In fact, from March to June there was hardly any rain at all, only a very few moderate showers. To make matters worse the end of April was hotter than anyone could remember. By July the canal's water stocks were seriously depleted and John Varley started work on heightening the dam at Pebley to increase the storage for future years. What a pity that the doubts voiced a year before had not been listened to. In January 1774, when Retford called a special General Meeting to force the resumption of work in Norwood Tunnel, they had also proposed that another reservoir be built. Retford lost that vote by 407 to

484, it had already become clear that the shareholders had made a crucial mistake.

The dry weather also aggravated the situation at Osberton mill. A common complaint against all canals was that water-powered mills suffered when water was taken from a river, the owners claiming that the remaining flow was insufficient to drive the machinery. Parliament acknowledged that such clashes of interest would occur and canal Acts are full of clauses protecting the interests of existing mills. They are indicative of the importance of water in the still infant steam age. Mr Foster was the owner at Osberton and he was making just such a complaint, he said the River Ryton was now a shadow of its former self. The canal already had two feeders from the Ryton so he probably had a reasonable case but such problems were difficult to resolve. The flow of rivers fluctuated according to the season and the weather, in addition the amount of damage done to the mill's power source could be defined in many different ways. Arbitration was usually called for as the two camps tended to became entrenched in their respective positions, and getting damage payments from the Chesterfield Canal Company was not easy; Anthony Lax usually saw to that. Foster's case was weakened as Osberton mill was not specifically covered by the Act of Parliament, but commonlaw would protect a business to some degree. After an initial investigation by John Varley and Richard Dixon a token payment was made, but the dispute went on for the next three years. The Company eventually agreeing to make a one-off payment of £30 to finish the matter.

By now the Company had built a small fleet of boats, many of which were used to carry construction materials. The expanded nature of the project meant that running such boats had become a substantial overhead and it was decided to lease the vessels to contractors who would run the operation themselves. The Company's Paymaster, John Peacock, was not slow in seeing that a profit could be made and together with Francis Grant he took over five of the boats. Peacock and Grant agreed to carry bricks, stone, lime and gravel anywhere between Sandhill (Worksop) and Hayton, the next village on the canal beyond Retford. They paid 10s a week to lease each of the prosaically named boats 1, 2, 3, 4 and 5 and earned 3s for carrying a thousand bricks, 1s.1d per ton of stone and lime, and 10d for each ton of gravel. It is probable that Peacock found the funds with Francis Grant actually supplying the crews and organising the work; it is certainly difficult to imagine the Rev. John Peacock actually boating down the canal in company with a load of bricks. Three other craft – known as 6, 7 and 8 – were leased by other contractors on the same terms, so as long as the water supply held out the problems of moving heavy construction supplies were a thing of the past. At least that was so in Nottinghamshire.

૨ૉ   ૨ૉ   ૨ૉ

Although making considerable progress in both directions, and already a working waterway of reasonable length, it was still a fact that the greatest engineering challenge on the Chesterfield Canal had still not been resolved. The workcamps, the brick-kilns, the spoil heaps were still strung out across a hilly ridge, surface evidence of years of ceaseless effort. Beneath the ground Norwood Tunnel was still unfinished.

The tunnel had always been the major work on the canal but over the intervening years the other achievements had increased the importance of its completion. It still sat there, a complete barrier between the navigable canal on the eastern side of the hill and the unusable Derbyshire sections to the west – sections still waiting for construction materials and a water supply to flow through the tunnel. The reason why there were no plans to feed water direct to the western end of the tunnel was because of a strict clause in the Act of Parliament. When the Don Navigation Company had asked that the River Rother be protected because it flowed into the River Don it was agreed that rain or streams that would naturally feed the Rother would not be prevented from doing so. If such water was diverted into the canal on the summit pound there would be nothing to stop it flowing eastwards through the tunnel and into a different valley and river system. However, there was no constraint on water being moved in the opposite direction. Therefore, Pebley reservoir had been built on the Ryton side of the watershed and its water was to supply the whole of the summit pound including the tunnel as well as the lock flights down both flanks of the hills.[*]

For all these reasons John Varley was told at the beginning of 1775 to complete the passage through Norwood hill as soon as possible. The date of completion was vital as public relations and Company politics demanded a grand opening ceremony for the longest canal tunnel in the country. To ensure reasonable weather and the attendance of many shareholders the celebrations were to coincide with the General Meeting in May. Heaven help John Varley if the tunnel was not finished in time. The shareholders were due to gather at Chesterfield's Angel Inn during the morning of Thursday the 11th of May, those that had a lengthy journey arriving the previous day. But the celebrations could not be on the 10th as the gentlemen of the Committee, together with their salaried servants Hugh Henshall, Anthony Lax and John Varley, were due to assemble as they usually did before facing the General Meeting. So the target date for the public opening of Norwood Tunnel was Tuesday the 9th of May 1775. John Varley's men finished the work two days before.

Notwithstanding the cold weather of the previous two months the first weeks of May were a spring-like contrast – the hawthorn bushes already in flower for some time, a circumstance not remembered by even the oldest local residents. In such weather the ladies and gentlemen attending the festivities made their way up the hill, past the still incomplete locks, to where the stone-clad western portal of Norwood Tunnel framed a black hole in the hillside. There was also a pool of still water, its furthest edge disappearing into the tunnel and the blackness – the remaining 200ft in the sunlight, enclosed by the towpath and the unfinished first lock. Floating there, moored next to the towpath, were three of the Company's narrowboats, suitably cleaned up from their usual trade. Six years ago many had disbelieved the claims that boats would float high in the hills; but here they were. The River Rother was down in

---

[*] Soon after the canal was finished it became apparent that Pebley reservoir could not supply all the water needed on the summit pound. As early as 1785 two more reservoirs were planned. Now known as Woodall Pond and Killamarsh Pond they did collect water destined for the River Rother. The feeder entered the canal near the western end of Norwood Tunnel, the method of preventing water flowing through the tunnel may have been some sort of gate or stop-lock, the Act certainly mentions this.

the distant valley bottom, and here were three boats disdainfully looking down from the peaks. It was an unbelievable, wonderful, awesome sight – it generated such pride, what could our countrymen not do? The inescapable speeches told the gathered visitors many facts, incredible though they were to the listeners. The other end of the tunnel was an amazing 2850 yards away, over one and a half miles. Throughout its journey through the hill it was 12ft high and 9ft 3ins wide; at its deepest it was 108ft below the surface. And it was so straight that if you stood at one end you could see daylight at the other. How stupendous, how were such things possible? Nowhere else in the country had such a feat been equalled. The Committee gentlemen of the Chesterfield Canal Company were rightly proud of their achievement.[6]

After the official opening Hugh Henshall led three hundred people aboard the narrowboats for a journey through the hillside – accompanied by the band that had been playing during the ceremonies. As they disappeared into the hillside there must have been some apprehension about what lay ahead. In keeping with most early canal tunnels Norwood had been built without a towpath so the means of propulsion was human, "legging" as it is now known. On each boat two or four men would have been lying flat on their backs, pushing their feet against the sides of the tunnel to "walk" the boats along. It is to be hoped that lanterns were provided otherwise the ladies and gentlemen would have sat in the dark for one hour and one minute, the time taken for the small convoy to reach daylight at Kiveton Park. A celebration it may have been but perhaps not enjoyed by all; over an hour in a crowded open boat on hard seats, shrouded in cold damp air, gazing through the dim light, loud music echoing and reverberating from the all-enveloping brickwork. It may be that more than a few were pleased to reach the comfort of their carriages, there to meet them at the other end of the tunnel.[7]

Two days later the General Meeting was a victorious occasion for Retford; official approval was given to building a wide canal to the Trent. It was of course just rubber-stamping the Committees earlier decision. In fact Varley had been working to the new dimensions for some time but it was important that it became official Company policy. Nine of Retford's finest representatives signed the agreement, pledging that a £500 donation towards the extra costs would be paid to the Treasurers before the 7th of September. Seth Ellis Stevenson was well pleased. His wife and three of his children had travelled to Chesterfield with him and were able to join in the celebrations that evening – and tomorrow a visit to Norwood Tunnel was to be the highlight of the journey home.

The Stevenson's travelled to Norwood the next day accompanied by Richard Dixon.[8] Although Dixon was the Company's Bookkeeper his knowledge of the canal's engineering was more than would be supposed from his pedestrian title. For the last nine months he had been assisting Varley in measuring all the open stretches of canal to be dug. Soon he was to be involved in checking the progress of the contractors working beyond Retford. It may seem an odd role for an administrative officer to be playing but it made sense in various practical ways. Planning ahead it would be necessary to replace Varley when the construction work was finished, the engineer going on to other schemes. It seems that Dixon was an acceptable candidate and as such it made sense for him to gain experience by working with Varley from now on. It also meant that now the works were geographically widespread Dixon could keep an eye on matters in the Retford area allowing Varley to spend more time on the Derbyshire sections. And of course it was politically astute; a Retford man as engineer/bookkeeper would balance the influence of Anthony Lax, Chesterfield's chief clerk and solicitor, during the coming years of running the canal business.

So it is likely that Dixon's presence on the Stevenson family outing was not just because he was also travelling back to Retford. He had probably learnt a reasonable amount about the tunnel's problems from Varley and was able to pass this information on to his companions. The party gathered at Norwood. Seth Ellis Stevenson with his wife Elizabeth and their children; William, who was twenty-four, nineteen year-old Polly, and little Kitty who was nine (almost ten) and learning to play the spinet. A journey through the hill was planned but narrowboats were too valuable to be kept at the tunnel waiting for visitors, no matter what their standing in the Canal Company. Nevertheless a small boat was found, maybe an inspection craft for the engineers, and Seth Ellis Stevenson and Richard Dixon set off through Norwood Tunnel. Not on their own of course;

"leggers" would be needed to move the boat along and it is hard to imagine two such august gentlemen lying on their backs with their legs in the air!

And the tunnelling navvies drifted away from Harthill to look for another job.

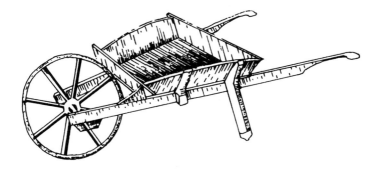

1775

Thursday Morning, near One o'Clock, as the Nottingham Coach was going for London, it was stopped by a single Highwayman on Wanlip Hill who rode round the Coach and ordered the Postilion to stand. The Boy took little Notice, on which he rode round a second Time and commanded the Coachman to stand, which he accordingly did. He then rode up the Coach Door and ordered the Window to be let down, but the Passengers did not immediately obey his Order. Upon which the Highwayman threatened if they did not instantly obey he would fire upon them. Accordingly they let them down and he said "Your money directly". The Passengers then collected him £4.14s.6d. A Female Passenger, who had a Guinea and two Shillings, cried out "Oh Sir, don't take my Silver', and to her agreeable surprise when she arrived at Northampton found she had given a Shilling to the Highwayman instead of the Guinea.

The robber was a little fat Man, in a light coloured Great Coat (with the Cape of which he had covered part of his Face) and rode upon a large Bay Horse.

It may not be improper to remind the Farmers to be particularly careful in having their Names upon their Carts and Waggons; as two or three Persons have been very busy, for these ten days past in the different Roads in this Part of the country, taking Notice of all the carriages they meet with, and lodging Informations against every Person whose Name is not upon his carriage.

DESERTED

FROM his Majesty's 35th Regiment of Foot, at Bristol.

Joseph Heath, aged 24 Years, 5 Feet 8 Inches high, pale Complexion, black Hair, hazel Eyes, and is much marked with the Small Pox. Born in Chesterfield, by Trade a Breeches-Maker. Went off from Bristol in his Regimental Cloathing, but changed them afterwards for a ragged brown Coat. Whoever will apprehend the above Deserter shall receive One Guinea Reward, over and above what is allowed by Act of Parliament, by applying to the Commanding Officer of the Regiment at Bristol; or to Lieutenant Colonel Heathcote at Derby.

1776

July; American Declaration of Independence – November; war with France and Spain thought to be imminent – Serious disruptions of trade.

M onday last a thorough Trial of Skill, Courage, and English Fortitude was displayed in the boxing Profession in Nottingham Park before near Two Thousand Spectators, who assembled to see a Battle fought according to the Rules of Art, between Thomas Hitchcock and William Clews, each in his nineteenth Year. The contest which was for a Wager of One Guinea began at Two O'Clock and did not conclude till near Six at Night; when neither of the Combatants yielding, tho' quite spent out with Blows, Falls and loss of Blood, the Seconds persuaded them to desist, and each acknowledged a drawn Battle. The Parties then adjourned to a neighbouring public-house with their Seconds and Friends, to enjoy themselves after their most terrible Struggle for Superiority. This Battle would have been much sooner decided, had not the Father of Clews attended and encouraged his Son to fight on manfully; when he found his Son's Strength exhausted and his Spirits fail, he told him that he should never enter his Doors again if he did not conquer. This Behaviour of the Father, together with allowing two Minutes between each and every fall, occasioned the Dispute for Victory to be thus held out to the uncommon Length of four Hours.

WANTED IMMEDIATELY

A Journeyman HAIR-DRESSER; one who can dress a Gentleman well, and assist in the Wig-making Branch, may have constant Employ, and Wages adequate to his Abilities by applying to SAMUEL JORDAN, Hair-Dresser, Market Place, Derby; who is also in want of an active, sprightly Boy, as an Apprentice to the said Branch. No Letters answered, unless Post paid.

CHAPTER TEN

Financial Crises

The great Norwood Tunnel was usable, the hill had been beaten and the public face of the Canal Company did indeed look confident. They had built the country's longest canal tunnel and a sensational flight of locks, a usable section was already earning income, and a visionary scheme for bringing wide-beam craft up to Retford had been realised. But behind the scenes financial problems continued to plague everyday actions. Since the construction work had begun the Committee had continuously brought in rules to contain spending and to improve the accuracy of their records, but usually after the event. What may now seem obvious and good business practice was still new and unlearned in the 1770s, in those early days of the Industrial Revolution no one had experience of running a large and complex Company. And some problems seemed unsolvable.

Poor John Varley! At the beginning of 1775 he was still in trouble with his paperwork. The Committee again told him to balance and settle the accounts still outstanding with various people and to produce the details for their inspection. He was also ordered to endorse all future bills with the name, date, purpose and amount, and no more than 1s.4d was to be paid for day labour during the winter months. Even Richard Dixon was under scrutiny; he was to make a list of all the bills received so that the Committee could check the items against the Paymaster's Cash Book, and authorise payment if satisfactory. No bills were to be paid until they had undergone this perusal. Other strict rules were enforced. Suppliers were told that if they wanted to be paid their bills must include where the materials were brought from and where delivered to. The bills of contractors were to include the exact location of the work done. The records of money paid out for damage done to nearby land were to show specifically whose land was involved and no such payments were to be made until approved by the Committee. In addition the Paymaster, John Peacock, was to show in his cash accounts to whom money had been paid, for what work done and for what materials supplied.

Extra income was earned by selling the engineering items that had been needed to complete Norwood Tunnel; machines, engines, wheels and other specialist implements which were now useless. As usual the parts were scattered about where they had last been used, the first task being their collection ready for storage in a secure area near Varley's tunnel-end house at Pennyholme. There everything was checked and catalogued. Anthony Lax arranged for two hundred handbills to be printed - a public auction was to be held at Pennyholme, starting at 11.00am on the 31st of July 1775. Mr Varley, the Company's engineer, would be present and would show the items as required. All had been used to build the great Norwood Tunnel.[1]

---

1 Horse Gin complete, wheel 14" diameter, pulleys 3'6"
1 Horse Gin complete, wheel 11" diameter, pulleys 3'6"
1 Horse Gin complete, wheel 10" diameter, pulleys 2'8"

1 Water Engine wheel, 20" diameter

1 Water Engine wheel, 16" diameter

1 Water Engine wheel, 17" diameter

9 Turn Barrels and Stand Trees

20 Yards of Pump Trees, 8" bore

4 Six inch Cast Metal working Pieces

1 Wind Engine

2 Pair of Smith's Bellows

4 Horse Water Tubs

A number of Rollers fixed in Frames for Slide Rods, Drum Wheels and Chains, and Slide and Pump Rod Joints.

But in spite of all the Committee's efforts major financial decisions could no longer be deferred. On the 25th of September 1775 the shareholders were due to pay the fourteenth and last Call. Allowing for the usual defaulters the full £100,000 capital had been raised. And it was not going to be enough.

The reasons for the overspending are not known, and it is difficult to pinpoint one major cause. Norwood Tunnel's greatly extended length must have increased costs considerably, tunnelling was by far the most expensive work on any canal. Staveley Puddlebank was not included in the original estimates, and Retford's contribution to the widening of the eastern section was not really sufficient. The involvement of the Varley family in the contracts for Norwood Tunnel must have resulted in some outlay as the shoddy work was redone, but in the context of the whole canal appears to be of lesser significance than previously proposed. Certainly, in hindsight, the Company could have been better managed but the gentlemen probably did their best, learning from their mistakes as they progressed. And they did not operate in a sealed vacuum, outside influences could not be ignored. The national economy was still badly affected by the revolution of the American colonies, not something that could have been foreseen. Even the weather had been against them, the work often delayed by some extreme spells – for many months too cold, too wet. It may be that a variety of reasons caused the shortfall in funds, some preventable, others not.

Whatever the excuses the Committee had to face the situation prior to the General Meeting in September, the shareholders would have to be told something. Obviously the canal could not be left as it was, it had to be completed and Henshall's estimate of the cost of doing so was £12,000. Ten members of the Committee met at the Castle Inn in Chesterfield to decide how to raise the extra money. Although it had recently been agreed to hold meetings alternately in Retford and Chesterfield it was noticeable that the Nottinghamshire gentlemen did not often venture into Derbyshire. Even for a meeting as important as this only the indefatigable Seth Ellis Stevenson and Carey Chambers, a new recruit from Worksop, were present to represent their county. Even so Stevenson did make an outing of it, taking his daughter Polly to see the market and buying a fine piece of worsted to be made up into breeches for himself.[2] If the alternate locations was a ploy to give Chesterfield control of at least half the meetings, it worked. Chairman Samuel Jebb wasted no time in raising financial matters, item one on the agenda. How was the extra money to be raised? The legal situation was that the Act of Parliament did allow for a further £50,000 to be obtained if necessary. It could be borrowed by pledging future tolls as security, or it could be raised from new or existing shareholders. It was obvious that new shareholders would be difficult to find in the current circumstances and an extra share issue would dilute future profits. The Committee therefore decided that the most proper method was to raise the sum as a loan from the current shareholders in the same proportion as their original subscription. Three extra Calls of £4 each share would raise the money. Anthony Lax was given the subtle task of writing to each shareholder to break the news; to explain how much of the canal could be finished with the current funds, how much it would cost to complete the rest, and how the money was to be found.

On the 7th of September 1775 the General Meeting assembled at The Crown in Retford. Hugh Henshall addressed the shareholders and told them the bad news that his estimate for finishing the canal had now risen to £14,000. It was proposed that this be raised as previously advised but it would now be two Calls of £5 and one of £4. A unanimous aye vote was recorded and it was agreed that the extra Calls be spread over six months, starting in the coming December. With past experiences in mind the Committee prudently made plans for non-payment. The first £5 would become due on the 25th of December and if this Call did not raise £5,000, as it should do, then the Treasurers were authorised to cover the deficiency by obtaining loans at 5% interest. Proving that their problems had not quashed their optimism it was also stated that if any shareholders wanted to pay the full £14 per share immediately they could do so. But the financial problems were acute. There was virtually no money in the Company coffers. Somehow they had to bridge the three months between the General Meeting and the first extra Call. Some payments could be deferred; by November £275.16s.5d was owed to twenty-two landowners for land taken to build the canal, but George Poplewell was told to pay them in three months time "on a Saturday only". Other more powerful creditors could not be delayed; the Duke of Norfolk claimed £33.18s for land damages and the Duke of Leeds received £346.7s for land purchases.

And no one wanted to defer John Hewitt's rent for his quarry! But eventually all the stop-gap measures were exhausted. The Company's cash-flow deteriorated to such an extent that there was no alternative to taking out short-term loans to bridge the gap until the end of December.

Unfortunately, but not surprisingly, there was a muted response to the first extra Call. The following month, January 1776, Anthony Lax was told to send circular letters to all the shareholders, advising them again of the order made by the last General Meeting and "earnestly requesting" them to pay. From this it is safe to assume that borrowings again had to make up for a substantial shortfall in the £5,000 that should have been raised. Indeed, in their role as local bankers, the two Treasurers themselves were made an offer by the Company. If they personally advanced £500 each they would be allowed 5% interest from the time of the advance and could deduct the interest and principal out of the next money received from the shareholders. So not only was the money from the shareholders not forthcoming, but when it was received it was already pledged to repay loans.

The tardiness of the shareholders is easier to understand when it is remembered that many of them were small local traders for whom £100 per share had been a considerable outlay. Now having scraped together the funds to pay all the original Calls, they were suddenly expected to pay even more. Like most of today's small shareholders they did not attend General Meetings nor did they use their proxy votes; as a result they had little insight into the Company's affairs. One such investor was Thomas Bailey, a saddler in East Retford. He had enthusiastically joined the great new canal age by buying one share, and dutifully paid the Calls. But he never saw any profits from his bold investment because he died before all the instalments were made. His widow Sarah successfully struggled to find the last scheduled Calls but the extra payments had come as a shock. Not being able to afford more she approached Richard Dixon and he arranged for the sale of the one £100 share, Thomas Lucus paying £85. Quite a loss for Mrs Bailey but the share price was bound to be depressed as £14 in extra Calls would have to be paid by the purchaser.[3]

❧   ❧   ❧

Serious though the financial problems were it was vital that the construction of the canal did not falter and in fact the opposite was the case; the geographical spread of the worksites was now at its greatest. Apart from the crucial opening of Norwood Tunnel the completed sections had not been greatly extended since the winter. But that was only because priority was being given to long-term projects further along the route in readiness for when the main line of the canal reached them. For instance Norwood was not to be the only tunnel on the Chesterfield Canal. After Retford the way east was blocked by a high ridge, forcing the canal's intended route to turn northward to run alongside it. As at Norwood the second tunnel was planned at a point where the ridge narrowed, allowing the canal to turn eastwards for its final approach to the River Trent. But Drakeholes Tunnel was not to be in the same league as its counterpart at Norwood; it would be only 154 yards long, much of it through solid rock without a brick lining. Nevertheless it would take some months to complete and as soon as the width of the canal from Retford had been established the work on the tunnel was open for tenders. Joseph Gregory won the contract, agreeing to blast a hole 16ft wide and 15ft 6ins high through the ridge for £2.2s per yard. The work was to be done in a proper and workmanlike manner, the Company supplying bricks and mortar as well as all the necessary tools. It was agreed that if he found it necessary Gregory could sink a shaft at the halfway point, for which he would be paid seven guineas. He was given until the end of September to complete the task, and to sharpen his mind a forfeit was to be deducted for every week his men worked beyond the target date. Every effort was to be made to reach the Trent by next spring and the contractors were left in no doubt that tardiness would be severely punished. Loans and extra Calls were unwelcome necessities; the source of revenue the Company really wanted was tolls for goods carried on the canal, and as soon as possible. A welcome amount was earned on the length between Norwood and Retford but the real prize was access to the area's main trade artery, the River Trent. It beckoned to the impoverished Canal Company like an oasis to a thirsty man in the desert.

John Varley was now under great pressure. As the Resident Engineer most of the everyday problems were his responsibility and during the crucial second half of 1775 he even had to leave his home. Such was the spread of the simultaneous worksites Varley had to be based in Retford, returning to his family would have to wait until the eastern end was finished. Fortunately swift progress could be made because in contrast to the early parts of the canal the route between Retford and the Trent was relatively flat and uncomplicated. Instead of tumbling down the Yorkshire hills with twenty-two locks in one mile, as in the great Thorpe and Turnerwood flights, the canal skirted the gentle hills of Nottinghamshire by following the contours. As it went deeper into the north-east of the county the influence of the Trent on the local geography became more apparent. From Gringley-on-the-hill, the village near the highest point of the Drakeholes ridge, vast lowlands could be seen. They spread to the northern horizon, crisscrossed by an intricate network of ditches – the great flood-plain of a great river, drained many years before by Dutch engineers. The original Brindley route to Bawtry would have taken the canal across the flat fields but now it was to run along the edge of the hills for as long as possible, eventually dropping down a further two locks to reach the lowlands of Misterton Carr. Two more locks would lower the canal to the level of Misterton Marsh, across which the canal would have to be raised on a lengthy embankment for its final approach to the Trent. The earthworks over the carr and marshlands would take some time to finish and the Committee, despite the cashflow problems, ordered in July that construction was to begin as soon as possible.

The work on the approach to Misterton appears to have been completed on time, but such was not the case on the far side of the village. The contractors, John and William Robinson, appear to have taken on more than they could cope with; by October it was obvious they would miss their deadline, and they were summoned to appear before the Committee in Worksop. They had to admit they could not meet their contract. The time for gentle management was past, the extra Calls meant that the pockets of the Committee gentlemen were feeling the strain. The Robinsons were ordered to allow another contractor to take on a portion of their work and John Varley was told to put as many hands on the job as he could spare.

All extra expense was to be charged to the Robinsons. Where the Committee expected Varley to find idle navvies is a mystery. However, advertisements appeared offering a daily rate of 2s to 3s for "good Hands", payable once a fortnight. Accommodation was another problem that had to be faced if men were to be gathered from outside the immediate area so the Company offered to pay 1s a week to anyone who would give lodgings to their workmen. A typical inexperienced applicant for the work may have been John Macfarland, a Scottish cattle-drover.[4] He used the old road through Blyth to walk the cattle from Scotland to London, therefore avoiding the heavy tolls on the Great North Road. As a result he knew the canal where it was crossed by the road and about this time he decided to become a navvy. He was a scruffy looking individual, his manners as rough as his appearance. Of moderate height and strongly built, when provoked Macfarland was able to use his fists better than most. During his twenty-nine years he had achieved very little formal education but he had learned about life and was to go on to reach other goals.[*]

ð¤ ð¤ ð¤

Out of the limelight, the neglected Derbyshire half of the canal was waiting its turn. After the euphoria of reaching the Trent it would need all the determination of the Chesterfield gentlemen to maintain the momentum towards their town. It had seemed sensible to give the Nottinghamshire section priority but now there was much work left undone and the money had run out. There was a real danger that Retford's considerable enthusiasm would disappear once their own goal had been reached – they would already have their link to the inland coalfields via Norwood Tunnel and coastal and river trade via the Trent. With Pebley reservoir supplying the water Retford would have a complete canal, the motivation to finish the route to Chesterfield would evaporate. It would be almost impossible to make them face another huge engineering

---

[*]   When the canal was finished Macfarland stayed on as a boatman based in Retford and he played a central role in bringing Methodism to the town. When Wesley visited there three years later it was Macfarland and his friends who ensured he had an unmolested hearing from the crowd.

challenge, but that was just what had to be done – just beyond the western portal of the tunnel Norwood locks were to take the canal down from the summit pound to the outskirts of Killamarsh. Wisely the Derbyshire interests insisted that no matter what the importance of the Nottinghamshire work Norwood locks would be built during that same summer. If everyone was to fall back into an exhausted state when the winter weather stopped progress then Chesterfield wanted to be sure that their share of the work had also been done. Very little is known about the construction of Norwood locks but they were still being built in June 1775 and probably finished by the end of November when the first lock-keeper was appointed. Certainly Varley could have spared little or no time to supervise the work, based as he was many miles away in Retford. He must have delegated the work to an assistant, some unknown engineer over-seeing the construction of a tremendous engineering challenge. Today there are thirteen locks – a top quadruple staircase set, followed by nine grouped as three triple staircases – but the original locks may have differed from this pattern.* It is possible that the use of so many staircase locks in such a short distance was a late strategy to save money. They were built during a financial crisis and when Henshall was on-site calculating the extra funds needed to finish the canal. One way he could have made a considerable saving would have been to pull the Norwood flight together into staircase sets instead of individual locks, most of the gates and sluices serving two locks instead of one. It would have meant a different, steeper drop down the hill but early plans did not include the solitary lock built a mile further on at Killamarsh and this may be an indication of a slightly different approach to that village. Whatever the saving in money the same could not be said of water – staircase locks are notoriously thirsty if the direction of boat traffic is not controlled. If the one reservoir at Pebley could cope with the Thorpe flight at the other end of the summit pound, it certainly could not supply a multi-staircase flight at Norwood as well. Water supply problems plagued the summit pound as soon as the canal was finished and the cheaper locks may have been a false saving.

Norwood was always going to be a busy place with both the one-way

---

*   See Appendix E for various configurations of Norwood locks.

tunnel and the locks causing a bottle-neck in the boat traffic.[5] As such it was an obvious site for Company officials and some of the one million bricks were used to build their offices and homes. A Tunnel-keeper's cottage was built just to the left of the entrance and there were stables for the horses waiting for their boats to be legged through.* Further down the flight, by the second staircase, was the house of Samuel Knock, the first lock-keeper to be appointed at Norwood. Knock had proved himself a trustworthy employee after his first involvement in the tunnel contracts scandal, since then he had been Overlooker of the Tunnel Arching, and Surveyor of the Brickworks. Now he was promoted, with wages of 15s a week, to Overseer of the Locks at Norwood, the solitary lock at Killamarsh also coming under his care. He was to look after the flight, keeping it in good order and repairing the damage done by the heavily laden boats. In addition Knock was to record all the boats that passed through, taking the opportunity to collect the tolls while they were "captured" between the gates.

Beyond Norwood plans were being made for extending the canal into Derbyshire. Negotiations were underway to acquire the land for Staveley Puddlebank, the great embankment that would carry the canal over the valley formed by the River Doe Lea flowing into the Rother. The amount of land required was quite substantial as the base of the embankment would have to splay out over the valley floor to prevent soil slippage. Luckily, for a cash-starved Canal Company, the landowner involved was the Duke of Devonshire. The Duke's Agents were not going to be obstructive; firstly their master was a major shareholder, and secondly the embankment was being built because of a clause in the Act of Parliament protecting the water supply to the family-owned Staveley Forge. Indeed they appear to have been very co-operative; preliminary agreements were made but land transfers and payments were postponed until the canal actually reached the area.

Another decision that was possibly made at the same time, about

---

*   It was rumoured, mainly by the boatmen, that there was an ulterior motive for the long delays waiting to go through the tunnel. They said it was so that a large number of unemployed horses would have a long stay in the stables, thereby increasing the amount of horse manure the stable-keeper sold for a good profit.

September 1775, was to save money by altering the final approach to Chesterfield. Instead of crossing the River Rother and building an extra length of canal as in Brindley's plan, it would be cheaper to have the two waterways merge with the boats using the River Rother for the last quarter of a mile. The change was not recorded in the Minutes but that is understandable as it could be argued that the proposal contravened the Act of Parliament.[6] The Committee had a tendency to use the powers in the Act when it suited them, and to ignore them on other occasions – unless anyone complained. From their point of view it was a reasonable policy, confident as they were that Anthony Lax could deal with disputes unless they involved a powerful landowner.

꒰Ꙭ ꒰Ꙭ ꒰Ꙭ

The eastern and western extremities of the current work were now forty miles apart; between them the various sections of the canal differed greatly – some completed, some still unturned soil. All along the extended line John Varley strove to continue the work. Constant supplies were needed despite the fragile and almost non-existent Company coffers – cordage, iron, coal, bricks, nails, paper, printing, lime, lead, pitch, fir and oak timber. In addition another item was proving to be surprisingly important, the rails for the fencing between the towpath and the adjoining land. In the naive days when the Act of Parliament was drawn up it was only foreseen that the towpath should be fenced or hedged to stop cattle and horses from adjoining fields wandering on to it. Typical Westminster legislators forgot to allow for human ingenuity, a failing not eradicated in later centuries. The towpath was extremely popular. Instead of struggling along the scandalous roads – up hill, down dale, through the tiring mud, dodging the heavy wagons and the pack-horse trains – why not use the lovely new, flat, dry, wide, empty route along the canal. Very soon the new "road" was no longer empty, much to the Company's dismay. The importance of the towpath is easily overlooked today but on the new canal it was the source of the only power that could move the boats. The heaviest work for a boat-horse was to start from a standstill, once a boat was moving one of the advantages of a canal became evident in that it required little effort to maintain a high speed. If that momentum was then lost by the horse slowing for local "road-users" then the efficiency of the operation was greatly impaired. For the same reason most of the wharfs that would eventually be built would be on the non-towpath side of the canal, well clear of the tow-ropes. By the time the canal was completed bye-laws would have been made to ensure a clear path for the boat-horses, but at this early and intermediate stage the Committee simply delegated the matter to Anthony Lax. Yet more handbills were printed and added to the growing collection of notices posted up along the canal; all unofficial users of the towpath would be prosecuted. Under what law is uncertain but doubtless Lax would have thought of something.

Regardless of too many towpath users and too few funds the engineers and the navvies worked on, toiling to connect the advance sites at Drakeholes and Misterton. Two locks were needed at Retford; the first brought the canal down so that it could cross over the River Idle on a stone aqueduct, the second was nearer the town and lowered the canal to a level which could be supplied with water by the new feeder from the River Idle. The work involved in building such locks was still hard, the navvies were more experienced than they had been four years before but accidents still happened. In the midst of a financial crisis the Committee's frugal opinion was that the workmen should set up a fund to pay for medical care, each man making a small weekly contribution. One of John Peacock's duties as Paymaster was to encourage such a fund – hopefully the Reverend Peacock had more success spreading other gospels as this message continually fell on stony ground. As did Joseph Platts, a mason working on one of the Retford locks, a broken leg being the unfortunate result. Platts was carried to the home of John and Ann Metcalf where he stayed for the next three months, recovering as best he could despite the medical services of the 1770's. The Committee grudgingly agreed to pay £2.13s for his board and lodging, but stressed it was "as a matter of charity", again chiding the navvies to look after themselves.

By July 1775 the line had been extended by another one and a half miles; filled with water for the first time on the 21st it was the first section to be dug to the new wide dimensions and it took the canal to the first wide lock – now famous for bearing the intriguing name Whitsunday

Pie.* At last Seth Ellis Stevenson could see a water-filled wide canal at Retford, eight years after his thought provoking visit to the Bridgewater Canal.[7] And the pressures dictated that no time was wasted in extending the canal still further. After Whitsunday Pie lock progress was rapid, the next nine miles were to be lock-free and through easily dug soil. Racing past Clarborough and Hayton the canal had reached Clayworth by the autumn. The versatile John Peacock again gained the contract to carry construction materials to the workcamps. Bricks at 3s per thousand, stone and lime at 1s.1d per ton – all to be carried anywhere between Brancliff (near the Thorpe and Turnerwood locks) and Clayworth. Obviously Peacock and his partners had been rather too efficient in the past because now they were warned that if they overloaded the boats so that they obstructed other vessels they would be fined £1 for each offence.

For many hundreds of years Clayworth had quietly straggled along its main street which was also the Roman road from Lincoln to Doncaster; the village's own history apparent in Clayworth and Royston Manors, the first a 17th century building, the latter Elizabethan. As in Harthill, four years before, the canal interrupted a quiet and mainly self-sufficient lifestyle, strangers rarely being seen until those fellows measuring the ground had come along. Almost all the households made cheese and butter and a great many brewed their own ale. Bees were kept and all gardens had space for vegetables, fruit trees and poultry; spinning and weaving were done as well as being available from craftsman in the village. Most of Clayworth's residents travelled very little, many lived and died without going more than a few miles away.[8] Although the impact of the canal's arrival was initially similar in Harthill and Clayworth the long term effects were to differ. Harthill had borne four years of intrusion from engineers, navvies and their families, but when all the activity at Norwood had ceased – tunnel, locks, reservoir – then all would be quiet once more. Perched high on its hill the village would again be remote from the harsher aspects of the new age. Clayworth on the other hand would suffer a short period of construction mania, difficult though that must have been, but would be forever influenced by the canal on its doorstep. It

---

* See Appendix F for reasons for the unusual name.

was to change the villagers lifestyle permanently, the outside world coming to them and trips to Retford market becoming a regular event.*

Skirting round the historical residences of Clayworth the canal passed to the west of the village, crossing the Roman road to the north before approaching Wiseton. Carefully avoiding Wiseton Hall, as previously agreed with its owner, Varley took the canal round to the already completed Drakeholes Tunnel, making a sharp turn to the right to pass through the hill.

The Committee closely monitored the progress of the canal as a way of maintaining the pressure on Varley and the contractors. At the beginning of October a list was made of all the locks and bridges contracted for completion during the month. The builders were told that the deadline was not to be missed under any circumstances, yet more extra hands being conjured up at their expense if they failed. Not that such haste was always productive, one bridge at Clayworth actually fell down only a month or two after it was finished. The cash-starved Company had no intention of paying for the repairs and the two contractors involved, William Parks and John Robinson – and the Company's Overlooker, William Singleton - were each ordered to pay one third of the £6.6s costs. Nevertheless such was the progress during the second half of 1775 that by the end of the year the canal between Norwood locks and Stockwith was almost complete, only the winter weather delaying the triumphant arrival at the River Trent.

The winter of 1775-6 was harsh, unremitting purgatory.[9] The central and eastern counties of England lay unmoving under a shroud of thick snow. Almost all roads were impassable. The high winds piled the snow into drifts too high to clear and froze the air until outside work became unbearable. All along the canal the temperatures plummeted. In Chesterfield thick, unmoveable ice covered everything, simply walking involved a high risk of injury. Elsewhere in Derbyshire a diligent

---

*   Set in the wall around Clayworth church is a very large boulder. In the village different tales are told of its origin, one of them about the canal. Mr Otter of Royston Manor used to tell his family that it had been dug up by the navvies. At their request it was placed in the churchyard wall in memory of one of their colleagues who had been killed.

meteorologist noted that at nine o'clock in the morning the temperature in his garden was 6°F (-14°C), and inside his house it was a shivering 24°F (-4°C). In Nottinghamshire it was no better. It was a fact of 18th century life that the abominable roads would be of little use in most winters, if not actually impassable. But it was usually safe to rely on the nation's water highways; the great rivers staying navigable as their volume and flow, and the sea's tidal influence, acted together to fight the effects of freezing temperatures. Not that winter. By the end of January the ice on the River Trent was so dense that all boat traffic had ceased, the last vessels struggling through several days before. And it was not surprising that the tide could not alleviate the problem – beyond the Trent its gateway to the sea, the River Humber, was itself frozen. The glacial conditions had formed a broad expanse of ice off Hull and even that near the sea the ferry boats could not cross to Barton on the other bank. In such conditions very little canal building could be done; Varley and his men had no option but to wait for the thaw before carrying on with their work.

However, not all was at a standstill. Although the freezing temperatures halted the canal's progress they also produced the conditions which clearly demonstrated the advantages of this new transport system. Before the cold had become too intense the Company had managed to keep the usable section of the canal open. And on the 9th of January a boat loaded with Killamarsh coal arrived in Retford.[10] Moving such tonnage in atrocious weather had never been seen before. An illustration of how bad the conditions were is that the boat arrived only two days after the Rev. Seth Ellis Stevenson had given up trying to reach his church, the snow making the journey impossible on foot or horseback. What the working conditions must have been like for the boatmen and their horse can only be imagined, but their efforts kept business flowing and proved the canal's worth beyond argument. And following such a fine example the Committee gentlemen endeavoured to keep active; somehow eleven of them managed to meet at Chesterfield's Castle Inn on the afternoon of the 30th of January. Nine were in their home town but the intrepid Seth Ellis Stevenson struggled across from Retford and the new recruit, Carey Chambers, was still keen enough to come from Worksop. John Varley also rode through the freezing, numbing cold; present to hear the Rev. Stevenson tell the Committee that Jonathan Acklom of Wiseton Hall was complaining about water flooding his land. The problem was a drainage channel dug to take excess water from the canal; it had been overwhelmed by the snow and ice and would have to be re-constructed to guard against such an event happening again. Although other tasks were still on-going Varley was told to allocate men to widen, deepen and build up the banking of the drain in whatever way Mr Acklom wished – the distinguished gentleman was not to be troubled further. It was accepted that the work would have to wait until the weather improved, but once in the area Varley was also to repair the road leading to the bridge near the Hall. The master of Wiseton Hall had set a good example; a quiet word with an influential member of the Committee had resolved two problems without fuss or undue expense. If the Company had maintained similar contacts with other landed gentry they could have avoided two disputes that were to take up much of their time in the near future. But they had not, and none of their three Worksop representatives noticed that the Duke of Norfolk's men were still watching every move the Company made. Watching, but not talking.

The Committee, under considerable pressure from their financial worries, did not need irate, powerful landowners added to their list of problems. Mr Acklom's complaints may have been dealt with but the corrective measures would cost time and money, both in very short supply. If such faults did occur – which they should not, but if they did – the Company's engineers should deal with the matter without bothering the Committee. For once it was the Chief Engineer and not John Varley who was the recipient of their wrath. Where was Henshall? He had not been on-site for some time. The Company was starved of cash but they still paid him a high salary – no arguments, they wanted to see their Chief Engineer and some value for their money. Everyone wanted the canal finished as soon as possible and time was not to be wasted waiting for their most august employee to earn his keep.

At the beginning of 1776 the current target was to make the canal usable to Killamarsh, the first village beyond Norwood locks and a coal-producing area. A prime reason for starting the project all those years before had been to link the coalfields with Nottinghamshire and the

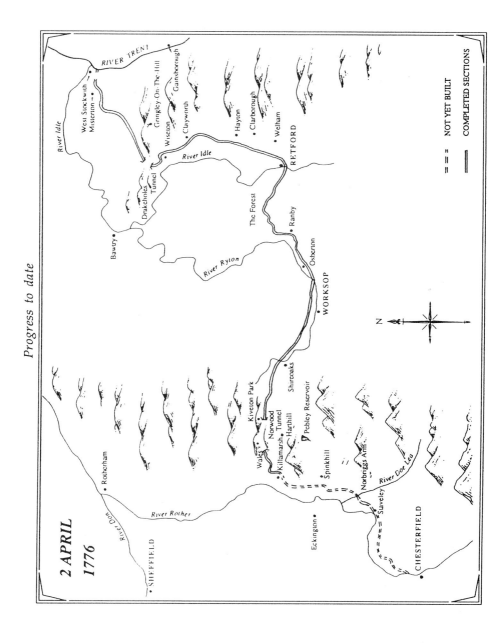

Progress to date

2 APRIL
1776

NOT YET BUILT

COMPLETED SECTIONS

Trent, now the Company was very close to achieving that target. Already the price of a ton of coal in Retford had come down from 15s to 11s, by the summer access to Killamarsh would reduce it still further to 9s a ton.[11] It was fervently hoped that the trade this would generate would bring in welcome funds and alleviate the financial pressures. Beyond Killamarsh detailed plans were already in hand for the final miles to Chesterfield. As early as November the previous year a contract had been given to John Allin to do the woodwork on the remaining six locks, and the constant need for timber had been satisfied to some extent by using trees from Birley Wood.[*]

At Norbriggs, a few miles before Staveley, the intended route passed near the turnpike and the Committee wanted a link between the canal and the road. As Hugh Henshall was present, having prudently responded to the abrupt summons he had received in January, the decision on whether the Norbriggs link should be a road or a side-cut was delegated to him. Whatever he thought most appropriate he was to do as soon as possible. As a water supply from the River Doe Lea was to be fed into the canal somewhere in the vicinity of Norbriggs Henshall cleverly decided to combine the two requirements – the link to the turnpike would be a side-cut formed by widening the last yards of the feeder. Such ingenuity in combining two functions to save costs was what the Committee expected of Henshall, when he was on-site he was well worth his salary. He was also good at forward planning to avoid obvious delays; the previous year he had organised the brickmaking so that stocks were built up and the slow production caused by bad weather avoided. Now as the canal progressed beyond Killamarsh 50,000 bricks were waiting at Renishaw, 50,000 at the Hague and 300,000 at Doe Lea – ready for the canal's dash to Chesterfield. If sufficient funds could be found the progress towards Chesterfield would be swift.

For the last miles to Chesterfield the pattern of the Company's activities was the same as in previous years; the surveyors marked the

---

[*]   The Minutes of the Canal Company clearly state "six locks to be made between Hollingwood Common and Chesterfield", but there are only five on the route as known now. They may have included the flood control gate where the canal was to end at the River.

route, followed by the administrators buying or leasing land and dealing with various legal disputes, followed in turn by the navvies doing the heavy work. Many of the administrative duties were now undertaken by William Skynner, leaving his superior, Anthony Lax – and very superior he could be – free to concentrate on the Company's critical finances. Skynner was a trusted employee and he was capable of dealing with most legal matters, only disputes with titled landowners warranting the involvement of Lax.

Most of the legal work involved in clearing the way for the navvies, and consisted of mundane tasks rarely acknowledged as a vital part of the history of our canal system. For instance payments to owners for damage done to their lands was usually only a matter of negotiating the values involved. The Act of Parliament was specific on such matters and the Company had little room for manoeuvre, no matter how astute their legal representatives may have been. The land involved was usually in the vicinity of the canal and had been harmed as a by-product of the construction work – crops trampled, paths widened into roads, drainage altered, fences or hedges removed, new access roads made for the heavy wagons carrying supplies. The payments were not always large amounts to powerful landowners, in some areas small parcels of land presented a complicated jigsaw to the Company's estate valuers. Killamarsh was a prime example and typical amongst a great list of those receiving damage payments were William Gee (17s.11d), John Marsh (£2.0s.11d), George Mallendar (3s.3d) and John Slagg (£3.3s.8d).

Also typical of Skynner's work was the resolution of a disagreement between the Canal Company and the Rector of Staveley.[12] In the 18th century most local clergy were financially supported by the community donating to them, voluntarily or otherwise, a tenth of the agricultural produce of the area. These donations were known as tithes and were collected with varying degrees of humility, depending on the nature of the churchman involved. It soon became evident to the Rector of Staveley that the canal was to go through his parish, in fact he could hardly miss the intended route as it passed within two hundred yards of his church. More to the point the Rector could see that many acres of productive land would be destroyed, acres currently growing wheat, oats, potatoes and peas. A tenth of those crops was a substantial part of his entitlement. After the canal had obliterated the fields a tenth of nothing would leave his table rather emptier than before. It was the Rector's opinion that the Canal Company would clearly be responsible for destroying the agricultural use of the land and his tenth of the produce. Therefore, they would have to compensate him for his future losses. It was worth a try but William Skynner had been well chosen by Lax, defending the Company against such claims was well within his capabilities. Skynner readily agreed that about forty acres would be lost to agricultural use within the parish and that the Rector would suffer a loss of tithes. What was not agreed was the liability of the Company to make good such a loss. A legal precedent was involved; if compensation was paid to the Rector a disturbing mental picture of the Company maintaining the clergy across three counties was only too clear. To counter the claim Skynner's argument was that tithes were payable on what was grown on the land and were not a "right". If a landowner did not wish to grow any crops then the Rector could not insist on his doing so. For instance, if a landowner chose to turn all his arable land "into fish-ponds or into a park to feed deer" the Rector would not be able to claim for his loss of tithes. The Rector thought little of this opinion; that was accepted Common Law but these circumstances were different as the Company was bound by the Act of Parliament that had created it. Within that Act was a clause ordering damages to be paid to any who suffered from the building of the canal. The Rector said that as his tithes would be reduced he would obviously suffer, so the Company was liable. Skynner was not impressed. He agreed that the Act made the Company responsible for payments to "those who were prejudiced", but his definition of that phrase was that a party would qualify for recompense only if "both a loss and an injury" had been sustained. The Rector's situation would not fulfil this criteria, he would suffer a loss only. To illustrate this subtle point of law Skynner used an ingenious example. The Canal Company had every intention of taking a substantial amount of the coal trade away from the Don Navigation – they fully intended their competitor to suffer a loss. No one could, or would, think that the Canal Company should recompense their rival – and as the Don Navigation would have suffered a loss, but not an injury, the Act would not require them to do so. The Rector would just have to bear his suffering with as much Christian fortitude as he could muster.

ﻉﻉ ﻉﻉ ﻉﻉ

The bad weather continued throughout February and March 1776 but nevertheless the surveyors, administrators, attorneys, engineers and navvies combined to extend the canal. By the beginning of April the vital first link to the edge of the Derbyshire coalfields had been completed and the canal was open from Killamarsh to Stockwith on the River Trent. To the Trent yes, but not into it. There is no evidence that anyone expected the canal's narrowboats to venture out onto the great river but the wide craft that Seth Ellis Stevenson envisaged using the canal to Retford would be river vessels. So part of the agreement to widen the canal was the creation of a large lock at Stockwith capable of bringing river craft up from the Trent to the canal. The lock would have to be considerably deeper than any other on the canal as the tidal river produced a considerable range of levels, and it would have to be sited so that the sail-powered boats of the day could enter across the Trent's fast currents. From an engineering point of view the construction of Stockwith lock would be a challenge but possible; from a political point of view it looked rather different. The Committee gentlemen of Chesterfield had no intention of allowing Stockwith lock to be built; not before their end of the canal was finished. Retford, and the Company, had already gained the benefit of the canal reaching the Trent. It was true that the busy river wharfs for the trading vessels were a quarter of a mile away near the mouth of the River Idle, but such a distance was infinitesimal compared with past times. It was already clear that the Retford members of the Committee were less interested in attending meetings now that the canal met nearly all their town's needs – they already had coal from Derbyshire and national trade from the Trent. If river craft could reach Retford what little interest they still maintained in the canal reaching Chesterfield would disappear altogether. Samuel Jebb and his colleagues in Chesterfield were shrewd enough to know that it was vital that the last link in Retford's canal was dependent upon the completion

226

of the whole project.

Everyone agreed, however, that as much profit as possible must be earned from the finished sections and that an advertising campaign was necessary. To extol the wonders of the new transport system they needed facts with which to amaze potential customers. A strong selling point would be the astonishing ability of the boats to carry heavy cargoes to a tight schedule no matter how bad the weather! Public transport timetables as we know them today had never been possible before the canal age. Stage-coaches called at inns somewhere near the time stated each day, the weather and God permitting, but general terms such as "late morning" and "early afternoon" were accepted as the best that could be expected. Even canal timetables were far from our standards, in an age when time itself had not been standardised throughout the nation it was not possible to state that a boat would arrive at a certain hour. But even so the ability of the canal to run a service throughout the year to some sort of schedule was an achievement incredible to 18th century minds. To check the facts John Varley sent a fully laden boat from Killamarsh to Stockwith, and back, and noted the time taken to reach the various wharfs, villages and towns. Anthony Lax published the information, being careful to stress that the Company had "appointed Proper Servants to pay due attention to the Goods committed to their Care" and that they would be carefully conveyed at the stated times. Having publicly stated the service available the next move was to ensure the boatmen maintained the Company's standards. The Act of Parliament contained many rules governing boats on the canal and these were drawn up into a list of regulations by Anthony Lax. Copies were distributed to all the Company's wharfs and toll-offices even though reading skills amongst the boatmen would have been slight. Nevertheless, the rules could be read to them and illiteracy was no excuse for non-compliance. Each boat was to have its number, and the name and address of its owner, painted on the outside in white capital letters on a black background. Priority at locks, and their usage, was strictly controlled. Penalties for boats damaging, obstructing or throwing ballast into the canal were detailed. Crews were not to help themselves to any fish or game, even having nets, traps, or guns on board was disallowed. And the rules for declaring cargoes, paying tolls and overloading, or underloading, boats were numerous.

Meanwhile most of the engineering activity was still involved in extending the canal beyond Killamarsh. The single lock in the village was the end of the descent from the hills at Norwood, now the canal could follow the valley of the River Rother all the way to Chesterfield. Because of the late clause in the Act of Parliament about maintaining a water supply to Staveley Forge the canal was to run along the valley side, and not along the floor as originally planned. After Killamarsh there would be no more locks for over seven miles, one level being maintained by using small embankments to even out the contours until reaching the start of the final climb to Chesterfield higher up the valley. But if the canal was to follow the valley side and go no lower a solution would have to be found to the problem caused by the River Doe Lea. Near Staveley the little river cut through the valley side on its way to the Rother, as a result the line followed by the canal dipped steeply. To keep the level a large bank of earth would be needed to carry the canal over the Doe Lea, joining the same contour on the other side of the cutting. The embankment, known as Staveley Puddlebank, was to take up much of the navvies time in the second half of 1776.

Very little is known about the construction of the canal between Killamarsh and the Puddlebank, only that the whole section was completed sometime between the 2nd and 16th of August 1776.[*] During the summer work had also started on the side-cut that Henshall had decided would be dug at Norbriggs, over half a mile long it joined the main line of the canal only a few yards from where the Doe Lea's deep valley was to be spanned by the Puddlebank. By the 17th of August the canal was open from Stockwith to Norbriggs. As a result of Henshall's clever planning Norbriggs Arm was to serve three important functions; it gave access to a turnpike road so that goods could easily be transhipped, it would soon be

---

[*] The route originally built followed a more winding course than seen in later years. The canal was realigned to make way for a railway, contour hugging loops near Renishaw being replaced by straight sections.

228

Progress to date

16 AUGUST 1776

NOT YET BUILT
COMPLETED SECTIONS

RIVER TRENT

River Idle
West Stockwith
Misterton
Gringley-On-The-Hill
Wiseton
Gainsborough
Clayworth
Hayton
Clarborough
Welham
RETFORD

Drakeholes Tunnel
River Idle
Bawtry

The Forest
Ranby
Osberton

River Ryton

WORKSOP

N

Rotherham

Kiveton Park
Shireoaks
Wales
Norwood Tunnel
Killamarsh
Harthill
Pebley Reservoir

River Rother
River Don

SHEFFIELD

Spinkhill
Eckington
Norbriggs Arm
Staveley
River Doe Lea
CHESTERFIELD

229

feeding water into the canal from the Doe Lea, and until the following year it would be an efficient head of navigation until the Puddlebank was finished.

The water to be fed into the canal from the Doe Lea was much needed because until Chesterfield was reached the only supply on the western side of Norwood hills was that coming down from the summit pound along the completed sections. It was too much to expect that source to fill the seven mile long bottom pound as well as operating the locks at Norwood and Killamarsh; that was the role planned for the water from the Doe Lea. The problem with getting a supply was the same as had been encountered in Retford; at the point where they crossed the canal was at a higher level than the river that was to feed it. Water will not run uphill so the same solution was used as in Retford; the Doe Lea was surveyed back along its course to find a point where, as it flowed down from the hills, it was higher than the canal. The river reached the required level some distance from the canal and the result was a requirement for a feeder channel nearly two miles long, linking the head waters of the river to the end of the Norbriggs Arm. Careful surveys were made to ensure an adequate flow of water, land was purchased, damages estimated and paid to landowners, bridges were built if necessary, shuttles were installed to control the flow, and overflow weirs were dug to drain excess water back to the river.[13] But in common with all the Derbyshire lengths of the canal, the Company left little or no details about how the feeder was built.

By now the driving force of the Committee was dwindling; five years of effort and the worsening financial problems had left the gentlemen jaded and careworn. The exhilaration and prestige of being involved in a breathtaking project had been dissipated by the day-to-day reality of the work involved. Their meetings were now usually held in Chesterfield and Worksop, the Nottinghamshire representatives only thinking the effort worthwhile when the venue was in their own county. Even Seth Ellis Stevenson succumbed to the malaise. Samuel Jebb kept the Chesterfield members involved, most of their meetings being recorded in minutes that

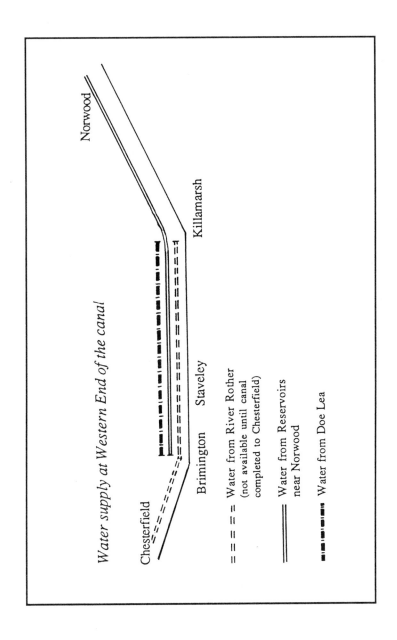

Water supply at Western End of the canal

Norwood

Killamarsh

Chesterfield

Brimington   Staveley

= = = = = Water from River Rother
           (not available until canal
           completed to Chesterfield)

Water from Reservoirs
near Norwood

Water from Doe Lea

are sketchy compared to the detailed notes kept in the heady days of previous years. In human terms the last few miles were to be the most difficult. Everyone was tired – and their tiredness led to errors of judgement. Retford's lack of involvement did not really matter when decisions were being made about the Derbyshire end of the canal, but without the advantage of their local knowledge the final land purchases at Stockwith were mishandled.

Although, for their own political reasons, Chesterfield's representatives wanted to delay the lock into the Trent they were keen to see adequate wharfs and a warehouse erected at the end of the canal. Stockwith had been a busy trading centre for as long as anyone could remember, its location at the junction of the Trent and Idle made it a natural stopping place for craft on both rivers. As well as being a trading post the village also had a thriving boat-building industry and as a result the residents could boast of many skills; they could make masts, blocks, ropes and sails, and there was not much they did not know about rigging and carpentry. Stockwith had been chosen as the canal's junction with the Trent because it was an established river-trading centre, activities that the Canal Company wished to augment. The negative side of choosing such a terminus was that owners of land near the Trent were well aware of its strategic value. It was unfortunate for the harassed and weary men in Chesterfield, struggling to complete their canal, that the land they chose for a wharf at Stockwith was owned by Nottinghamshire's local grandee, the Duke of Newcastle.

When the Committee met to discuss the purchase of land on which to build the wharf, all but two of those present came from Chesterfield. If informed Retford representatives had been present, as they should have been, they could have told the meeting that the Duke of Newcastle had already made his opinion clear. Informally, but clear – no sale. But without such insight the Committee voted to force the matter. Instead of using the quiet methods that had placated Jonathan Acklom at Wiseton Hall they simply passed the problem on to their administrators. So into this fragile situation strode Anthony Lax, not the most tactful of men and at that time distracted by the Company's financial cares. Lax was told to write to the Duke asking his consent to the Company "taking the piece of land belonging to him at Stockwith". But consent he did not.[14] Lax then went to see William Mason, the Duke's agent, and stated the Company's case clearly, and bluntly; if an amicable agreement could not be reached then the Act of Parliament would be used to force the issue. It took only two weeks for Mason to tire of such treatment, the agent complaining bitterly to his Grace that the Company's attitude was uncivil and high-handed. The Duke and his agent were well aware of the strategic importance of the piece of land as a trading point; they did not need an upstart Canal Company to teach them that. The Duke would not sell for the same reasons the Committee wanted to purchase. Today we are used to the concept of "compulsory purchase"; it is now an unpleasant legal fact of life since long distance routes cannot be diverted around every complaining householder. But it should be remembered that the necessity for such legal powers was first recognised for the building of canals, before that ownership of land was generally sacrosanct. So early Canal Company's, such as the Chesterfield, were wielding a new and dreadful legal weapon and it was not easy for those in the firing line to come to terms with such a modern concept. Difficult enough for an average landowner, but for a Duke it was even more of a culture shock. Offensive though they were Mason knew the facts were clear; the wishes of Parliament could not be ignored by the aristocracy and, after all, the Duke was a shareholder in the Canal Company so improved trading facilities were welcome. In the circumstances William Mason's advice was that a compromise should be offered – the Company could use the land but it would stay the Duke's property. That was rejected as too constrictive, a similar spirit of moderation not being evident in the mood of Anthony Lax. He was an attorney with the law on his side and he was going to force the issue. No other solutions were forthcoming. Stalemate. An impatient Lax referred the matter to higher legal levels. What was the general opinion on using the Act of Parliament to force the Duke of Newcastle to sell his valuable land? Older and wiser heads counselled caution – although Duke's were not above the law the cost of fighting such a case, both in time and money, would be unacceptable to a Company in dire financial straits. And did the Committee wish to make a powerful enemy, especially when he was one of their own substantial shareholders? So the year progressed but the

233

dispute did not. By the autumn it became irrelevant who wanted Stockwith lock built and who did not; it was held up by the uncertain land availability. Perhaps the whole matter could have been avoided if the Retford members of the Committee, many of whom had recently visited Clumber Park as the Duke's guests, had taken their rightful responsibility for canal matters in Nottinghamshire. All in all it was yet more proof that disagreements with Dukes were best avoided. The Committee would not have been pleased if they had known that in Worksop the Duke of Norfolk was still doubtful about the amount of his land taken by the Canal Company and had just commissioned an independent survey to clarify matters.

❧ ❧ ❧

Throughout 1776 the financial health of the Company continued to give cause for concern. During the first six months the payment of the extra Calls asked of the shareholders should have brought in the £14,000 specified by Henshall, his estimate of the additional money required to complete the canal. But it soon became evident that such an amount was far in excess of actual receipts. The first extra Call should have brought in £5,000 but the response was disappointing and the letter sent to the shareholders to encourage payment had little effect. In March the Committee acknowledged the shortfall and took the only course open to them; the missing funds had to be borrowed. It was the start of a slippery slope down which the Company would slide for many years, most of the early profits going to repay debts before any genuine benefit could be enjoyed. But the canal had to be completed if it was to realise its full potential, and it could not be finished without the extra funds. If the shareholders would not provide then the money market was the only option. The Committee gave Anthony Lax the authority to borrow £2,000 or £3,000 for one year against the credit of the Company. He was allowed to offer the usual 5% interest and on receiving the Treasurers' receipt for the money he could put the Company's Seal to any security that had to be given.

The second extra Call on the shareholders, due to be paid on the 25th of

April, was as disappointing as the first; a second scheduled £5,000 failed to materialise. Early in the following month Anthony Lax was again authorised to borrow money. This time the amount had increased to £6,000, the loans to be secured against future income from tolls levied on canal users. As shareholders themselves it may be safe to assume that the gentlemen of the Committee set a good example by paying the extra Calls on their shares, and some risked even more of their own money. Edward Brown was one of Retford's most conscientious Committee representatives, his involvement in the project going back to the very earliest days. His commitment had been increased by the canal cutting through his land and he had been very quick to see the commercial possibilities, building a wharf upon which many of the goods for Retford were landed. For the next three years Brown made annual loans to the Company, eventually amounting to £200. It was agreed that repayment, plus 5% interest, would be made by assigning "tolls, rates and duties" to him. The loans were still outstanding twenty-two years later.[15]

The third and last extra Call, this time for £4,000, was scheduled for the 24th of June 1776. The Company's books were ruled off on that day and Richard Dixon took his records, and those of John Peacock, to prepare them for inspection. On Tuesday, 9th of July some of the Retford members of the Committee and Messrs. Storrs, Wilkinson, Jebb and Twigge met at the Angel in Chesterfield to scrutinise the accounts. The figures did not look good. The Company still had insufficient funds to complete the canal and extra expenses were accumulating all the time. More land damage payments were due to be made the following month, and construction materials were still required – iron, cordage, lime, nails, timber, the canal's appetite for such items appeared insatiable. Some bills could be deferred, Leonard Halley would have to wait for his £93 for posts and rails, but others would wait no longer. And the usable part of the canal, although earning income, was also incurring extra costs. For instance, a lock had been damaged by a boat taking a gate off its hinges and repairs had had to be done immediately or the canal would have come to a standstill. The boat owners, MacPherling and White, were responsible but recovering the costs would take time as they would probably have to be sued before agreeing to pay. There was also a suspicion that the Company was receiving less than it should as income from the boats. One thought was that the markings on the side of the boats, showing how deep they were in the water and therefore how many tons they were carrying, had not been correctly calculated. As a result Richard Dixon was told to re-gauge every boat to ensure that the standard weight used was the ton as defined in the Act, and not one of the many local variations. It was also possible that the wharfingers were not collecting payments from every boat – so just in case it was true they were all threatened with instant dismissal if they did so, "never afterwards to be employed by the said Company of Proprietors". The wharfingers were well paid and losing such employment was a serious threat; John Windle at Stockwith earned £50 a year, Joseph Hill at Norbriggs £45, and John Best £20 at Retford.* Their salaries were justified because they played a crucial role in the Company, dealing directly with customers and taking responsibility for the goods entrusted to their care. And if they failed in their duties the penalties were financially severe; John Windle had to pay £11, a good part of one years salary, to Messrs. Cliff of Brigg because a parcel of rabbit skins left in his care got wet at Stockwith. Perhaps the temporary shed/warehouse was not all it should have been.

By now the twice-yearly General Meetings of proprietors were a shadow of those held in more vigourous days. The great majority of shareholders were not involved in the everyday running of the Company and showed little interest beyond authorising proxy votes on their behalf. On the 5th of September 1776 only twenty-four of their number met at the White Hart in Retford, all but four past or present Committee members. And an intense, joyless gathering it was. The project had reached the difficult stage that afflicts all substantial long-term developments, especially those dealing with new challenges and attitudes. Between the euphoria of inauguration and the prestige of completion is a period when dogged determination is the prime, but tedious, requirement. The same malaise still strikes in the

---

* Best was paid a lower rate as he was also wharfinger for the Corporation of Retford.

20th century, and probably will in the 21st; it is a fact of human nature. The gentlemen at the White Hart did not care to remember past glories, nor did they enthuse about future hopes; the present was all too stark. Income was disappointing and expenditure was eternal. The profitability of the completed section was already suffering; boats were being hindered by an insufficient supply of water to the summit pound and a reduction in goods carried meant a reduction in the tolls levied. Some work had been done to rectify the situation; during the summer Varley's men had been improving the wall of Pebley reservoir so that more water could be stored, but now the matter was urgent. In addition to everything else John Varley was told to give the work a very high priority and to report the latest situation at every Committee meeting. Such measures would, hopefully, improve income. The other side of the equation was expenditure. Another estimate of the cost of finishing the canal was needed and with Hugh Henshall again conspicuous by his absence the task was, of course, given to John Varley. The overworked Resident Engineer was allowed fourteen days to inspect every detail of the work still outstanding, and to put a value on the land and materials yet to be purchased. Even with Richard Dixon helping with the paperwork the meeting recognised that the assignment would take up much of Varley's time. Again the impatient shareholders demanded to know why they had seen so little of their Chief Engineer – once again, where was Henshall? Anthony Lax was told to send a messenger to find him. And, having found him, the reasons for his non-attendance were to be demanded. Not only that, Henshall was to come to the canal without delay and when he arrived he was to busy himself making the same survey and estimates as Varley. No excuses would be tolerated and in fourteen days time the Committee expected to be able to compare two sets of figures from their two engineers.

Even without the latest estimates the meeting knew that still more money would be required, it was only a question of how much. Further loans would have to be arranged, this time Lax was authorised to raise up to £10,000. But by this time the Company's credit was running low, much of the security that could be offered was already covering previous loans. Now the only options acceptable to the money-market were the personal guarantees of the Committee gentlemen – they would have to put their names to legal Bonds which would make them responsible for repaying the money. Not surprisingly the meeting voted that the very highest priority be given to settling these loans. Other repayments could wait, no matter what had been said in the past all profits would be channelled to alleviate this situation before anything else!

At this fraught stage of the proceedings some light was seen when a new proposal was put on the table; an offer that was to become controversial, some shareholders stridently disagreeing with the concept. But to a drowning Canal Company any lifeline was welcome, especially when it was being kept afloat by the contents of personal pockets. Chesterfield controlled the General Meeting with the 210 proxy votes in their hands and they thought the idea worthy of consideration.[*] It involved a colliery owned by the Duke of Portland. Mr Cleaver, the Duke's agent, suggested that it would be of mutual benefit if the Company agreed to lease the colliery – the crucial point being its location near the end of the side-cut at Norbriggs. That meant the Company would make a good profit from selling the coal as the transport costs would be minimal. And the boat traffic would generate toll payments. Why carry other people's goods, why not carry your own? It was worth investigating at least, anything that would earn money was to be considered. Anthony Lax was sent to negotiate.

❦ ❦ ❦

But not everything was doom and gloom. Although the Canal Company was a source of strain and disappointment at the moment those involved still had hopes for the future – even if that future appeared distant and the hopes elusive. And canal building was not the only thing in life, although to a toilworn John Varley it may have often appeared so. The canal was certainly an important development in the area but it was only

---

[*] A shareholder had one vote for each share owned, up to a maximum of 35. The limit was contained in a clause of the Act of Parliament designed to prevent undue control of the Company by one or more wealthy individuals. The maximum number of shares that could be held by one person was 50, but the maximum number of votes was limited to 35 per person. Three shareholders are known to have had 50 shares – the Duke of Devonshire, Phillips Glover of Lincolnshire and Charles White.

one aspect of the local scene, many people having no involvement with it at all. So life carried on as normal during the summer of 1776. In Chesterfield the usual activities were taking place. The annual Florist Feast flower show was held at a local inn; the morning judging followed by the prize ceremony and a celebratory meal. Three of the canal's supporters had another cause for congratulation – Adam Slater, the influential Samuel Jebb, and Treasurer Allwood Wilkinson were all made Justices of the Peace in Derbyshire. The Manor Court met and issued edicts with its usual flair, some of the canal proprietors again featuring in the list – Saltergate had become rather wet and unpleasant and Joseph Storrs was told to solve the problem by clearing the drain on his property. And of course the town would hardly seem like home without Samuel Towndrow's rubbish strewn about; this time the scruffy grocer was told he had three days to clear a pile of hogsheads from the Shambles. On the last day of July the parish church was the place to be, especially if one needed to curry the favour of the visiting Bishop of Lichfield and Coventry. A few days later a different religious creed was on offer; luckily the Bishop had left before John Wesley preached to the citizens a little distance from the centre of town. The crowd listened to him attentively and the Methodist left much to be discussed when he continued his journey to London. If neither of the two religious messages found favour then perhaps faith could be found in Mr Page's Restorative Medicine, guaranteed to cure almost everything – all you had to do was go along to the Castle Inn and buy a bottle of it, or perhaps more. Thus restored perhaps energy could be found for two days of horse racing at the local course. Or perhaps a more refined evening concert in the Assembly Rooms; harpsichord and violin or a group of Italian opera singers.

In Harthill village life was beginning to return to normal, most of the navvies having left when the work at Norwood was finished. Some had remained in the area employed as canal officials or maintenance men, and as residents they went to Harthill church for religious services. John and Hannah Varley still lived nearby, the Company's house at Pennyholme sheltering a growing family. In June they made the journey from their tunnel-end home to Harthill's parish church for the baptism of their first son, also called John.[16]

In Retford the London Evening Post could be obtained for the first time, from now on it was to be delivered as often as three days a week.[17] Now local gentlemen of influence and ideas could keep up to date with national events at Westminster – and what those colonists in America were up to. It was irritating to read that the rebels had had the gall to declare themselves independent on the 4th of July. Independent! The word for it was treason – 'pon my soul, what was the world coming to? And the weather did not help to cool tempers, at the beginning of August it was as hot as anyone could remember. Luckily it was cooler for the celebration of the 21st birthday of Seth Ellis Stevenson's daughter Polly, now a fine young lady. Many of the canal gentlemen also took advantage of the warm weather to visit the Duke of Newcastle at his new home in Clumber Park. Indeed it was so modern that a visitor from further afield noted "we expected an old magnificent house . . . but everything is new; the house is just built, the woods just planted, and the walks just planned. Clumber Park will hardly be worth a traveller's notice before the next century." It is certainly worthy of note now. Today's visitors to Clumber's 3,800 acres of park and woodland, 80-acre lake and 13 miles of paths would find it difficult to recognise such a description.

A few miles away at the next ducal home, Worksop Manor, the summer visitors were the Lord Chancellor and his Lady. The Duke of Norfolk was not in residence, having returned to London for a few months, so Henry Howard was the host on behalf of his lordship. A grand dinner was served in honour of the distinguished guests, with many other dignitaries also invited.[18] Such social contacts with the head of the English judiciary made the Duke of Norfolk a powerful legal foe. And the Canal Company had seen the ability of the Duke's agents during the Worksop Common dispute with John Hewitt; the stubborn stance taken to win that battle was indeed noteworthy. Everything would seem to have sent a clear message to the canal proprietors – avoid legal arguments with Dukes, especially the Duke of Norfolk. But no, at the end of 1776 the Committee walked straight into a dispute they could well have done without. And to make matters worse the Duke of Norfolk himself returned to Worksop Manor just as the first disagreements were being aired. Just in time to take a personal interest in matters.

1777

The American war rages on all year

We hear from Chesterfield that on Saturday last, being Market Day there, a farmer named Tagg of Normanton was artfully decoyed into an Inn amongst a set of sharpers. One of them performed the part of Squire. Upon the farmer being introduced to the company, the "Squire" pretended to take great umbrage at his permission not being first asked but after a slight apology, a few glasses of liquor soon reconciled everything. Cards being proposed the unthinking farmer proved at first very lucky and was thereby induced to play deep, by which these knowing gentry soon stripped him of notes and cash (most of which he borrowed in Chesterfield by persuasion of his pretended friend) to the amount of upwards of sixty pounds. Then the Squire, pretending to call some ladies downstairs, left the room and his companions soon followed. Thus they all got clear and left the unsuspecting farmer to lament his credulity.

To the PRINTER OF THE DERBY MERCURY

Mr Drewry,
I am a very tall young Woman, of fifteen, that am so unfortunate as to be under the Care of an old fashioned Aunt who will not suffer my Head to be dressed like other young Women's, from a prudish Notion that Men-Hair-Dressers are indecent. I hope some of your Readers will consider my Case, and write something to convince my Aunt of the absurd Vulgarity of her Opinion – I forgot to tell you that my Aunt would have no Objection to Hair-Dressing, if the Hair-Dresser would wear a Silk short Apron while the Operation is performed.

Yours
BIDDY LANGUISH

CHAPTER ELEVEN

Final Stages

As 1776 entered its last two months it became impossible for any business venture to ignore the national crisis caused by the rebellion in the American colonies. The initial skirmishes had developed into a serious war. For some time there had been a suspicion that Britain's old enemies would take advantage of the situation; by November war with France and Spain was expected before the end of the year. As in all times of international tension the effects spread far beyond the men in the fighting services. Commerce and profits suffered as the free flow of trade was disrupted by the use of convoy systems to protect vital coastal shipping from attack. Further interference was caused by the Royal Navy's need for 10,000 extra men if it was to fulfil its widespread commitments. Warships were sent not only to America but also to blockade French ports, others going to South America to protect Portuguese settlements from the Spanish. Press-gangs were out in force, even taking the crews from merchant vessels. Warehouses were still full of goods that the American colonies refused to buy, now trade with Europe was almost impossible. The effect on the national economy was ruinous. None of this could have been foreseen by canal enthusiasts forming their plans eight years before. Now it was the misfortune of the Chesterfield Canal Company to have their waterway nearing completion in the midst of a national crisis.

The circumstances were difficult but a fact of life and the Company had to deal with them as best they could. With the approach of winter, and the usual cessation of large-scale construction, the Committee busied itself with promoting what trade there was. One positive aspect was that the market for Derbyshire coal had been improved by the crisis. Most of the substantial supply from Newcastle was shipped to the rest of the country down the east coast, now it had been curtailed along with everything else using that route. The canal's ability to take coal to the Trent meant that inland towns in the midlands could be supplied but access to the main area of acute shortage, London, was no easier for Derbyshire's coal than for Newcastle's. Prices were booming in the capital city but Trent ships going down the coast to the Thames were hampered by the same regulations and port controls; the southern part of the east coast bearing the brunt of the defensive measures against France. Nevertheless, all the Committee could do was improve the ability of the canal to seize whatever trade there was, local and national. Offices, warehouses and wharfs had already been installed at most of the major centres along the route. Stockwith and Retford, Norbriggs and Killamarsh – the latter having a side-cut in which loading and unloading could take place without obstructing the main canal. Worksop had received less attention and as a result was a little lacking in facilities. In September the Committee ordered that a warehouse be built as soon as possible, much valuable trade would be lost if customers goods could not be protected from the winter weather.

It seemed a simple enough decision to erect a warehouse on the Company's own land but as soon as building work started a complaint was received from Henry Howard, the Duke of Norfolk's distant relative and Chief Agent.[1] But nothing in the plans was changed and within two weeks the wharf at Cow Moor near Worksop contained an almost finished warehouse. In the meantime Howard had made no more comments as he knew the Duke would soon be arriving for a four-month stay at his Nottinghamshire home. What he had been doing was collating the evidence produced by the painstaking investigations carried out during the past year; the quiet watching, measuring and checking activities that no one on the Committee had noticed. He had never trusted the Canal Company and had always expected a dispute to occur at some time. Now it had and the matter would be handled in Howard's usual efficient manner. Only two months before he had employed an esteemed local surveyor, Mr Kelk of Carlton, to accurately measure the land that had been taken from the Duke to build the canal. Kelk marked the area on a current map of the Worksop estate and made two copies to different scales; comparisons had been made with the landsale documents signed by the Canal Company and opinions stored for the future.*

As in the dispute with John Hewitt about Worksop Common the Duke's legal representative was John Mander, the attorney from Bakewell. The case presented by Mander and Howard contained two distinct objections to the Company's actions. First - the stated use for the land bought from the Duke was the construction of a canal and a towpath, a wharf had not been included. The specific grievance was against items associated with trade; there had always been a tool store on the site but that was accepted as a necessary maintenance feature of the canal. But a wharf was not an essential item and was therefore subject to different legal controls. Second – the warehouse was being built adjacent to the wharf and on land still owned by the Duke, a situation covered by the Act of Parliament. They quoted a clause that said the first option for erecting buildings for trade on private land belonged to the landowner. If he did not take up his right then the Company could build a wharf, warehouse, crane, landing-place or weighbeam after giving one year's notice. By immediately constructing the warehouse the Company had usurped the Duke's rights. The Company disagreed. They said they had bought the land and on it they could erect buildings associated with the business of the canal and that included trading facilities. By its very nature a canal was a commercial waterway, trade and profits were the reasons for its existence. Defying the Duke's wishes the Committee authorised the completion of the warehouse.

Once again the Duke of Norfolk's representatives obtained legal advice and then took decisive action – they went to the canal and pulled the warehouse down.

If nothing else their actions brought matters to a head, it had gone beyond being an administrative headache and was now an altogether more serious problem. Winter was approaching and there were no storage facilities at Worksop. As a result customers would not deliver items into their keeping and badly needed wharfage and toll fees would be lost. The key question was – who did own the land? The original sale agreement had been personally drawn up by Anthony Lax, in the aftermath of the

---

* No effort or expense was spared in such investigations, an example being the considerable fee of £101.1s.6d paid to Kelk for his work.

previous conflict it had been deemed prudent for the Company's senior administrator to handle the matter. Now Lax was told to go and check his paperwork and settle the controversy as soon as possible. But if Anthony Lax thought he could easily find a resolution then he was mistaken for Mr Kelk had done his work well. The maps drawn by the local surveyor showed that the Company had indeed used more land than they had purchased. A second survey confirmed the embarrassing truth. Lax had no alternative but to acknowledge the error on behalf of the Company before asking to purchase the extra land. Permission was denied.

By now there was very little Nottinghamshire influence on the Committee; during the whole of 1776 the only meeting held in Retford was that immediately prior to a General Meeting, the venue of which was fixed by the Act. Retford still had half the Committee appointees but they rarely chose to attend. So there were no informal contacts between the two groups in dispute, Henry Howard knowing little of Chesterfield and the active members of the Committee knowing even less about the agents of the Duke of Norfolk. So everything was on a formal basis and up to now the Canal Company, under the influence of Anthony Lax, had dealt with the matter in their usual high-handed style. And once again it was to be counter-productive when dealing with the representatives of powerful men. Henry Howard now insisted on compliance with the Act; that the Company could only build a warehouse on what was now agreed to be the Duke's land if his Grace had been given one year's notice and did not wish to erect such a building himself. There would be no compromise because the Company had "treated with neglect and even positive denyal the frequent applications, both verbal and written, made to them to stop their irregular and wilful proceedings". But Lax was not a man to be brow-beaten either and he persuaded the Chesterfield-dominated Committee to fight. This they did by ordering the reconstruction of the warehouse on the same site, followed by a published intention to start legal proceedings against the persons who pulled the original one down. Both parties now retired to seek higher legal advice and a state of cold-war existed between the Duke of Norfolk and the Chesterfield Canal Company.

The warehouse was rebuilt to stress the Company's legal point of view but it was incomplete at the end of November 1776 and the dispute was still unresolved, indeed it was about to enter a more bitter phase. The cause was the Committee's decision, almost as a side issue, to take down the unfinished warehouse and to store the bricks and materials out of the winter weather until "they shall be wanted in the spring". As Varley was in Derbyshire dealing with Staveley Puddlebank and complaints about the feeder to Norbriggs side-cut the task was given to Richard Dixon, now very much more than the Company's Bookkeeper.* Dixon gathered together a work gang, went to Worksop and innocently carried out the order he had been given. The Duke's men saw these actions in a completely different light and were not pleased. As the warehouse had been built on the Duke's land they considered it to be under his control, no matter who had put it there. More to the point the materials from which it had been built had been forfeited by the Company as a result of their illegal actions. They had no right to move them. The attorney John Mander wrote:-

> "Persisting in their obstinacy and contempt of the Duke and his Agents
> . . . they have come in a clandestine manner very early in the day and
> with a multitude of people suddenly pulled the building down . . . and
> suddenly removed and carried away the materials. One Richard Dixon,
> who is a Clerk to the Company, bore a principal part in this pulling down
> . . ."

An interesting legal situation now existed. At different times both parties had pulled down the same building and both were planning to prosecute the other for doing so! If it ever came before a court it would need the judgement of Solomon, or the cold reality of common sense, to decide the matter. Few citizens could remember seeing much of either in 18th century courtrooms.

The year changed but entrenched opinions did not. Incensed by the attitude of the Duke's men, and needing to keep their customer's goods dry, the Company started to use their tool store as a temporary warehouse.

---

*   In the future, May 1778, Richard Dixon would be made "Superintendent of the Canal and Bookkeeper". By that time Varley had left the Company and had gone to work on other new projects. It was acknowledged that Dixon had been trained as Varley's replacement for some time and that his duties had been far in excess of those expected of a Bookkeeper. Therefore, his appointment and salary were backdated to March 1776.

When this was discovered a bad situation worsened still further. Such a change of use was not appreciated by Henry Howard, nor the cranes and wharf timbers lining each side of the canal. It was admitted that the damage done to the area was not great and that the site was fit and proper for a trading centre but that was not the point. The Company did not have permission for such activities.

By now the Duke of Norfolk had taken a personal interest in the dispute and John Mander wrote that ". . . these arbitrary, stubborn and obstinate proceedings of the Company are by the Duke regarded as very insulting." This exacerbated the pain caused to his faithful servants. The Duke of Norfolk was a tolerant, charitable and kindly old man, but shaken by the death of his beloved Duchess four years before. The heirs for whom he had started to build Worksop Manor had died before her and life held little promise for the future. He had always generated great loyalty in the people who served him and now in his final months men such as Henry Howard and John Mander felt overly protective towards him. They were indignant that the Duke knew of the Company's disrespectful and discourteous attitude. After all the canal men were only jumped-up money makers who thought their Act of Parliament a wondrous means of riding roughshod over traditional values.

Eventually, in February 1777, Howard and Mander sought the opinion of the Duke's senior legal advisers in London. Feelings were still running high but this time the Duke of Norfolk did not achieve an outright win, a drawn match would be a more accurate assessment. The London attorneys did not think the Duke had much of a case against the Canal Company. The strict interpretation of the trading clauses in the Act may not succeed, on the other hand a court would think reasonable the Company's admission that they built by "mistake" and not on purpose. A similar view would be taken of their offer to buy the extra land. So a stalemate was reached and there is no evidence of legal action being taken by either side, but the dispute had obviously soured the Company's relationship with the most powerful landowner in Nottinghamshire. The Duke of Norfolk died later that same year, aged 91, and his heir never lived at Worksop Manor. This must have been a relief to the Canal Company and as a result the dispute dwindled. But as late as August 1777 they only had a wharf and crane at Worksop, indeed it was not until March 1778 that the Committee again thought about building a warehouse on Worksop Common.

⁊ₐ ⁊ₐ ⁊ₐ

But the warehouse dispute was only a distraction from the major achievement now within reach; at long last the end of the canal was in sight, metaphorically if not quite actually. The navvies were now working well into Derbyshire; only six miles from the outskirts of Chesterfield where the canal would end by merging with the River Rother. From the current head of navigation at Norbriggs, over the River Doe Lea on the Puddlebank, past Staveley, then a climb via a number of single locks to the end. They were almost there. The remaining miles would follow the Rother's valley with the river never far away, the two waterways eventually becoming one. And at that junction the canal would take its final, or first, water supply from the river. Boats would emerge from the canal and use the river for the last quarter of a mile to the site of Chesterfield wharf which would eventually be enlarged into an off-river basin. But there were no funds for such fripperies now, the major task was to make the canal navigable from Stockwith to Chesterfield, and that was close to becoming a reality.

Unfortunately it appears that those last triumphant months of canal construction went unrecorded, if documents ever existed they have yet to be discovered. By now no one was in the mood to write copious notes about what had become routine. After six years of effort, digging soil and building bridges was mundane, even if they were approaching Chesterfield. What we do know is that by October 1776 the feeder from the Doe Lea had been completed and was bringing much needed water into the canal via Norbriggs Arm. And work on building the Puddlebank must have been underway during the winter of 1776-7 because it was a substantial embankment by early March, although still unfinished. At the same time the canal was being extended on the far side of the Puddlebank and by December 1776 it had reached Staveley. There a side-cut had been

dug the previous October, ready to link the canal with the main road.*
The Committee had ordered it built "as soon as the farmers have sown
their land", referring to the wheat seed that was sown between September
and November. The reason for this may have been that the construction
work would hinder the farmers at a busy time, or it may have been that
the manpower was fluctuating between the farms and the canal, the
farmers paying more for labourers when they needed them most? After
sowing the crops was the canal money better than the normal farm wages?
Either way the Committee – well at least the Chesterfield members of it –
had ensured that the work was completed ready for instant access to the
road when the main canal reached the area, as it now had.

Having passed Staveley the canal came to the end of the seven mile
pound from Killamarsh and commenced the climb to Chesterfield; ever
since the start of the project the canal had been built downhill from the
summit pound at Norwood, now it was to rise again. Although there is no
proof it is probable that the downhill principle was used again for the
last miles. Boats could only be used to carry construction materials if water
was flowing into the completed sections behind the navvies, and water
only flowed downhill. The sole supply for the last climb was to come from
the Rother at the end of the canal so the only way Varley could use the
methods that had already proved their worth was to go to Chesterfield
and work back towards Staveley, meeting the main section of the canal
somewhere in that vicinity. We do know that early in December 1776
urgent orders were issued for the building of three boats, and these may
have been the craft needed at Chesterfield on the new isolated section of
canal. Because of the magnitude of the challenge the Puddlebank may
have been the last part of the canal to be finished.

As speed was vital the advantage of having the Duke of Devonshire as
a substantial shareholder now became clear. The Company's financial
worries were alleviated by the Duke allowing construction work to go
ahead in the Staveley area without waiting for the legal niceties of land
purchase to be formalised.[2] This was another example of the Committee

---

*   The location of this side-cut is now marked by Wharf Lane, Staveley. The deep railway
    cutting at that site is the line originally followed by the canal arm.

gentlemen's local contacts smoothing the path of the canal and allowing progress to be maintained without delay. But even so matters were not as cosy as they had once been. At the beginning of the canal project the fact that the Duke of Devonshire's Chief Auditor was a Chesterfield man, Godfrey Heathcote, had proved to be very useful. But after Heathcote's death the post had not passed to his assistant, Anthony Lax; instead it had gone to John Heaton, an astute and extremely able administrator based at Lincoln's Inn in London. Because of the Duke's large shareholding in the Canal Company Heaton was amenable to the work progressing before the land purchase documents had been drawn up, but beyond that his first duty was to safeguard the Duke's financial affairs. Therefore, he sent one of his local assistants, John Barnes, to the Puddlebank to form an opinion on the Company's offer for the land taken for the embankment. And Heaton was wise to check because although embankments had been built in great numbers from the earliest days of the canal age no systematic approach to their construction had yet been adopted. When he arrived Barnes found that Lax and his men were up to their usual sharp practices and that the Company was only offering to pay for the area taken up by the actual canal and the towpath. The fact that many more acres had been taken up by the base of the embankment necessarily splaying out across the fields was being dismissed. This time the Company was represented by Thomas Fletcher, another of Anthony Lax's able assistants. Fletcher told Barnes that it was not reasonable to expect the Company to pay for the total acreage taken as most of that land would be replaced by the sides of the embankment. When the Puddlebank was finished Varley would have his men spread soil over the banking thereby making it usable land. John Barnes was not that much of a fool. He reported to John Heaton that such land would be worthless and that furthermore the Company did not intend to pay anything for the inconvenience caused to the Duke's tenants in the area. The farmers had shown him that the canal had cut their fields of wheat, oats, potatoes and pasture into pieces. Many had been left with no road at all to their land, others had to go more than a mile around canal obstacles. All were very unhappy and all were of the opinion that unless Heaton intervened little would be done to alleviate the problems.[3]

The Duke's tenant farmers were probably correct. Only two months before, in January 1777, there had been a battle about access a little distance away near Staveley church.[4] The canal had cut straight across a well-used footpath that connected Staveley and Handley. A bridge had not been erected and this was in direct contravention of the Act which stated that the canal could not be made until the Company had installed a means of crossing where the canal would cut a "publick footpath". In their usual high-handed way the Company did nothing to alleviate the situation until the local residents, led by the landowner General Gisborne, took legal advice on the possibility of forcing the Canal Company to comply with their own Act of Parliament. William Manley, a Chesterfield solicitor, was instructed to draw up a case and to approach a barrister, Mr Balguy of Alfreton. The legal case was watertight, and everyone knew it. So when Manley met Anthony Lax and presented the barrister's opinion to him Lax was quick "to undertake to make good the same." And a footbridge was built a few days later but, as usual, the Canal Company had done as little as possible until forced to do so by others more powerful.

ⅇ ⅇ ⅇ

During the first months of 1777 the Company's financial situation was still difficult but there were signs of relief. The canal had now been earning money for nearly fourteen months and the tonnage earned to date was £1981.2s.7d, mainly for coal and lime carried to the Retford area from Yorkshire and Derbyshire. As a result plans were made to pay the outstanding interest on the shareholders' extra Calls and the many mortgages issued. And at the start of the year Allwood Wilkinson was told to ensure that in future all interest payments were made promptly – an optimistic aim, money was not that plentiful. Matters soon took a turn for the worse and as early as February a revised scheme was devised, this time paying the two years' interest due by offering more mortgages on the canal income. This amounted to giving new mortgages to pay the interest on current mortgages! A further condition was that a mortgage would be offered only to those shareholders who were due £50 or more of outstanding interest payments. Those who were owed less than £50, and who did not pay the shortfall to the Company, would be paid the interest owed "as soon as the convenience of the Navigation will permit". Anthony Lax sent circular letters to the shareholders concerned, having inserted the respective amounts for each investor as shown in Richard Dixon's accounts. One such mortgage, for £1240, was made out to the Duke of Devonshire.[5] In general the financial quagmire was still as waterlogged as ever.

As the year progressed financial matters settled into a familiar pattern. As usual the Committee eventually realised that large amounts of the supplies purchased were scattered along the canal, unused and unwanted. This time it was boat-building materials and these were to be collected together and sold for the best price available. At the same time extra supplies were still being purchased – timber, bricks, nails, clay, cast metal, oak trees, cordage, lead, ironwork and furniture. The canal had certainly brought prosperity to local traders if not yet to the Canal Company itself. Sometimes a cashflow crisis would necessitate a special solution; on one occasion Anthony Lax agreed to supply the money for some limestone by transferring the contract to his own name, then holding the stone in trust until the Company could reimburse him.

But despite the Company's parlous financial situation, the canal was almost complete. At long last the dispute with the Duke of Newcastle about the land at Stockwith had been resolved and by April work could at last start on the great lock down to the River Trent. Poor John Varley, he had a tight deadline to meet and the two active workcamps were forty miles apart. Although the materials for Stockwith lock had been taken to the site many months before it is unlikely that the work was finished by the beginning of June – making Stockwith lock the last part of the Chesterfield Canal to be completed. The crucial point was that the rest of the canal should be finished by the King's birthday; all that was needed was for a boat to arrive in Chesterfield having carried goods all the way from Stockwith, the fact that the canal was not yet linked to the Trent was unimportant in the context of the celebrations planned. The final month of construction was exhausting for John Varley and his navvies as they made a prodigious effort to meet the deadline set by their Committee. And somewhere near Staveley they must have had their own private ceremony as the water was fed into the last section – just before the 4th of June 1777.

On the great day a large crowd of people waited at the lock nearest to Chesterfield, waited for the first boat to arrive in the town loaded with a cargo from Stockwith.[6] Of course for such a stage-managed event the boat must have been waiting a few miles away since at least the day before, but nevertheless its arrival was symbolic of a new age. For the first time in its history Chesterfield would be free of a dependency on atrocious roads and slow wagons and packhorses. Now bulk transportation of goods was a fact, cheap and capable of use in all weathers. Although the first flush of canal fever had abated, and general business and trade had been badly affected by the revolution in the American colonies, the canal was still an almost unbelievable achievement. Boats were floating in the Derbyshire hills, the old farmers had not believed it possible when the plans were first published – but now the proof would soon be seen.

The narrowboat came into sight around the final bend, passed under the bridge carrying Lockoford Lane and through the open gates into the lock. The excited onlookers saw it rise up, probably the first time many of them had seen a boat go "uphill", and then followed down the towpath as the boat-horse pulled the vessel along the last few yards of the canal. Just before the junction with the Rother the horse, and the crowd, crossed over a bridge as the towpath changed to the left bank and suddenly, there was the end of the canal. The new, brash waterway merged with the old River Rother. The new, stark, muddy, barren, clay-lined canal towpath gave way to the old grass-covered, tree-lined path alongside the river. The exact site of the first wharf is not known, it may have been where the first basin was eventually built or it may have been nearer to the end of the canal. Wherever it was, the boat stopped and with flags flying, guns firing, and a band playing the goods were unloaded and put into wagons which were drawn along the road to the town centre by the navvies. Ahead of them walked the gentlemen of the Committee and other shareholders, and in front of all the band marched and played.

It is pleasing to know that the navvies were not forgotten during the celebrations, especially as their trade had already gained an infamous reputation elsewhere. But on that Wednesday in Chesterfield nearly three hundred of them sat down to a handsome feast, paid for by the shareholders. For the rest of the day the men who had built the canal continued to be orderly and polite, dispersing early in the evening without making any disturbance whatever. The day finished with the canal celebrations merging with those for the King's birthday; the church bells were rung, bonfires were lit, and fireworks sparkled in the evening sky. Perhaps some of those present remembered other fireworks; those that had welcomed Anthony Lax when he arrived from Westminster with news of the Royal Assent to the building of the Chesterfield Canal. Six years, two months, and six days before.

EPILOGUE

The celebrations continued the next day. The boat which had brought the first cargo was decorated with streamers and, as at the opening of Norwood Tunnel, a band joined the passengers. The Committee gentlemen and other shareholders had arranged a boat trip for their female relatives and over one hundred ladies embarked for a daring voyage not only to, but through, the first lock.[1]

After that the Chesterfield Canal began its chequered career of almost two hundred years of commercial carrying. Work continued on building the extra facilities that had been deferred until the canal had been completed. In May 1778 a warehouse, accounting office, and house for the wharfinger were ordered for Chesterfield. In June 1779 the Committee was thinking about a side-cut at Stockwith. By March 1781 a basin had been built at Chesterfield and was already in use.[2] But some problems were to plague the canal even during those early years. One of the most serious was the condition of the great Norwood Tunnel. The first trouble was recorded as early as September 1777; the Duke of Leeds' tenants in the area had dug coal from the ground over the tunnel and as a result nineteen yards of the roof had been damaged by the lessening of the weight compressing the arch. The Committee ordered that the arching be repaired and that Anthony Lax tell the Duke's Agent that the Company would pay for the damages on this occasion. However, they hoped there would be no further instances. But the tunnel was never to be secure – over the centuries the coal seams permeating the hill were to cause endless structural problems. Between 1871 and 1906 £21,000 was spent on remedial work but all to no avail. On the 18th of October 1907 a large section of the roof again collapsed, blocking the tunnel and leaving a large crater in a field near the road to Harthill. Three days later senior officials of the railway company then owning the canal came to see the damage and decided not to spend any more money on repairs.[3] The official decision to abandon Norwood Tunnel was made in 1908.

Staveley Puddlebank also caused continuing headaches. In 1806 it was reported as losing its water and soaking and injuring the lands below.[4] And in later years the feeder from the Doe Lea was guilty of the same fault – the whole two miles was repaired in the spring of 1834, but local landowners still complained. By that time the Canal Company's chief engineer was Mr Gratton and he drained the feeder so that a close inspection could be made. Faithful to the memory of those who had gone before him Mr Gratton duly stated that the structure was in good condition and that the trouble was caused by the landowners' cattle. He himself had seen a dozen beasts standing in the feeder to drink and, therefore, the Company could not be responsible for damage to the clay lining of the channel.[5]

But by far the most serious problem was a shortage of water in the summit pound. This had become apparent before the canal was finished and it was to cause many headaches. In May 1778 a regulation was made that no one but the lock-keeper at Norwood could draw water out of the Company's reservoir. It was also made an offence for a boat to use more than the minimum amount of water when passing through a lock and the only people who could use water from one pound to fill another where the level was low were the wharfingers and lock-keepers. The usual routine for a boat in a low pound was for as much cargo as necessary to be unloaded so that the boat could pass over the lock entrance. Richard Dixon later reported that lack of water had adversely affected the Company's trading figures since 1779. Elsewhere on the canal it was satisfactory but the summit pound could only cater for boats carrying £5,000 of goods each year, even though there was the trade available to earn the Company £7,000-£8,000.[6] In March 1785 plans were made for two more reservoirs to be built in the hills at Norwood – now known as Woodhall Pond and Killamarsh Pond they fed their water into the canal by a feeder to the western end of Norwood Tunnel.[7]

But not all was doom and gloom. Trade in the country gradually recovered from the dire effects of the American War of Independence and the fortunes of the Chesterfield Canal improved accordingly. By the 1790s the second great age of canal building was reflecting the recovery and in 1795 the Company was able to pay a 6% dividend to its shareholders.

Until the middle of the 18th century the canal enjoyed a moderate prosperity until progress took another leap forward and the railways came along as the heralds of another new age. Commercial carrying continued until the 1950s, since then the Chesterfield Canal has become a lovely waterway for leisure use. Looking like a natural part of the countryside it shows little sign of its man-made beginnings, little sign of the effort and ingenuity of its creators.

ta ta ta

And of those men we know little more.

Hugh Henshall went on to become the General Manager of the Trent & Mersey Canal Company. He died on 16 November 1816, aged 82. He was buried in the churchyard of St. James at Newchapel, Staffordshire just one grave away from his old tutor, James Brindley.

The gentlemen who served so long on the Committee mostly continued as the management of the Canal Company, living locally and carrying on their various trades. The names Jebb, Heathcote, Wilkinson, Storrs occur throughout the intervening years of Chesterfield's history. In Retford – Simpson, Sutton, Bright, and Brown.

A memorial to Godfrey Heathcote can be seen in the Baptistry of Chesterfield's famous "crooked spire" parish church, St. Mary's. Not far away in St. Katherine's Chapel is another memorial, this time to his junior partner Anthony Lax. Known as Anthony Lax Maynard from 1784 he became a Deputy Lieutenant of Derbyshire in 1796. He was still the Canal Company's senior administrator in June 1806, although Richard Dixon had taken over most of his duties after the canal had been completed. Anthony Lax died on 3 July 1825, aged 83.

Seth Ellis Stevenson continued as a churchman and the headmaster of Retford Grammar School until his death in 1793, aged 69. His memorial is to be seen in Retford – a canal that passed through his town only because of his efforts. Progress has left behind Stevenson's original reasons for the waterway, but his vision and energy are still evident in a canal which now brings great pleasure to its many leisure users. And if further testimony to a remarkable man is required it can be found in the six wide locks between

Retford and the River Trent.

After the completion of the Chesterfield Canal John Varley immediately moved on to build the Erewash Canal, just fifteen miles further south near Nottingham. Throughout the 1780s he was involved with the Erewash with varying degrees of success. He and his family continued to live in their house at Pennyholme and three further children were christened at Harthill, Betty (1778), Thomas (1781) and Francis (1784). After the Erewash Varley was involved in various canals; in 1792 working under William Jessop to survey a line from Leicester to the Grand Union Canal, with a branch to Market Harborough. His son John drew the maps for this project and John Senior eventually became Resident Engineer. The digging of Saddington Tunnel presented familiar problems. During the 1790s Varley was still involved with the Erewash on a consultancy basis, the partnership eventually dissolving in 1798 when Varley started legal proceedings for the payment of a disputed bill for his services. In 1800-01 he was working on the Huddersfield Narrow Canal – supplying mortar, doing repairs, sub-contracting the work to finish Standedge Tunnel. He was not happy with the six year deadline set for the tunnel and eventually the contract was revised and given to another engineer. On 3 May 1808 a petition was presented to the Erewash Canal Company on behalf of Varley who was "in a very infirm and distressed state and soliciting an Annuity from the Company". It was refused but a one-off donation of twenty guineas was made.[8] John Varley died on 16 February 1809, aged 69, and was buried at Harthill; less than a mile from Norwood Tunnel.[9]

In the past many have written of the Chesterfield Canal's Resident Engineer as a failure and a cheat. They point to the problems with Norwood Tunnel and the inadequate water supply, and to the work contracts issued to his relatives. But after Brindley's sudden death Varley did complete one of the earliest large reservoirs in the country, two tremendous flights of staircase locks, and a canal tunnel that was then England's longest. It was Varley's misfortune that such achievements were, and still are, overshadowed by exploits on other more central and prestigious waterways.

John Varley has no fancy church stone with his name upon it, no faded monument that has toppled and become unreadable; more than two hundred years later his memorial is plain to see. It covers forty-six miles of England and is made of stone, brick, clay, lead, iron, timber, water – and human vision, ingenuity and effort.

LOCATIONS OF SOURCE DOCUMENTS

Abbreviations

BL	British Library
BM	Bassetlaw Museum, Retford
BMM	Brindley Mill and Museum, Leek, Staffordshire
CHAT	Chatsworth House. Archives of His Grace, the Duke of Devonshire.
CL	Chesterfield Library, Local Studies
DCL	Derby Central Library
DRO	Derbyshire Record Office, Matlock
DM	Derby Mercury, newspaper. CL, microfilm copy.
HLRO	House of Lords Record Office
NCL	Nottingham Central Library, Angel Row.
NRO	Nottinghamshire Record Office
NU/MD	Nottingham University, Department of Manuscripts & Special Collections, Hallward Library.
PRO	Public Records Office, Kew
SAO	Sheffield Archives Office
SBT	Shakespeare Birthplace Trust

SOURCE REFERENCES

Details of Chesterfield and the inhabitants have been built up from separate items in contemporary editions of the Derby Mercury and the records of the Manor Court. Both available on microfilm in the Local Studies section of Chesterfield Central Library.

SES.   Unless otherwise noted details of the Rev. Seth Ellis Stevenson and Retford life are from his diary. The diary of the Rev. Seth Ellis Stevenson 1760-77. Ref FR/73, Nottingham University, Department of Manuscripts & Special Collections, Hallward Library.

MINS.   Unless otherwise noted details of the Canal Company's meetings, decisions, purchases, appointments are from the Minute Book of the Company. Minutes of the Chesterfield Canal Company, April 1771 to May 1780. PRO, ref RAIL 817/1. CL, microfilm copy.

Chapter One   A Canal for Chesterfield

1   Philip Riden, An Eighteenth-Century Proposal for the Navigation of the Rother, The Derbyshire Archaeological Journal, CIV(1984), 68-70.

2   DM, 4 Nov 1775.

3   Ibid.

4   Chesterfield Manor Court Records. CL, microfilm.

5   SAO. Notes on the Intended Navigation. Ref MD3707.

6   Rotherham Central Library. Records of Harthill Church, 16 Feb 1809.

7   SAO. Notes on the Intended Navigation. Ref MD3707.

8   Ibid.

9   L. Stedman, Mapping History, New Civil Engineer, June 1991, 24-29.

10   Map in private ownership. Copy at DRO.

11   SAO. Notes on the Intended Navigation. Ref MD3707.

12   Ibid.

13   SAO. Wentworth Woodhouse Muniments. Refs MP47b and MP47c.

14   SAO. Wentworth Woodhouse Muniments. Refs MP47d.

Chapter Two   What about Retford?

1   NU/MD. Clumber Estate Weighing Book. Ref N-eX-685.

2   SES, pp235.

3   DM, 4 Aug 1769.

4   DM, 6 Oct 1769.

5   Ibid.

6   DCL. Pamphlet, A Cursory View of an Intended Canal, 1769.

7   DCL. Pamphlet, Seasonable Hints relating to the Intended Canal from Chesterfield in Derbyshire to the River Trent below Gainsborough, 1769. Also SES, pp250.

8   DM, 22 Dec 1769.

9   DM, 2 Feb 1770.

Chapter Three   Selling the Idea to the Public

1   DCL. Pamphlet, Seasonable Hints relating to the Intended Canal from Chesterfield in Derbyshire to the River Trent below Gainsborough, 1769.

2   Ibid.

3   DM, 2 Feb 1770.

4   DM, 1 Aug 1770.

5   DM, 25 Jan 1770.

6   HLRO. Journal of the House of Commons, Vol.33 Part 1, 9 Feb 1770.

7   NRO. Letter, Saville to Acklom, 24 Feb 1770. Ref DD277/4.

8   Ibid.

9   DM, 11 May 1770.

10   Ibid.

11   DRO. The Report of John Grundy, Engineer, Respecting the Proposed Navigation from Chesterfield to the River Trent, 22 Aug 1770. Strutt Library, ref A66.

Chapter Four   An Act of Parliament

1   DM, 1 Aug 1770.

2   SES, pp275.

3   DM, 11 Jan 1771.

4   Philip Moritz, Description of the House of Commons 1782, Contained in English Historical Documents, Vol.X, 1714-1783.

5   HLRO. Journal of the House of Commons, Vol.33 Part 1.

6   Ibid.

7   Ibid.

8   SES. 19 Feb 1771.

9   DM, 15 Feb 1771.

10   DM, Aug 1777.

11   HLRO. An Act for Making a Navigable Cut or Canal from Chesterfield in the County of Derby, through or near Worksop and Retford, to join the River Trent at or near Stockwith in the County of Nottingham. 28 Mar 1771.

12   HLRO. Journal of the House of Commons, Vol.33 Part 1.

13   Ibid. 19 Mar 1771.

14   SES, pp293.

15   HLRO. Journal of the House of Commons, Vol.33 Part 1. 22 Mar 1770.

16   Ibid. 27 Mar 1770.

17   DM.

18   SES, pp293.

Chapter Five   Final Arrangements

1   NU/MD. Clumber Estate, No.4 Receivers Accounts, George Mason. Ref N-eX-162-175.

2   Pressnell, L.S; Country Banking in the Industrial Revolution; Oxford Clarendon Press; 1956.

Chapter Six   Start at the Top

1   DCL. Map of canal route and rise/fall data, Kitchen, 1769.

2   George Alexander Cooke, Topographical & Statistical Description of the County of Nottingham, 1804, London.

3   DM, 17 Nov 1771.

4   SES, pp 305.

5   Rotherham Central Library. H Garbett, The History of Harthill.

6   DM, 15 Nov 1771.

7   SES, pp 329.

8   Receipts are in various archives. Two examples are: handwritten, DRO, Pashley Papers, ref D267/67c. Printed, Shakespeare Birthplace Trust, ref DR4/134.

9   On-site measurements taken by ex-British Coal engineers.

10   DM, 24 Jan 1772.

11   Rotherham Central Library. Records of Harthill Church.

12   DM, 12 Jun 1772.

13   DM, 31 Jul 1772.

14   SAO. Worksop land damage survey, 1774. Ref ACM W166.

Chapter Seven   The First Crises

1   SES, pp330.

2   DM, 30 Jul 1773.

3   PRO. Vallancey quoted in; M W Baldwin, Soil Mechanics as Practised by the Engineers of the Early English Canals, dissertation, University of London. Ref ZLIB/15/52/7.

4 SAO. The dispute is covered in various documents in the Arundel Castle Manuscripts, refs D107, W166, WD577a.

5 SAO. Land sale contract. Arundel Castle Manuscripts, ref WD5776.

6 PRO. M W Baldwin, Soil Mechanics as Practised by the Engineers of the Early English Canals, dissertation, University of London. Ref ZLIB/15/52/7.

7 PRO. Vallancey quoted in; M W Baldwin, Soil Mechanics as Practised by the Engineers of the Early English Canals, dissertation, University of London. Ref ZLIB/15/52/7.

8 SES, pp382. Also NU/MD, Day Book, Kirke W, 1759-73, ref Ki 106/3.

Chapter Eight   Norwood and Retford

1 DM, 10 Dec 1773.

2 SES, pp 362.

3 Ibid.

4 SES, pp 364.

5 SAO. Letter, Owen to Charge. Arundel Castle Manuscripts, ref W166.

6 DM, 19 Sep 1774, and 26 Sep 1774.

7 SES, pp 369.

8 NU/MD. Letter, Bright to Duke of Newcastle, Nov 1774. Ref NeC 2720/11/34.

Chapter Nine   Through Norwood Hill

1 John Farey, General View of the Agriculture of Derbyshire, 1817, Vol III, p475.

2 SAO. Notes on the Intended Navigation. Ref MD3707.

3 NRO. Memo Books of W Holland. Ref DD590/2.

4 NRO. Memo Books of W Holland. Ref DD590/4.

5 Ibid.

6 DM, 26 May 1775.

7   Ibid.

8   SES, pp 382.

Chapter Ten   Financial Crises

1   NU/MD. Cresswells Nottingham Journal.

2   SES, pp 388.

3   DRO. Share transfer, Jan 1776. Pashley Papers, ref D267/67c.

4   B J Biggs, The Story of the Methodists of Retford and District, 1970.

5   John Farey, General View of the Agriculture of Derbyshire, 1817, Vol III.

6   Bill of Complaint, In Chancery, The Manchester Sheffield and Lincolnshire Railway Company v The Mayor Aldermen and Burgesses of the Borough of Chesterfield. No.148, filed 5 Dec 1874 and 18 Jan 1875. See also, Appendix G.

7   SES, pp 384.

8   Elizabeth Perkins, Village Life from Wills and Inventories; Clayworth Parish 1670-1710. Centre for Local History, University of Nottingham, Record Series 1.

9   DM, various items January 1776.

10   SES, pp 399.

11   SES, pp 409.

12   CHAT. Various letters, ref L/60/18A.

13   CHAT. Land sale agreement, Duke of Devonshire and the Canal Company, 25 Mar 1777. Ref L/60/18A.

14   NU/MD. Letter, Mason to the Duke of Newcastle, 18 Jun 1776. Ref NeC 3465/21/67.

15   DRO. Loan assignment, Brown to Pegge, 6 Jun 1798. Pashley Papers, ref D267.

16   Records of Harthill Church. Rotherham Central Library.

17   SES, pp 406.

18   SAO. Worksop Manor Account Book. Arundel Castle Manuscripts, ref W82.

Chapter Eleven   Final Stages

1   SAO. The warehouse dispute is detailed in various papers, all to be found in the Arundel Castle Manuscripts, ref W166.

2   CHAT. Letter, Barnes to Heaton, Mar 1777. Ref L/60/18A.

3   Ibid.

4   DRO. Manley's legal services invoice, Dec 1778. Ref 459 M/2P 42.

5   CHAT. Loan agreement, Duke of Devonshire and the Canal Company, 25 Jun 1777. Ref L/23/24.

6   DM, 13 Jun 1777.

Epilogue

1   DM, 13 Jun 1777.

2   DRO. Sale of boat, Gee to Snibson. Pashley Papers, ref D267.

3   Office diary of Kiveton Park Colliery, 1907-8.

4   CHAT. Report, Gratton to Canal Company. Ref L60/18A.

5   Ibid.

6   CHAT. Letter, Dixon to Heaton, 8 Feb 1785. Ref L/60/18A.

7   CHAT. Letter, Heaton, 18 Mar 1785. Ref L/60/18A.

8   PRO. Minutes of the Erewash Canal Company. Ref RAIL 828/1.

9   Rotherham Central Library. Records of Harthill Church.

Appendix G

1   Bill of Complaint, In Chancery, The Manchester Sheffield and Lincolnshire Railway Company v The Mayor Aldermen and Burgesses of the Borough of Chesterfield. No.148, filed 5 Dec 1874 and 18 Jan 1875.

Table of £.s.d / £.p equivalents

Because all costs and prices in the book are taken from pre-1972 sources, they are quoted in £.s.d currency; however, it was felt that it would be helpful to include this conversion table giving decimal currency equivalents.

s.	d.	£p	£	s.	£p
	1d			2s	10p
	2d	1p		3s	15p
	3d	1p		4s	20p
	4d			5s	25p
	5d	2p		6s	30p
	6d			7s	35p
	7d	3p		8s	40p
	8d	3p		9s	45p
	9d	4p		10s	50p
	10d	4p		11s	55p
	11d			12s	60p
1s (12d)		5p		13s	65p
				14s	70p
				15s	75p
				16s	80p
				17s	85p
				18s	90p
				19s	95p
			£1	(20s)	100p

APPENDIX A

A canal lock allows a boat to move from one level of canal to another, either higher or lower. It consists of a brick or stone sided chamber wide enough to take one narrowboat, or in a wide lock two narrowboats side-by-side. At each end of the chamber are wooden gates to allow boats to enter. Also at each end are sluices, now known as paddles, which can be opened or closed to allow the water to flow into, or out of, the chamber.

After a boat has entered the lock the gates are closed behind it and the appropriate paddles opened to empty or fill the chamber. The boat then rises or falls to the new level of the canal outside the lock. The gates are then opened at the other end allowing the boat to leave.

Canal Lock

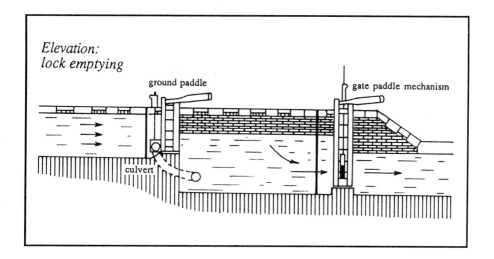

APPENDIX B

Summary of the options and costings contained in Grundy's report.

— — — — — — — — —

To carry vessels the same as those currently on the Idle trade. Capable of navigating the Trent and Yorkshire rivers, cutting out trans-shipping.

First Alternative

Shireoaks – Carlton – Blythe – Bawtry – River Idle – Stockwith

Lengths	–	Varley	27m	0f	4ch
		Grundy	21m	5f	4ch
		Difference	5m	3f	0ch

Cost of Varley route Chesterfield – Stockwith	£94908.	17.	0d

— — — — — — — — —

Cost of Grundy route:-

Varley's route Chesterfield – Shireoaks	37667.	1.	3
Shireoaks – Gateford	3140.	10.	0
Lock at Gateford	856.	0.	0
Gateford – Oldcotes	5115.	16.	0
Lock & bridge at Oldcotes	650.	0.	0
Oldcotes – Bawtry wharf	7276.	4.	0
Lock at Bawtry	680.	0.	0
Contingency sum	1617.	0.	0

— — — — — — — — —

Total –– Chesterfield to Bawtry	£57002.	11.	3
Improving the Idle, Bawtry - Stockwith	7688.	0.	0
Contingency sum	767.	0.	0
Total – Chesterfield to Stockwith	£65457.	11.	3

— — — — — — — — —

LESS THAN VARLEY ROUTE	£29451.	5.	8
Giving the canal an additional use of draining the lowlands	2929.	5.	0
Total – Chesterfield to Stockwith, plus drainage	£68386.	16.	3
LESS THAN VARLEY ROUTE	£26522.	0.	8

continued . . .

Appendix B (cont)

Second Alternative

Varley's route to north of Chequerhouse – along the Ryton valley to Blythe – join route of first alternative at Oldcotes.

Cost of Varley route Chesterfield – Stockwith	£94908.	17.	0d

– – – – – – – – –

Cost of Grundy route:-			
Varley's route Chesterfield – Shireoaks	37667.	1.	3
Varley's route Shireoaks – Chequerhouse	17987.	0.	4
Chequerhouse – Oldcotes	6736.	8.	0
Lock & bridge at Oldcotes	650.	0.	0
Oldcotes – Bawtry wharf	7276.	4.	0
Lock at Bawtry	680.	0.	0
Contingency sum	860.	0.	0
Total – Chesterfield – Chequerhouse – Bawtry	£71856.	13.	7
Improving the Idle, Bawtry – Stockwith	7688.	0.	0
Contingency sum	767.	0.	0
Total – Chesterfield to Stockwith	£80311.	13.	7

– – – – – – – – –

LESS THAN VARLEY ROUTE	£14597.	3.	4

– – – – – – – – –

Giving the canal an additional use of draining the lowlands	2929.	5.	0
Total – Chesterfield to Stockwith, plus drainage	£83240.	18.	7
LESS THAN VARLEY ROUTE	£11667.	18.	4

Continued . . .

Appendix B (cont)

Third Alternative

Same as first alternative to Bawtry but including – a new cut to the Trent to bypass the River Idle, and side-cuts to Worksop and Retford.

Cost of Varley route Chesterfield – Stockwith	£94908.1	7.	0d
_ _ _ _ _ _ _ _ _			
Cost of Grundy route:-			
First alternative, Chesterfield – Shireoaks	57002.	11.	3
New cut, Bawtry – Stockwith	14476.	15.	6
_ _ _ _ _ _ _ _ _			
Total – Chesterfield – Stockwith	£71479.	6.	9
_ _ _ _ _ _ _ _ _			
LESS THAN VARLEY ROUTE	£23429.	10.	2
_ _ _ _ _ _ _ _ _			
Side-cut, Scrooby – Retford	5540.	0.	0
Contingency sum	554.	0.	0
Total – Scrooby – Retford	£6094.	0.	0
Total – Chesterfield – Stockwith (& Retford)	£77573.	6.	9
_ _ _ _ _ _ _ _ _			
LESS THAN VARLEY ROUTE	£17335.	10.	2
_ _ _ _ _ _ _ _ _			
Varley route, Shireoaks – Worksop 3 miles @ £2116. 2. 4d per mile	6348.	7.	3
Total, Chesterfield – Stockwith (& Retford & Worksop)	£83921.	14.	0
_ _ _ _ _ _ _ _ _			
LESS THAN VARLEY ROUTE	£10987.	2.	11

APPENDIX C

Circumstantial evidence of wide canal at time of Act.

The Act refers to "wide burthen" vessels; Grundy's option was for a wide canal, would he have done this if it was to meet with a narrow Varley canal at Shireoaks? Did they change back to narrow when Norwood Tunnel was replanned to be much longer? Or did the Staveley Forge amendment mean that an enhanced water supply for a wide canal could not be found? Was the cost of the Puddlebank saved by making it a narrow canal instead? Would Seth Ellis Stevenson with his knowledge not have planned for a wide canal from the start?

Narrow canals were a compromise. Normally 5-6ft deep, width on waterline 40ft across, width 20ft across bed. Cheaper to build than a wider waterway but could still carry narrowboats; Brindley planned vessels 7ft by 70ft, loaded draft 2ft 6ins, rudder transferable to each end, therefore double-ended, flat-bottomed, cabin and towing masts, hull form may have followed the tunnel boats at Worsley. The length was determined by the horse's ability to pull it and handleability. Could carry 20 tons, very good compared with wagons and packhorses.

APPENDIX D

Subjects covered in the Act of Parliament, illustrating the complexity of such legislation.

List of Proprietors.
Declared a Corporation.
Power to Make a Canal.
Access Roads to the Canal.
Prevention of Waggon Roads near Harthill and Wales.
Canal not to Pass through Certain Gardens.
Mills on the Canal and Cutting Wood not allowed.
Not to Alter the Course of Bonder (or Boundary) Beck.
Wharfs Not to be Made on Certain Lands.
One Towing Path only, on Opposite side of Canal to Certain Lands.
No Building to be on a Certain Stretch at East Retford.
Towpath Limits.
Proximity of Canal to Wiseton Hall, Manton Farmhouse.

Water Supply, Safeguards for – Staveley Forge, Mills on the Rother, River Don Navigation, River Rother Water to go no further than Norwood Hill, Worksop Manor, Duke of Norfolk's Water Engine, Kiveton House (Hall), Mills, Thorpe Hall, River Idle Navigation.

Maps and Book of Reference.
Construction in Accordance with Plans.
Omissions from the Book of Reference.
Lands may be Entered for making Surveys.
Breadth of the Canal and Towpath.
Purchase of Land.

Dispute Procedures – Commissioners.
Commissioners – Elections & Qualifications.
Commissioners Meetings.
Dissatisfaction with Commissioners Rulings.
Penalties – Sheriffs, Coroners, Jurymen, Witnesses.
Expense of Calling a Jury.

Appendix D (cont)

Time Limit on Complaints.
Verdicts to be Recorded.
Fines, Convictions, Appeals.

Right of Construction.
Valuations and Damages.
Purchase Money paid to Corporations and Trustees.
Shares of Purchase Prices or Damages.
Non-Payment of Awards or Damages.
Non-Payment by the Company of Annual Rents.
Punishment for Destroying the Works.
Penalty for Obstructing the Works.

Coal and other Minerals found during Construction.
Owners of Mines may make Drains into the Canal.
Coal Mines not to Prejudice the Canal.

Shareholders may Raise Extra Money.
Shares.
Not to Construct until £100,000 Subscribed.
Interest at 5% to be Paid until the Works are Complete.
Shareholders Votes.
An Extra £50,000 may be Raised.
Transfer of Securities.
Mortgage Interest to be Paid Half-Yearly.
General Meetings – Schedule and Committee Election.
Committee to be Directed by the General Meetings.
Books to be Kept.
General Meetings to be not Less than 400 Shares.
Power of General Meetings and Committees.
Notice of Forfeiture of Shares.
General Meetings may make Bye-Laws.
Death of Shareholders.
How Shares may be Disposed of.
Appointment of Clerks.
Proceedings to be Entered in the Company Books.

Appendix D (cont)

Tonnage Rates.
Exemptions from Tolls.
Tolls Free from Taxes.
Rates for Goods remaining on Wharfs.
Wharfage Rates.
Rates to be the Same throughout the Canal.
Declaration of Cargoes by Boatmen.
Estimate of Tonnage.
Differences in Weight Estimates.
Navigation on Payment of Tolls.
Vessels under 20 Tons.

Drainage of Lands.
Provision of Cattle Watering Places.
Land Drainage, Dinnington, Anston, Todwick.
Towpaths to be Fenced off.
Bridges for the Dukes of Norfolk and Leeds.
Private Bridge, Gates, etc may be Built.
Warehouses, Wharfs, Cranes, etc may be Built.

Boat Regulations – Boat Markings, Damage done by Boat Crews, Turning
    Points and Passing Places, Lock Regulations, Boats Obstructing the
    Canal, Boat Overloading, Boat Ballast thrown into the Canal,
    Catching Fish or Game, Pleasure Boat Usage.

Preserving Rights in Law.
Fishery Rights.
Sewer Laws not to Apply.
Unused Land.
Stamp Duty.
Milestones.

APPENDIX E

The Canal Company left no details of the original Norwood locks and they may have been built to a different configuration than known today. A report by John Farey in 1817, surveyed in 1806/7, describes the locks, from the top, as three staircase sets of 4, 2, 6. If correct the last group of locks at Norwood were the only six-rise staircase ever built in England, five being the maximum known elsewhere. The current site is large enough for such a pattern to have been built but a search for definite evidence is a future project.

If Farey is accurate then Norwood locks must have been built as he saw them in 1775. Such a configuration would have saved on construction costs but in use would have consumed a great deal of water, especially if boat traffic was allowed to use them in alternate directions – staircase locks without sideponds using much less water if traffic is one-way only. Farey said that for some reason he did not understand all traffic through the tunnel and locks was east to west one day, and west to east the next day, and so on. Certainly this would have considerably reduced the amount of water going down the staircase locks, especially as Thorpe flight at the other end of the summit pound would save water for the same reason. Farey reported that such traffic management caused considerable delays and it may be that when Company profits increased in the first half of the 19th century Norwood locks were changed to allow two-way traffic – they would still have to be staircase locks to manage the descent but smaller groups and sideponds, as seen today, would make water usage a good deal more efficient. If the locks were altered it must have been between the date of Farey's visit, 1806/7 and the date of the earliest map showing the new formation, 1845. A clue may be the date in the keystone of the bridge near the bottom of the locks, 1833.

At the moment the evidence for this theory is inconclusive and further investigation is required.

APPENDIX F

The research for this book disproved the two most widely quoted reasons for the name Whitsunday Pie.

The first version was that sometime during the working days of the canal there was a stoppage at the lock and a back-log of boats built up. As the working boats of the Chesterfield Canal were not designed for living on for long periods they did not carry a large stock of food and the boatmen solved this problem by arranging with a farmer's wife to bake them a pie on Whit Sunday. The second version was that during the construction of the canal the navvies finished building the lock on Whit Sunday and a farmer's wife living nearby baked them a pie to celebrate.

The real meaning of the name may never be known but it is unlikely that a pie was involved. The name was in use before the canal arrived and the most likely explanation to date is that offered by Edwin Shearing of Malvern in response to an article I wrote on the subject in the magazine Waterways World. Consulting John Field's English Field Names, 2nd impression 1982, Mr Shearing found (p254) that "Whitsunday Pasture" and other Whitsun names related to land changing use or tenancy at Whitsun. John Field explains that field names are usually of two or more words, the second or denominative component such as Close, Furlong, Field etc being common to many different first word "qualifiers". The denominatives have become modified over the centuries and place name scholars seek out the earliest versions through old deeds and plans when interpreting the names. It seems quite probable that we have here a field originally called "Whitsunday pightle", pightle being a small enclosure or croft; the "tle" sound may well have got lost over the years with disuse of the word in general speech.

APPENDIX G

In 1874 the Manchester, Sheffield and Lincolnshire Railway Company (MSLR), then the owners of the canal, prosecuted Chesterfield Borough Council because the water in the River Rother was polluted. They complained that the water was then taken into their canal and the pollution spread along to the first lock.[1]

Included in the Borough's defence argument was the following:-

"The said canal was not made in accordance with the Act and the plans therein referred to by which the canal as authorised to be made is defined and described. The canal authorised by the Act . . . was made to take a route entirely independent of the River Rother which it was to have crossed at the place then and still called Rickett's Mill and thence to have proceeded to its terminus on the north-west side of the town of Chesterfield opposite to the point where the Rother intersects or touches the town which is on the south-east side. No junction with the river was authorised by the Act nor . . . was any right given to the Canal Company to supply themselves with water from the river. The Canal Company instead of causing their canal to cross the River Rother by Rickett's Mill effected a junction with it at that point in violation of their Parliamentary contract . . . and now take their first supply of water from the river which is similarly a violation of the said Act of Parliament. The Canal Company . . . used the river in common with all the subjects of the Crown for their navigation for a distance of about a quarter of a mile towards Chesterfield and without Parliamentary authority constructed a basin opening into the river and connected with it by a lock. Their basin is therefore separated from their canal by the intervening portion of river. The River Rother is a public navigable river in both directions from Rickett's Mill and the supply of water which the canal . . . has taken from the river at that point has considerably injured the navigation thereof in the northward direction and has also diminished its volume and natural scour and thereby augmented the injurious effect of the sewage which has passed into the river from the town and above it."

BIBLIOGRAPHY

Ashton, T S; *Economic Fluctuations in England 1700-1800*; Oxford Clarendon Press; 1959

Bailey's British Directory; 1784;

Bailey's Northern Directory; 1781

Beckett J V; *A Regional History of England – The East Midlands from AD1000*

Beestall J M & Fowkes D V; *History of Chesterfield; Vol II,Part 2*

Bickley, Francis; *The Cavendish Family*

Biggs, B J; *Nottinghamshire Countryside; Vol 28, No.2;* 1967: Macfarland

Biggs, B J; *The Story of the Methodists of Retford and District*; 1970

Bird, Anthony; *Roads & Vehicles*; London 1969

Bode, Harold; *James Brindley, An Illustrated Life of*; Shire Publications; 1980

Borer, Mary Cathcart; *People of Georgian England*

Boucher, Cyril T G; *James Brindley, Engineer*; Goose & Son, Norwich; 1968

Boynton; *The Chemistry of Lime and Limestone*

Bradbury, David J (comp); *Clumber Treasures*; Wheel Publications

Bradshaws; *Canals & Navigable Rivers of England and Wales;* 1904; (Incorporating De Salis, H R; *A Handbook of Inland Navigation*; 1901)

Burke's Landed Gentry

Burke, Sir Bernard; *The General Armory of England, Scotland, Ireland and Wales;* 1884; London

Burton, Anthony; *The Canal Builders*; Methuen; 1972

Canals & Waterways; Trent Number; Sep 1921

Cartwright, F F; *A Social History of Medicine*

Chambers Biographical Dictionary

Chambers, J D; *The Vale of Trent 1670-1800;* 1957; Cambridge

Chapman S D; *A Business History of Stanton & Staveley*

Chapman, William; *Observations on Canal Navigation;* 1797; London

Cooke, George Alexander; *Topographical & Statistical Description of the County of Derby; 1804;* London

Cooke, George Alexander; *Topographical & Statistical Description of the County of Nottingham; 1804;* London

Cooper, Roy; *The Book of Chesterfield*

Cox; *Three Centuries of Derbyshire Annals*

Cresswells Nottingham Journal; The name of this newspaper changed quite often, this ref includes *Cresswells Nottingham & Newark Journal, Cresswell & Burbages Nottingham Journal*

Davis, Dorothy; *A History of Shopping*; 1966

De Salis, Henry Rodolph; *A Chronology of Inland Navigation in Great Britain*; London; 1897

Derbyshire Countryside; Vol 19, No.4; Christian, Roy; *The Chesterfield Canal*

Derbyshire Times; *Chesterfield Canal, Some Thoughts on its History*; 5 Feb 1937

Farey, John; *General View of the Agriculture of Derbyshire*; 1817

Ford, Thomas; *History of Chesterfield*; 1839

Fox-Davies, Arthur Charles; *The Book of Public Arms*; 1915; London

Garbett, H; *The History of Harthill*

Gatty, Rev Alfred; *Family of Howard*; 1879

Glover, Stephen; *History & Gazetteer of the County of Derby*; Vols 1 & 2; 1829; Longmans

Gray, J; *Reflections on Inland Navigation*; London; 1768

Grounds, A D; *A History of King Edward VI Grammar School, Retford*; Worksop; 1970

Hadfield, Charles; *Canals of the East Midlands*; 1959

Hall, Rev George; *History of Chesterfield*; 1823

Hanson, Harry; *The Canal Boatmen 1760-1914*; 1984; Alan Sutton Publish.

Harrison's Derby Journal

Hemingway G Y; *East Midlands Canals*

Hey, David; *Packmen, Carriers and Packhorse Roads*; Leicester University Press; 1980

Hibbert, Christopher; *The English, a Social History*; 1987

Hill, C P; *British & Social History 1700-1982*; Fifth edition

Holland, Derek; *Bawtry & The Idle River Trade*; *Museum & Art Gallery*, Doncaster; 1964

Holland, John; *The History of Worksop*; 1826; Sheffield

Hopkinson, G G; *Development of Inland Navigation in South Yorkshire & North Derbyshire 1697-1850.*

Jacks, Leonard; *The Great Houses of Nottinghamshire and the County Families*; 1881; Nottingham

Jackson A; *History of Retford*; 1971

Jackson, M J; *Worksop in Times Past*

Jackson, M J; *Worksop of Yesterday*

Kelly's Directory of Nottinghamshire; 1888

Kelly's Post Office Directory of Derbs & Notts; 1864

Lloyd, Nathanial; *A History of English Brickwork*; 1925; Blom, New York

Longman's Atlas of Modern British History

Lowe, Robert; *General View of the Agriculture of the County of Nottingham*; 1794; London

Malcolmson, R W; *Life and Labour in England 1700-1780*; Hutchinsons; 1981

Marshall, Dorothy; *18th Century England*; 1974; 2nd Edition; Longman

Meaby, K T; *Nottinghamshire County Records of the 18th Century*; Nottingham

Moritz, Philipp; *Description of the House of Commons*; 1782; Contained in English Historical Documents X 1714-1783

Morris & Co's Commercial Directory & Gazetteer; 1869

Otter, Anthony; *From Atoms to Infinity*; Arthur James Ltd; 1977; Evesham

Paget-Tomlinson, E W; *The Complete Book of Canal & River Navigations*; 1978

Peck, W; *A Topographical History and Description of Bawtry & Thorne*; 1813; London

Pendleton; *Old and New Chesterfield*; 1882

Phillips, John; *A General History of Inland Navigation*; 1792; London

Piercy, John S; *History of Retford*; Sep 1828

Pigot & Co Directory; 1822 & 1831

Pigot & Co Notts Directory; 1828

Pigot National Commercial Directory; 1835

Pigot's Directory of Nottinghamshire; 1830

Practical Diabetes; Nov/Dec 1990

Pratt, Edwin A; *Canals & Traders*; 1910

Pressnell L S; *Country Banking in the Industrial Revolution*; Oxford Clarendon Press; 1956

Priestly, Joseph; *Historical Account of the Navigable Rivers, Canals and Railways throughout Great Britain; Second Edition*

Raistrick, Arthur & Jennings, Bernard; *A History of Lead Mining in the Pennines*; 1965

Rawsley, John E; *Antique Maps of Yorkshire and Their Makers*

Reed, Michael; *The Georgian Triumph 1700-1830*

Rees, Abraham; *Cyclopaedia, Vol VI*; 1819; Article "Canals", c1806; 84th page from beginning

Riden, Philip J; *Tramroads in North East Derbyshire*

Robinson J M; *The Dukes of Norfolk*; 1982; Oxford University Press

Robinson, Philip; *The Smiths of Chesterfield*; 1957

Searle, Alfred B; *Limestone and its Products*

Shimwell, Thomas Haydn; *A History of Killamarsh*

Skempton, A W; *British Civil Engineering Literature 1640-1840*

Smiles, Samuel; *Lives of the Engineers*; London; 1861

Sutcliffe, John; *A Treatise on Canals and Reservoirs*; 1816; Rochdale

Universal British Directory of Chesterfield; 1794; Vol 2

Universal British Directory of Trade, Commerce & Manufacture 1791-98

White's Directory of Nottingham

White's History, Gazetteer & Directory of Notts; 1832

White's Notts History, Gazetteer & Directory; 1864

White, Robert;Worksop, *The Dukery & Sherwood Forest*; 1875

Whitworth, Richard; *The Advantages of Inland Navigation*; London; 1766

Williams, E N; *Life in Georgian England*

Wood, A C; *The History of Trade and Transport on the River Trent*; Thoroton Society Transactions; 1950,Vol 54

Yeatman J P; *History of the Borough of Chesterfield*

Yorkshire Arch.Soc; *A Descriptive List of the Printed Maps of Yorkshire*; Record Series, Vol LXXXVI; 1933

Young, Arthur; *A Six Months Tour through the North of England*; Vol 1; 1771

INDEX

Acklom, Jonathan, 57, 65, 67, 221
Act of Parliament, 63, 65, 73-87, 178, 188,
      192, 199, 209, 216, 227, 233, 251,
      274-6
Allin, John, 169, 223
Anston, 61, 124
Arthur, Robert, 177

Babworth Hall, 48
Bailey, Thomas & Sarah, 210
Ballington, Jonathan, 176
Barber, John, 115
Barker, Alexander, 30
Barnes, John, 250
Bawtry, 18, 27, 34, 68
Best, John, 133, 188, 236
Blake, George, 121
boats, 41, 55, 70, 155, 167, 189, 198, 218, 220,
      226-7, 249
Bough, James, 168, 170
Brancliffe Grange, 150
brick-making, 113-4, 121, 155, 170, 172, 175,
      196, 223
bridges, 169, 176, 183, 196, 219
Bridgewater Canal, 23, 27
Bridgewater, Duke of, 23, 43
Bright, John, 48, 68, 148, 183
Brindley, James, 23, 33, 42, 50-1, 61, 71, 75,
      91, 95, 116, 125-7, 174
Brown, Edward, 94, 195, 235
Brown, George, 48
Brumby, Thomas, 48, 148, 195
Bunting, Edward, 133

calls – (See Share Payments)
canal - construction Costs, 42, 53, 75, 89,
      103, 156-164, 176, 194, 208, 211
    – dimensions, 41, 75, 118, 190-5, 273
    - official opening, 253-5
    - routes considered, 32, 49, 51, 55, 57,
      68, 270-2
    – vandalism, 177
Canal Co Management, 50, 90, 95, 104, 109,
      129, 130, 150, 154, 156-164, 173,
      206
Cargoes, 54, 59, 188
Cavendish, Elizabeth, 80
Cavendish, Lord George, 28, 67, 74, 83

Cavendish, Lord John, 28, 74
Chambers, Cary, 208, 220
Chesterfield, 87, 123, 239, 253, 255
    – description, 14, 19, 20
Clayworth, 218
Clumber Park, 48-9, 240
Cockshutt, Rev. Thomas, 48, 172
construction - brickwork, 113, 156
    – clay puddle, 142, 146
    – ironwork, 171
    – organisation, 101, 107, 117, 119
    – standards, 108, 156-164, 167
    -- supplies, 70, 102, 105, 114, 117,
      125, 129, 143, 145, 155, 175, 179,
      216, 235, 252
Cowley, William, 32
currency, 92

Day, John, 170, 172, 175, 181
dental treatment, 119-120
Devonshire, Duke of, 28, 89, 90, 215, 249
Dixon, Richard, 104, 109, 125, 134, 145, 159,
      162, 202, 210, 236, 246, 252, 256
Doe Lea, River, 35, 77, 84, 215, 223, 228
Don Navigation, 28, 35, 43, 54, 61, 68, 77,
      225
Downes, William, 177
Drakeholes Tunnel, 211

Erewash Canal, 258
Eyre, Anthony, 48

financial problems, 143, 155, 173, 206-240,
      251
Fletcher, Samuel, 161, 176
Frith, George, 133
Frith, John, 31, 94

Gainsborough, 51, 54, 61, 96, 109
Gamble, Stephen, 90, 96, 140
Gillott, Thomas, 171, 181
Grant, Francis, 198
Gratton, Mr, 256
Greasbrough Canal, 43, 53
Great North Road, 46, 48, 76
Gregory, Joseph, 211
Grundy, John, 68, 270-2

Haggonfield, 138-141
Handbury, John, 161, 173, 176
Harthill, 105, 116, 129, 218, 239, 258
Hayton, 198, 218
Heathcote, Godfrey, 30, 65, 95, 125, 147, 164, 257
Heaton, John, 250
Henshall, Hugh, 130, 154, 156, 166, 174, 194, 201, 209, 221, 223, 237, 257
Hewitt, John, 136-141, 145, 149, 178, 179
Hill, Joseph, 236
Holmes, John, 196
Holmes, Joseph, 181
Howard, Henry, 138-141, 243-248
Hutchinson, John, 132

Ibbotson, Henry, 167
Idle, River, 18, 21, 27, 37, 46, 55, 68, 80, 192, 226
international events, 15, 115, 154, 174, 240, 242

Jebb, Samuel, 31, 159, 165, 209, 226, 230, 235, 239
Jones, Charles, 133, 161, 176

Killamarsh, 35, 196, 215, 221, 224
Kinder, Charles, 130, 140
Kirke, William, 49, 94, 147
Knock, Samuel, 156, 160, 215

land purchase, 63, 67, 123, 136-141, 149, 224-226, 232, 250
Lawrence, Fortunatus, 167
Lax, Anthony, 31, 78, 86, 90, 122, 125, 136-141, 165, 227, 232, 243-8, 257
Leeds, Duke of, 61, 65, 78, 105, 109, 114, 209, 255
Lewis, Edward, 170, 172, 175, 181
Lister, John, 68, 80
locks, 135, 168, 235, 269
   – Forest, 170
   – Lockoford Lane, 253
   – Norwood, 80, 214, 277
   – rebuilding, 167
   – Thorpe/Turnerwood, 117-8, 134
   – Retford, 149, 172, 183, 217
   – West Stockwith, 226, 232, 252
   – Whitsunday Pie, 217, 278
Lucus, Thomas, 210

Macfarland, John, 213
Mander, John, 139-141, 244-8
Manley, William, 251
Mason, George, 49, 94
Mason, John, 49
Mason, William, 233
medical treatment, 132, 171
Metcalf, John & Ann, 217
Mettam, Robert, 197
Milnes, Richard, 32
Misterton, 212
Moody, Edward, 178
Morton, Thomas, 175
Mosman, Sampson, 49, 94, 109

Nall, Richard, 90, 94, 140
navvies, 102, 105-6, 112, 133, 146, 186, 213, 253
   – accidents, 132, 217
Newcastle, Duke of, 48-9 61, 74, 89-90, 183, 186, 232
Noake, William, 168, 170
Nock, John, 183
Norborne, Mr, 180, 197
Norbriggs, 223, 228, 238
Norfolk, Duke of, 61, 65, 78, 124, 138-141, 209, 240, 243-8
Norwood, 37, 80, 96
Norwood Tunnel, 37, 65, 101, 103, 111, 124, 175, 255
   – construction problems, 156-164
   – opening of, 200
   – sale of equipment, 207
Osberton, 149, 160, 198

Palmer, William, 28
Parker, John, 49, 94, 195
Parks, William, 219
Parliament, 66, 73
Peacock, Rev. John, 68, 73, 95, 104, 145, 198, 217-8
Pebley (See Water Supply)
Pennyholme, 164, 167, 172
Platts, Joseph, 217
Poplewell, George, 49, 90-1, 125, 195
Portland, Duke of, 61, 238
public meetings, 51, 53, 57, 66, 73

Read, John, 183
Renishaw, 196

Reservoirs (See Water Supply)
Retford, 50, 57, 87, 183, 186, 192-5, 220, 240
   – Description, 19, 43
river navigation, 16
roads, 15, 60, 76, 84, 86
Robinson, John & William, 212, 219
Roe, Richard, 95
Rogers, Robert, 149
Rother, River, 28, 34, 77, 83, 199
   – junction with canal, 216, 248, 279
Ryton, River, 136, 142, 146, 198

Saville, George MP, 67
Scarsdale, Lord, 90
Seddon, Thomas, 170
share payments, 66, 86, 89, 91, 109, 143,
   155, 174, 209, 234
Shilleto, Mr, 47
Shireoaks, 37, 60, 136, 145, 155, 170, 175,
   181
Simpson, Lindley, 48, 90, 94, 109, 126, 194-5
Singleton, William, 219
Skynner, William, 224
Slater, Adam, 147, 239
smallpox, 123
Smeaton, John, 43, 53
Staveley, 196, 249
   – footbridge dispute, 251
   – Forge, 80, 228
   – Puddlebank, 84, 215, 228, 248-250,
   256
   – tithes dispute, 224-6
steam power, 78, 113
Stevenson, Rev Seth Ellis, 46, 49, 55, 59, 73,
   84, 87, 90, 94, 105, 108, 119, 126,
   129, 159, 171, 175, 190-5, 257
   – family, 47, 76, 148, 202, 240
Storrs, Joseph, 31, 90, 94, 130, 140, 235, 239
Story, John, 196
surveying, 38, 43, 50, 67-8, 111
Sutton Robert, 48, 94
Sykes, Thomas, 115

Taylor, John, 94, 195
The Forest, 149, 162
The Hague, 196
Thompson, Francis of Ashover, 113
Toft, John, 196
Towndrow, Samuel, 32, 94, 140, 239
Trent, River, 49, 51, 55, 220, 226, 232

tunnel – Castle Hill, 54-5
   – Drakeholes, 211
   – Norwood, 65, 101, 103, 111, 124,
   156-164, 175, 200, 207, 255

Twigg, Nicholas, 32, 235

Varley, Francis, 156-164, 173
Varley, John, 33, 83, 85, 104, 108, 119, 128,
   136, 173, 206, 237, 258
   – family, 33, 116, 172, 239
   – map making, 40, 43
   – surveying, 34, 38, 43, 50, 67, 69
Varley, John Snr, 156-164, 173
Varley, Thomas, 156, 161, 173, 176

Walker & Co, Messrs, 125, 155
water supply, 35, 78, 83, 108, 143, 199, 214,
   230, 256
   – feeders, 142, 192-5, 223, 256
   – mills, 78, 83, 198
   – reservoirs, 80, 103, 105, 142, 160,
   197, 237, 256
weather, 101, 115, 141, 159, 181, 194, 197,
   219
Weights and Measures, 189
West Stockwith, 38, 51, 55, 57, 232, 236
wharfingers, 188, 236
Wilkinson, Allwood, 30, 91, 94, 125, 147,
   239
Wilkinson, Isaac, 30, 147, 235
Wilson, Joseph, 95, 129
Windle, John, 236
Wiseton Hall, 57, 65, 67, 219
Worksop, 50, 53, 68, 169, 176
   – commonland dispute, 138-141, 150
   – warehouse dispute, 243-8
Worstenholme, Martin, 181
Wray, Sir Cecil, 49, 51, 159

York, Archbishop of, 65, 73
York, Dean of, 73